The Sacrament of Baptism

Lex Orandi Series

John D. Laurance, S.J.
Editor

The Sacrament of Baptism

Michael G. Witczak

LITURGICAL PRESS
Collegeville, Minnesota

www.litpress.org

Cover design by Greg Becker.

Cover illustration: Alberto Arnoldi (fl. 1351–64). Baptism, Museo dell'Opera del Duomo, Florence, Italy. Scala/Art Resource, New York. Used with permission.

1   2   3   4   5   6   7   8

Library of Congress Cataloging-in-Publication Data

Witczak, Michael G.
      The sacrament of baptism / Michael G. Witczak.
            p.   cm. — (Lex orandi series)
      Includes bibliographical references and indexes.
      ISBN 978-0-8146-2517-0 — ISBN 978-0-8146-3946-7 (e-book)
            1. Baptism—Catholic Church.   2. Catholic Church—Doctrines.
      I. Title.

BX2205.W58   2011
234'.161—dc22   2010032484

To my parents
Ronald and Mary Louise Witczak
and to my godparents
Peter Traudt and Geraldine Waldoch
who launched me into life and the life of faith

Contents

Preface to the *Lex Orandi* Series   ix

Acknowledgments   xii

Introduction: A Note about Method   xiii

Part One: The Shape of Baptism   1

Chapter One:
   The Shape of Adult Initiation   3

Chapter Two:
   The Shape of Children's Baptism   49

Part Two: The Words of Baptism   69

Chapter Three:
   The Scriptural Readings in Baptism   71

Chapter Four:
   The Words of Prayer at Baptism   98

Part Three: The Theology of Baptism   143

Chapter Five:
   Themes of Baptismal Theology in Historical Perspective   145

Chapter Six:
   A Theology of the Celebration of Baptism   180

Conclusion   199

Index of Documents   201

Index of Scripture References   203

Index of Proper Names   207

Index of Subjects   209

Preface to the *Lex Orandi* Series

The theology of the seven sacraments prevalent in the Catholic Church through most of the second millennium interpreted those rites more as sacred objects to be *passively* received than as *active* participations in Christ's paschal mystery. And their meaning was to be derived, not from the shape of their liturgical celebration, but from the Church's official teaching, teaching typically occasioned by historical challenges to her faith. Whereas in patristic times Church writers expounded the theology of the sacraments from the rites themselves, with the later expansion of Christianity into central Europe confidence waned that the form and enactment of the liturgy in any way *manifested* the Mystery it contained. As the *Adoro Te Devote*, a medieval hymn on the Church's use of bread in the Eucharistic Liturgy, puts it, "Seeing, tasting, touching are in Thee deceived."

In recent times, however, there has been a kind of "Copernican revolution" in sacramental theology. Not only have sacraments come to be understood as actions of God *and* the Church, the truth of the ancient adage, *lex orandi, lex credendi* (how the Church prays expresses what she believes), has also been seen in a new light. Theologians have come to realize that if all Church dogma is rooted ultimately in her faith-experience of God, so too must her understanding of the sacraments derive from her experience of their liturgical celebration. Sacraments, too, must *manifest* the Mystery they contain. Consequently, in the tradition of ancient mystagogies, "liturgical theology"—that is, God's word ("first theology") to the Church through her worship—has come to be understood, along with official Church teaching, as an indispensable source for sacramental theology. And sacramental theology itself has returned to its proper place within a larger "theology of liturgy." The works of theologians such as Guardini, Casel, Rahner, Schmemann, Kilmartin, and Chauvet mark various stages in this historical development.

Although much has been written on the role of the celebrating Church, up until now no set of studies on all seven sacraments that we know of has attempted to exegete their meaning primarily from their typical celebrations. The aim of this present series, then, is precisely to investigate the sacraments as liturgical events in order to discover in them the faith understanding of Christian life of which they are both the source and the summit (SC 10).

However, since the theology of liturgy is but one part of the whole of systematic theology, liturgical events can be adequately interpreted as witnesses to the Church's faith only in light of the other ways she experiences God's word. Accordingly, individual volumes in this series analyze typical experiences of the rites they cover against the background of the rest of the Church's traditional life and teaching, and they do so guided by the unique synthesis of that tradition that each author, as theologian, brings to the work. To do anything less would be to fail in the task of theology. On occasion, then, authors will offer their own critique, whether of the rites themselves or of how they have experienced their celebration, doing so on the basis of other theological sources as well (including, for example, the official instructions introducing each rite).

Sacraments as liturgical *events* are not understood by most theologians today as they once were, that is, as so-called moments of consecration (the "This is my Body"; the pouring of water "in the name of the Father . . ."; etc.). Rather, similar to how Aristotle's *Poetics* envisions Greek tragedies, sacraments are seen as events extended through time, having beginnings, middles, and ends. True, as protracted events they include indispensable high points, but separated off from the whole liturgical celebration, those key moments, at least in the short run, lose much of their intelligibility and intensity and, therefore, their efficacy as well (see SC 14). Accordingly, volumes in this series attempt to study each sacrament as it unfolds through its total performance, discerning especially its basic structure and how various elements contribute to its overall faith meaning.

The motivating purpose of this new series on the sacraments is ultimately a pastoral one: to help foster the fuller liturgical participation called for by Vatican II, and not necessarily to "break new ground" in sacramental theology. The readership envisioned by the series, therefore, is a broad one, not confined just to liturgical experts. Individual volumes presuppose only a beginner's familiarity with Christian theology, such as that possessed by university upper-level undergraduate or master's level students.

Finally, the rites studied in this series are those of the Roman Rite of the Catholic Church in use today. As valuable as a comparison of various Christian liturgies would be, no one series can do everything. At the same time, it is hoped that efforts made here toward understanding the Roman Rite might help inspire other, more explicitly ecumenical studies of Christian liturgy.

John D. Laurance, s.j.
Marquette University

Acknowledgments

No book is written in isolation, and this one is no exception. I would like to acknowledge several colleagues and friends who have read and commented on the chapters of this book over the period of many years that it has been in the making. These clear-eyed readers who have read all or part of the manuscript include: Rita Ferrone; Stephen Lampe; Steven Malkiewicz, OFM; Andrew Nelson; David Stosur; Barbara Turner; and Paul Turner. John Laurance, SJ, has exercised a light but guiding hand as series editor. Their concerned comments have saved me from numerous errors and have challenged me to clarify my thoughts. Many of the strengths of this work are due to their attention. The errors that remain are, as is always the case, mine alone.

With profound gratitude for a life lived in the Body of Christ through baptism, I dedicate this book to my parents, Ronald and Mary Louise Witczak, and to my godparents, Geraldine Waldoch and Peter Traudt. Their love and example led me into the mysteries of God's grace.

Introduction: A Note about Method

Every book needs a method, and this one will follow a method of liturgical theology as developed by several theologians.[1] Peter Fink proposes an analogy for an approach to theological method, that of language. Language communicates, and the liturgies of the sacraments communicate as well. They communicate God's grace to us and they communicate our praise and worship to God. The liturgy uses three languages (at least) to communicate: the language of action, symbol, and objects; the language of story, poetry, and song; and the language of reflective theology, rooted in philosophical categories. This book will attempt to analyze the liturgy of baptism along this threefold category.

Part 1 will explore the basic structure of the action of baptism: the people, what they do, the objects they use, the movements they make. Chapter 1 explores in the celebration of the initiation of adults, starting with its historical context. Chapter 2 does the same for the baptism of children.

Part 2 will explore the language of Scripture. Chapter 3 explores the Word of God, using the lectionary (the list of readings) assigned to be used for the celebration of baptism. This will allow us to get at the narrative of salvation history that baptism is telling us. That narrative continues in the texts of the prayers that are used for the celebration of baptism, the topic of chapter 4. The poetry and Scripture contained in the prayers will help us gain some understanding of how the Church has and currently does articulate its faith about the meaning of baptism.

Part 3 allows us to offer some systematic reflections on the celebration of baptism, paying attention to issues that emerge from the tradition and that also are of importance to us today. Chapter 5 gives an account of how the theology of baptism has developed in history. Chapter 6 concludes the whole work by presenting a theological reflection on baptism as it emerges from the celebration of the rites.

When we start trying to read the liturgy using these three languages, it is important to recognize that we need to do so with a plan in mind. Paul Ricoeur[2] offers a way of reading these languages. He says that we approach the experience of the sacrament with a first naïveté, an openness to the moment that allows it to speak to us with no necessary prior knowledge or experience. That is how we often experience baptism, or, really, any liturgy. We bring little or nothing to the experience and it just washes over us. In this book, however, we try to organize these first naïve impressions. This organization is made more difficult because we are not used to using the languages of ritual and story. We are more used to the language of logic and analysis. We are not used to seeing the liturgy of the sacraments as "communicating" to us. The language of that communication is one that is part of our regular experience, but one that we seldom reflect on. It is the experience of awe, of something more behind the symbols, the emotional impact of the action on us.

This language, though, the language of symbol and story, emerges from antiquity. The use of oil and the stories that come from the first-century Mediterranean world are far distant from our twenty-first-century sensibilities. Part of the task of this book is to help the reader to bridge the centuries and understand the issues and themes in the light of contemporary concerns.

The final goal of reading the language of the liturgy, coming to it with a first naïveté and letting it speak our heart and soul, and then stepping back from it to see its history, its context, its theology—the final goal is to return to the liturgy and experience it again in a second naïveté. This is an openness to the emotional and aesthetic power of the experience but now informed by study and reflection.

At the end, the liturgy is God's language. In the liturgy, God the all-powerful Father reveals his plan of salvation for us in Christ, who lived and died and rose for our salvation and who gave us the gift of the Holy Spirit to remain with us. The study of baptism is the study of how this plan of God's unfolds each day in our world among those who pray to God, call Jesus their Lord and Brother, and live the gifts of the Spirit.

Two Different Ways of Celebrating Baptism

The Roman Rite has two different rituals for celebrating baptism. One is the Rite of Christian Initiation of Adults.[3] This ritual is designed to initiate adults who have never been baptized and now have come to believe in Jesus Christ as God's Son and our Savior. The celebrations take place over a period of months or even years and have several liturgical steps. One who celebrates the adult rite is baptized, confirmed, and receives First Communion in the same ceremony. Adults enter the community of faith in stages but fully.

The other liturgy is contained in the Rite of Baptism for Children.[4] It provides the ritual for those who become members of the Church in infancy, whose parents are believers and want to share God's divine life with their children. In contrast to the rite for adults, this ritual takes place in a single liturgical action and anticipates a long period of coming to adult faith afterward. Those baptized as children receive confirmation and the Eucharist later in life after they have begun to assimilate their faith.

These two ways of bringing new members into the Church have histories that diverge at a certain point and today offer different theological perspectives and pastoral problems. We will explore these two rituals in this book.

Notes, Introduction

[1] See Kevin W. Irwin, *Context and Text: Method in Liturgical Theology* (Collegeville, MN: Liturgical Press, A Pueblo Book, 1994); Peter E. Fink, "Three Languages of Christian Sacraments," in *Worship: Praying the Sacraments* (Washington, DC: Pastoral Press, 1991), 29–44; Irwin, *Liturgical Theology: A Primer*, American Essays in Liturgy (Collegeville, MN: Liturgical Press, 1990); Joyce Ann Zimmerman, *Liturgy and Hermeneutics*, American Essays in Liturgy (Collegeville, MN: Liturgical Press, 1999); Salvatore Marsili, "La Liturgia, momento storico della salvezza," in *La Liturgia, momento nella storia della salvezza*, vol. 1, *Anàmnesis: Introduzione storico-teologica alla Liturgia*, ed. M. Augé et al. (Casale Monferrato: Marietti, 1974), 31–156; Alceste Catella, "Theology of the Liturgy," in *Fundamental Liturgy*, vol. 1, *Handbook of Liturgical Studies*, ed. Anscar J. Chupungco (Collegeville, MN: Liturgical Press, A Pueblo Book, 1998), 3–28; Irénée Henri Dalmais, "Theology of the Liturgical Celebration," in *Principles of the Liturgy*, vol. 2, *The Church at Prayer: An Introduction to the Liturgy*, new ed., ed. Aimé Georges Martimort (Collegeville, MN: Liturgical Press, 1987), 227–80.

[2] The reflection here is based on Fink, "Three Languages," and Wendy Wright, "Reading the Spiritual Classics" in *Francis de Sales: Introduction to the Devout Life*

and Treatise on the Love of God, The Crossroad Spiritual Legacy Series (New York: Crossroad, 1993), 17–28.

[3] The text can be found in *The Rites of the Catholic Church*, vol. 1 (Collegeville, MN: Liturgical Press, A Pueblo Book, 1990), 15–356. We will cite this book as *The Rites* and refer to it throughout the text.

[4] The text can be found in ibid., 359–465.

Part One

The Shape of Baptism

In this first part, we will explore the shape of the celebration of baptism. The ritual and the symbols that constitute the initiation of adults and the baptism of children, and the people who act in the ritual and use the symbols of the various celebrations are our focus of attention.

Chapter One

The Shape of Adult Initiation

Introduction

Scriptural Data about the Conversion and Initiation of Adults[1]

One of the things that we know about Jesus is that he was a very attractive person. From the beginning of his public ministry, he attracted attention by his words and by his actions. He called certain men to be his followers and others followed him of their own accord. He called fishermen (Mark 1:16 par.) and tax collectors (Mark 2:13; Matt 9:9; Luke 5:27) who left their work to follow him. Sometimes others, like John the Baptist and his disciples, pointed Jesus out to others (John 1:35-37, 40-42). From the gospel accounts, we find that the only "initiation" into this following of Jesus was the act of responding to the call, either direct or indirect, of Jesus. It is not clear that the apostles, the Twelve, and the women who followed Jesus were baptized. Some were baptized by John the Baptist and then became followers of Jesus. But it seems that once they responded to Jesus, they simply followed him.

After his death and resurrection, Jesus gave the gift of the Spirit to all who gathered together. The original followers of Jesus were gathered in the Upper Room on the first Pentecost when they received the gift of the Spirit. How this Lukan story of the gift of the Spirit (Acts 2) relates to the Johannine story of Jesus giving the Spirit on Easter night (John 20) is not clear. What is clear is that the gift of the Spirit was a key element in the early community.

3

With the impetus of the Spirit, the members of the early community continued the work of Jesus, preaching his message and doing his works. Those who met them were attracted to the person of Jesus through them, beginning that first Pentecost. The Acts of the Apostles tells several stories of how new members came to follow Christ. The pattern seems most clearly outlined in Acts 2:36-42. Peter proclaims Jesus as the fulfillment of all the promises of the Scriptures. Those who hear are deeply moved by his words and are called to follow. This leads them to be baptized with water for the forgiveness of sins and to receive the gift of the Holy Spirit. Then they enter life in the Christian community that includes preaching (*didache*), community (*koinonia*), breaking of the bread (*klasis tou artou*), and prayer (*proseuchai*).

Why baptism emerges as the ritual for this entrance into the Body of Christ is not entirely clear. We know that baptism had become an important part of religious life in Palestine at the time of Jesus. Jesus himself had been baptized by John at the Jordan (Mark 1:9-11 and par.) and some of his disciples may first have been followers of John (John 1:35-37). Jesus and his disciples may have baptized some followers as well (John 3:22; 4:1-3). For whatever reasons, this action becomes the defining one for the Christian community.

This basic pattern laid out in Acts 2 has several variations. In fact, the Acts of the Apostles does not repeat itself in telling how new members come to Christ. Sometimes it is not clear that they entered into the Christian community. (The Ethiopian eunuch immediately returned home, where there was no Christian community, although he may have become a preacher of Christ Jesus to those in his home country [8:26-40].) Some were baptized but did not receive the gift of the Spirit until they received the laying on of hands by the apostles (8:14-17; see also 19:1-7). Some received the gift of the Spirit first and then were baptized subsequently, because who can withhold baptism when the Spirit is already present (10:1-48, esp. 44-48)? Despite all this variation of details, the basic elements of preaching, the response of conversion, the act of baptism in water and the Holy Spirit, and the entry into Christian living seem to be at the heart of the process of coming into the Christian community.[2]

When individuals decided to follow Christ, their whole family would come with them. Acts tells us that households came to the faith and received baptism (e.g., Cornelius's household, 10:44, 48; Lydia's household, 16:14-15; the jailer's family, 16:25-34). This action by a whole family when the head had come to faith was a characteristic of the ancient Mediterranean world where the father spoke for and acted on behalf of the family. It would also imply that children and slaves were part of the mix in the early Christian community. The path to belief taken by an adult and taken by a child is different. We will have a chance to explore the implications of this in part 3 of this work when we discuss the theological and pastoral issues that we encounter in baptism today.

The Early History of Baptism until the Peace of the Church (to AD 313)[3]

We learn bits and pieces about the celebration of baptism in the early centuries from documents and writers from different times and places. The Didache, possibly from about the year 100 in Syria or Egypt, tells that, after a period of preparation learning the "two ways," that of life and that of death, a new member of the community would be baptized. The baptism would take place in running water if available, or else in other water, and this would be done "in the name of the Father and of the Son and of the Holy Spirit" (Didache 7; see Matt 28:16).[4]

Justin, a Samaritan convert to Christianity and a philosopher who settled in Rome, wrote about baptism in an apologetic work he addressed to the emperor Antoninus Pius around the year 150. He described the baptism and how it concluded with the celebration of the Eucharist.[5]

Tertullian is credited with creating much of the technical language for theology in Latin. He wrote a treatise on baptism, which is a treasure trove of information about the details of the celebration in North Africa around the year 200. There was an anointing with oil and a clothing with a white garment as well as other ceremonies. Tertullian highlighted the paschal character of baptism (following the theology that St. Paul develops in Rom 6), noting that Easter's fifty days are the ideal time for baptism, and indeed any Sunday is, since it is the day of the Lord's resurrection. Then he commented that, in fact, any day is appropriate, because every day is the Lord's Day.[6]

One of the most famous documents of this period is the *Apostolic Tradition*, often attributed to Hippolytus of Rome and ascribed to the year 215 or 220.[7] We find quite an elaborate description of how those new to the faith were to be admitted into the community. There was a lengthy questioning about their moral uprightness, and they were to have sponsors present them and testify that they were worthy to begin the process of entry. Then there was a time of catechetical preparation, lasting three years, though the document reminds us that it is not the time that was important, but the person's readiness (remember the Ethiopian eunuch!). When they were ready, another inquiry was conducted to satisfy the leaders of the community of their readiness. The newcomers fasted for several days before their baptism and gathered on Saturday morning for a final exorcism. Then, in the night between Saturday and Sunday, the newcomers rejected sin and were anointed with the oil of exorcism. They entered the water and as they professed their faith by responding to the threefold creed (Do you believe in God? . . . Do you believe in Jesus Christ? . . . Do you believe in the Holy Spirit? . . .), they were three times immersed. When they emerged from the water, a priest anointed them with oil of thanksgiving. They clothed themselves in a white garment and were led to the gathered community where the bishop welcomed them and anointed them on the forehead with the oil of thanksgiving and shared with them a sign of peace. The newly baptized then shared in the Eucharist with the rest of the community, although they also shared in a cup of milk and honey and a cup of water in addition to the bread and cup of wine. The notable things in this document are the lengthy preparation, the three anointings, and the extra foods at Communion. Unlike Tertullian, the *Apostolic Tradition* contains no mention of Easter as the likeliest time for baptism.[8]

In eastern Syria, there was originally but a single anointing done for the gift of the Spirit, before baptism in water. This is a very different pattern from the *Apostolic Tradition*, for instance. Later, in the eastern Syrian tradition, we find a ceremony at the font (a source of water or a baptistery), not at the church, beginning with an exorcistic anointing before water baptism, then a Christic anointing at the font by a presbyter immediately after baptism, and finally a third anointing in the Holy Spirit by the bishop, now in the body of the church.[9] Just as the Acts of the Apostles did not give a single pattern for becoming a follower of Christ, so too the early Church did not have a single pattern. The important thing is to come to Christ. The pattern takes time to develop.

The Emergence of Medieval Patterns of Baptism: From Baptizing Households to Baptizing Adults to Baptizing in Danger of Death— The Decline of Adult Baptism (313–1500)[10]

The legalization of Christianity (313) led to important changes in life for the Church. From a small persecuted, but growing, group of believers, Christians now became the privileged public religious group. The Roman emperor Constantine (+ 337) built churches throughout the empire and gave civil honors to the leaders of the Church. By the end of the fourth century, paganism had been outlawed and Christianity had become the official religion of the empire.

At the beginning of this period (in the mid-300s), a curious pattern developed. Parents would enroll their children as catechumens but then would not have them baptized immediately. Two things seem to have led to this development. First, there was a fear that in their adolescence they would "sow their wild oats" and so be unworthy of their baptism. The second point is related. The practice of reconciliation after baptism for those guilty of serious sins was extremely rigorous, so much so that many postponed their reconciliation until on their deathbed to avoid the rigors of the penances imposed. As a result, baptism, which wiped away all sin and included no requirement for further penance, was a much more palatable choice but one better put off till the youthful ardors had run their course. Famous figures who followed this pattern include Ambrose, Augustine, Basil, and Gregory Nazianzen.[11]

By the year 500, the situation had changed. The ritual was more elaborate. Now most of the newcomers to the faith were not adults but the children of adult believers. We find evidence for this evolution in the successive descriptions of baptism by the Roman deacon John in his letter to Senarius (about 500) and the ritual documented in the *Old Gelasian Sacramentary* (some Roman material from as early as 550–600).[12]

The letter of John to Senarius reveals a situation in which adults were still the focus of initiation but in which many children were also baptized. There were still catechumens who received instruction and exorcism. They had salt placed on their tongues as a sign of the wisdom they imbibed. They received the Creed and were scrutinized. They were anointed with oil in a ceremony that touched their ears and nostrils with oil so that they would only hear and smell what is holy; and they were anointed again with the "oil of sanctification" or oil of catechumens. They stripped themselves naked and were immersed three times as they professed their faith in the Father, the Son, and the Holy Spirit. They were then dressed in white and anointed on the head with chrism (scented oil, different from the unscented oil of catechumens). At Communion, they received milk and honey as well as the consecrated bread and wine.

The *Old Gelasian Sacramentary* blends both Roman and Gallican material. Its material dates from the mid-seventh century, blending earlier customs with later ones. (For instance, there are three scrutinies prescribed for Sundays, but there are also scrutinies on weekdays, a situation that makes more sense when dealing principally with infants, as was then the case.) The rituals include a rite for making a catechumen, when the names of those to be baptized were written down and the salt was placed in their mouths. There was a series of exorcisms for men and women with the imposition of hands. The elect received the four gospels, the Creed, and the Lord's Prayer. On Holy Saturday morning, there was a final exorcism, the Effeta ceremony when their nostrils and ears were touched with spittle,[13] and the elect were anointed with the oil of catechumens and renounced Satan. At the Easter Vigil, after the readings, the Litany of the Saints was sung during a procession to the font. The water was blessed with a long prayer of blessing. Each person was immersed three times as they professed their faith in the Father and the Son and the Holy Spirit. Each one was then anointed with chrism on the head. The bishop then imposed hands on each one with a prayer, signed them with chrism, and gave them the sign of peace. The litany was chanted again as the bishop went to his chair, then the Gloria was sung and the rest of the Mass celebrated.

Another document, the *Ordo Romanus XI*, with material from around the year 700, organizes this same material in a more cohesive way into seven celebrations culminating at the Easter Vigil.[14]

All these documents presuppose that baptisms were celebrated at Easter. We know, however, that this was not always the case. A high infant mortality rate made many parents want to have their children baptized as soon as possible after birth, especially since they had the conviction that they would not be saved if they were not baptized. This theology was rooted in the arguments of St. Augustine, who, in the midst of his debates with the Pelagians, opined that since baptism is for the forgiveness of sins, and the Church exorcises and baptizes infants, they must be guilty of sin. Since they are incapable of personal sin, they must bear some other sin, most likely that of Adam, passed on from generation to generation.[15] Later, the chronology of Augustine's theology was reversed: in the Carolingian period (700–850), the opinion was expressed that the Church baptized children because children participated in Adam's original sin.[16]

The lengthy ceremonies during Lent and at the Easter Vigil arose when large mixed groups of adults and children were being baptized. When mostly children came to be baptized Sunday by Sunday, though, such a long ceremony came to be condensed. Since the children were baptized because they were in danger of dying, the rite of baptism for those in danger of death seemed the best solution. The ritual that became the standard for baptism, then, was the rite for a catechumen about to die. It was the old set of rituals for adult catechumens adapted to a single ceremony.[17]

The celebration of baptism saw a shift from a lengthy preparation and set of rites for adults over several months during Lent and the Easter Vigil, to a rite for infants in a single ceremony, usually on Sunday. While this fit the situation of the predominantly Christian Europe of the tenth to the fifteenth centuries, it was not a rite that worked well when once again the majority of those to be baptized were adults, as will be the case in the subsequent process of European discovery and colonization.

This period, from the legalization of Christianity under Constantine (313) to the European discovery of the "New World" (ca. 1500), began with an intense attention to the baptism of adults and the need for instruction prior to their entrance into the Church. It then evolved to a period focused on the needs of families and children in a Christian world, when children first were baptized and then trained in the practice of the faith. The rituals of baptism went from an elaborate series of rites over a period of months or years to an elaborate rite done in one ceremony. The theology of baptism went from one of new birth or of dying to sin and rising to life in Christ as articulated by the Mystagogical Catecheses, to one of removing original sin and entering the Christian community.

The New Situation: Missionary Zeal (1500–1962)

The European discovery of America sparked a tremendous desire to spread the Gospel to peoples who had never heard it. The established religious communities of the Franciscans and the Dominicans and new communities like the Jesuits committed many of their members to the spread of the Good News. In turn, this led to a rethinking of how the rites should be celebrated in the situation when adults are catechized and baptized. Missionaries adapted the rites to the realities of the situation they found themselves in. The sixteenth century, marked by intense religious debate sparked by the Protestant Reformation, also involved a renewal of the rites. Castellani's *Liber sacerdotalis* (1523) and Santori's *Rituale* (1593–1602) both made provision for the rite of baptism. Santori's included a celebration of the catechumenate in stages over a period of time.[18]

The debates of the Protestant Reformation and the Catholic reaction led to a reform of the theology and the rituals of the Roman Catholic Church. All the Protestant leaders accepted that baptism was a sacrament (though they did not accept confirmation as one). Baptism was clearly attested in the New Testament. There was an institution by Christ with a promise of grace (see, for example, Matt 28:16-18). Where there was not unanimity, however, was in the question of who should be baptized: only adult believers, or also children? Luther and Calvin clearly accepted the baptism of children. Others, given the name "Anabaptists" since they seemed to favor "re"baptism, insisted that personal adult faith was necessary for baptism. One needed to be able to respond to Christ personally to be baptized.[19]

The Roman Catholic response was that of course children could be baptized. The pope also produced a reformed ritual to replace the hundreds of local rituals in dioceses and monasteries throughout Europe and the new world. The rituals of Santori and Castellani mentioned above were sixteenth-century way stations to the ritual that finally appeared in 1614. Pope Paul V did not make this book mandatory, as Pius V had so made the Roman Breviary (1568) and the Roman Missal (1570). But Pope Paul V did say that it should be used as a point of reference.[20] The rite of baptism had two main sections: a rite of baptism for infants and a rite of baptism for adults. The 1614 ritual eliminated Santori's celebration in stages and presented both the children's and the adult's rituals in a single ceremony.[21] See the following chart for an overview of the shape of the 1614 ritual:

Outline of the 1614 Rituale Romanum, *on the Baptism of Adults*

At the foot of the altar, the priest in surplice and violet stole and ministers pause in private prayer

- Baptismal office (Pss 8, 28 [29], and 41 [42], with baptismal antiphons, followed by Kyrie, Pater)

- Three prayers

Procession to the doors of the church, the priest standing on the threshold, the catechumen outside the doors

- Dialogue with catechumens about their Christian names, and their reason for presenting themselves, followed by an exhortation of the priest

- Renunciation of Satan and profession of faith, question-and-answer form

- Exsufflation

- Imposition of the sign of the cross on the forehead, with a text for the renunciation of former religious adherence (e.g., Jewish, Muslim, or Protestant)

- Prayer followed by the signing of the senses with the cross (forehead, ears, eyes, nostrils, mouth, chest, shoulders, over the whole body)

- Three prayers follow, with an imposition of hands on the elect during the third prayer

- Blessing of salt, and then placing it in the mouth of the catechumen (the nomenclature is not consistent between "elect" and "catechumen" at this part of the rite)
- Prayer
- Recitation of the Lord's Prayer followed by a series of exorcisms, first for the men and then for the women, with a final prayer over both men and women

The priest then leads them *into the church*, whereupon they prostrate themselves

- They rise, receive an imposition of hands, and recite the profession of faith, using the Nicene Creed
- Another imposition of hands and exorcism
- Epheta rite, using saliva placed on the ears and noses
- Renunciation of Satan
- Anointing of the chest with the oil of catechumens

Procession to the *baptismal font*

- If necessary, new baptismal water can be blessed by the priest

At the font, the profession of faith is recited in dialogical form

- The person is baptized with the pouring of water three times on their forehead, while their godparents touch them
- The anointing of the crown of the head of the elect [sic] by the priest
- Vesting in a white garment
- Giving a lighted candle
- There follow rubrics for baptism by immersion
- Dismissal

As the centuries progressed, and especially with the rise of the biblical, patristic, and liturgical movements in the nineteenth and twentieth centuries, the ritual for adults came under increasing criticism since it did not celebrate the incremental growth in faith of those who were being evangelized. A celebration in steps such as that found in the *Apostolic Tradition* (newly identified as such in 1910 and 1916) and in the *Old Gelasian Sacramentary* seemed to be a desirable change in the ritual and pastoral practice of the mid-twentieth century, and missionaries began to petition Rome for some changes. At the same time, the celebration for children came to seem less and less effective, since it was a rite intended originally for adults and the parents and godparents only spoke on behalf of the child. The rising catechetical movement led to concerns about both adult catechesis (that of the parents) and the need for a catechesis for the children that was adapted to their needs.

The ferment in Scripture, patristics, and liturgy received recognition in a series of three encyclicals of Pope Pius XII on the Mystical Body of Christ (*Mystici Corporis*, 1943), on Sacred Scripture (*Divino Afflante Spiritu*, 1943), and on liturgy (*Mediator Dei*, 1947). He established a special commission on liturgical reform that issued revised rites, first for the Easter Vigil (1951) and then for all of the Holy Week services (1955) and other reforms as well.

Pope John XXIII called a new ecumenical council (1959), and liturgy emerged as a key topic for that gathering.

Finally, in 1962, the Sacred Congregation of Rites published a revised rite of baptism for adults in stages to be used as an option. It retouched several elements of the prayers and rubrics but essentially left intact the 1614 ritual but spread it over seven steps.[22]

The devastation of two world wars and a depression led to profound theological soul-searching. What did baptism actually mean? How could baptized persons treat others in so unchristian a way? How could one explain the horrors of the death camps, the saturation bombings, the use of atomic weapons? What did baptism mean when parents had their children baptized but made no effort to train them in the faith, so that whole generations came to see their Christian life in terms only of baptism, marriage, and funerals?

The Swiss Reformed theologian Karl Barth opened an intense theological debate in the 1930s, which continued after the Second World War, with Oscar Cullman, Joachim Jeremias, and Kurt Aland. Roman Catholics in Europe were caught up in the same dynamics and concerns. This was the context that preceded the discussions and votes at the Second Vatican Council.[23]

Vatican Council II (1962–65)

The Second Vatican Council called for the reform of the liturgy and, in particular, for a reform of the way in which baptism is celebrated.

The first chapter of the Constitution on the Sacred Liturgy (*Sacrosanctum Concilium*; SC), the first document to be issued by the bishops of the council (December 4, 1963), presented the principles for reform.[24] In particular, these principles were both theological (e.g., the primacy of the paschal mystery, the mystery of Christ's dying and rising, SC 5–8) and practical. These latter include the full, conscious, active participation of all the faithful (14); that ministers should do everything but only those things that pertain to their ministry (28)—this is especially concerned with changing the law that the priest must recite every text of the Mass, even if someone else says it (for instance, if the choir would sing the Gloria, the priest would still recite it); that the vernacular could be used in the celebration (36); that Scripture should be a part of every liturgical celebration (24, 35); and that the liturgy should be adapted to the culture of the various peoples (37–40).

One of the emphases of the constitution was on the role of the signs used in celebrations. For instance, "In the liturgy, by means of signs perceptible to the senses, human sanctification is signified and brought about in ways proper to each of these signs" (7). The liturgical rites are to be reformed, in part, in order that "they express more clearly the holy things they signify" (21). The sacraments, because they are signs, instruct. "They not only presuppose faith, but by words and objects they also nourish, strengthen and express it" (59).[25]

The bishops at the council made some specific provisions for the celebration of baptism. They continued to distinguish two separate circumstances: the baptism of adults and the baptism of children. They first called for the restoration of the catechumenate in distinct steps. Since the Congregation of Rites had just issued a revised rite for the baptism of adults in stages, something more, clearly, was meant by the conciliar mandate than simply dividing the ritual in yet another way. The concern was that the period of the catechumenate: "which is intended as a period of well-suited instruction, may be sanctified by sacred rites to be celebrated at successive internals of time" (64). The bishops went on to say that initiatory rituals from mission lands could be incorporated into the new rites, as long as they conformed to the concerns about adaptation presented in SC 37–40 (65). They further stipulated that both the simpler and the solemn forms of baptism must be revised to take into account the time of the catechumenate. Hence, the reform was to be not simply window dressing but a thorough rethinking and revising of the rites so that the catechetical concerns and needs of the catechumenate were taken into account (66).

In addition to the adult rite, the children's rite was also to be revised. One of the underlying principles of the reform was that the rites work through the signs themselves. Things that had crept in or been retained that did not clearly express the meaning of the rites were to be eliminated or changed (62). Hence, the Rite of Baptism for Children, which was for the most part the rite of baptizing a catechumen in danger of death and in which the godparents simply answered on behalf of the children, was now to be revised so that it is clear that children are being baptized (67). The bishops asked that certain pastoral adaptations be built into the new rite. There should be a special rite when a very large number are to be baptized. There should be a rite for catechists to use, especially in mission countries where there are not enough priests. New rites should be drawn up to supply ceremonies for a child baptized in danger of death and for the welcoming of an already baptized Christian into full communion in the Roman Catholic Church (68–69). Finally, the bishops required that new water be blessed for each celebration of baptism outside the Easter season (70). This would avoid the problem of water (mixed with chrism) being kept for the whole year between Easters, turning moldy and smelly as the year wore on.[26]

The rest of this chapter will focus on the rite for adults. Chapter 2 will offer an account of the rite for children.

The Post–Vatican II Rite (1972): An Overview of the Introduction and of the Overall Structure

Pope Paul VI quickly moved to implement the will of the council fathers. On January 25, 1964, he issued a *motu proprio* establishing a special commission (called the Consilium) for the implementation of the Constitution on the Sacred Liturgy.[27] Two groups of experts began work on the new Rite of Christian Initiation of Adults (RCIA) in September 1965. In 1966, a draft was ready for experimental use and was introduced in a number of countries. A new draft was prepared in 1969 in the light of the comments made by those who had used the experimental version. Further discussion with the Congregation for the Doctrine of the Faith followed, and the final version of the Rite of Christian Initiation of Adults was promulgated on January 6, 1972.[28]

The first English translation of the Latin text came out in 1974. The bishops of the United States approved it for interim use. After a decade of experience with the texts and rituals, a revised edition was prepared and published in 1988. This edition incorporated not only changes in the pastoral ordering of the ritual but also some particular prayers and rites for use in the United States. The Code of Canon Law had been issued in a new edition in 1983 and certain changes were made in the rite based on the new law. The commentary that follows uses the 1988 version for the United States.[29]

The basic structure of the celebration of the Rite of Christian Initiation of Adults is a series of "periods" and "steps." The image of "steps" implies a journey along the path of conversion to Christ, leading someone from life outside the Church to one inside, becoming a member. The "periods" are lengths of time during which the one seeking faith comes to a deeper and deeper relationship with the Lord. The "steps" are liturgical events in which the person moves from one way of being in the Church to another. The pattern looks like this:

Rite of Christian Initiation of Adults

First Period: Evangelization and Precatechumenate (over an indeterminate time)

First Step: Acceptance into the Order of Catechumens (celebrated at any time)

Second Period: Catechumenate (perhaps several years)

Second Step: Rite of Election or Enrollment of Names (celebrated on the First Sunday of Lent)

Third Period: Purification and Enlightenment (Season of Lent)

Third Step: Celebration of the Sacraments of Initiation (celebrated at the Easter Vigil)

Fourth Period: Postbaptismal Catechesis or Mystagogy (Easter Season and beyond)

This bare-bones outline can only give a hint of the richness contained in this process of conversion and coming to faith in Christ Jesus. In the sections that follow, we will explore the steps and the various rites celebrated during the periods to discover how the Church structures the ongoing encounter with God in Christ in the community of the Church.[30]

The Rite of Acceptance into the Order of Catechumens

Overall Shape: From Outside the Church to Inside (A First Reading)

The rite of becoming a catechumen takes place when someone who has felt called by Christ and has begun to inquire about him and his

Church finally decides that the time has come to act on the call. The pastor and others involved with the inquiry sessions in the parish help the person discern their readiness to take the step of formally entering the community of believers in Jesus Christ in the Catholic Church. The criteria are found in the ritual:

> The prerequisite for making this first step is that the beginnings of the spiritual life and the fundamentals of Christian teaching have taken root in the candidates. Thus there must be evidence of the first faith that was conceived during the period of evangelization and precatechumenate and of an initial conversion and intention to change their lives and to enter into a relationship with God in Christ. Consequently, there must also be evidence of the first stirrings of repentance, a start to the practice of calling upon God in prayer, a sense of the church, and some experience of the company and spirit of Christians through contact with a priest or with members of the community. (RCIA 42)

The basic structure of the Rite of Acceptance into the Order of Catechumens is a journey. Someone comes to the Church and is admitted into it. This occurs literally. The rite falls in three main sections: first, the receiving of the candidates at the door of the church where they accept the Gospel for the first time and receive signing with the cross, the mark of salvation in Christ. Next, they go into the body of the church for the first time as those who have taken on this sign of Christ in order to hear the Word of God proclaimed. Finally, the candidates are sent forth to continue the journey. The basic movement of the rite is: being outside the church, accepting the Gospel and being signed with the cross, entering the church and hearing the Word of God proclaimed, and returning to the world. Here is a complete outline of the rite:

Rite of Acceptance into the Order of Catechumens (nn. 48–74)

Receiving the candidates at the door of the church

    A greeting

    An opening dialogue between the celebrant and the candidates

    Candidates' first acceptance of the Gospel

    Affirmation by the sponsors and the assembly

    Signing of the candidates with the cross

    Concluding prayer

Invitation to the celebration of the Word of God

Liturgy of the Word

Introduction of the Word

The readings themselves, with psalms and acclamations

A homily

Presentation of a Bible to the catechumens (optional)

Intercessions for the catechumens

Prayer over the catechumens

Dismissal of the catechumens

A Second Reading

Who Are the Actors?

Telling the sequence of events does not exhaust the meaning of the signs and symbols of the ceremony. The first symbol of the Rite of Acceptance is the persons involved. Since this is a celebration of a first entrance into the community of the Church, the various actors are crucial to understanding the rite.

Inquirers

It is during this ceremony that inquirers become catechumens and begin their formal membership, even if not complete, in the Church. Their gathering outside the church, their first acceptance of the Gospel and receiving of the sign of the cross on their bodies, the invitation to hear God's Word proclaimed in the church, and being sent forth at the end is the heart of the celebration.

Sponsors

No one can come into the Church unless someone who is already a member stands as his or her sponsor. Throughout the time of the catechumenate, the sponsor will walk with those coming to faith, answer questions, explain various aspects of the faith, and simply be there for them. They can serve as a catalyst for the dynamics of conversion that are taking place.

The Faithful

The faithful followers of Christ constitute his body in the world. The catechumens feel a call to membership in that same body. Hence, the current members are duty-bound to participate in the process of welcoming new members. In this very act, the community will find its own faith articulated anew and challenged to grow.

Celebrant

The celebrant, whether a priest, deacon, or catechist, represents the local Church of the diocese. He takes the lead in the dialogues and the signing, gives the homily, and leads the prayers. In this role he offers cohesion and legitimacy to the proceedings.

Others: Readers, Cantors

Other ministers serve principally in the celebration of the Liturgy of the Word. They share their faith in the proclamation of the Word of God and in leading the response to the reading in the psalm. Their principal task is to help those gathered to experience the presence of God in the Word through their work.

What Do They Do?

Gather at the Door

Doors are powerful symbols, not just practical forms of passage and security. A closed door speaks of shutting out and shutting in while an open door welcomes and allows passage. Gathering at the door implies the start of a movement and transition—from outside to in, from exclusion to inclusion (or vice versa!). Other rituals include stations at the door: marriages, funerals, dedicating a church. In each of these cases, a significant transition is enacted: from single life to married life, from life to death to eternal life, from profane to sacred.

The symbolism of doors can be instructive for reaching some of the richness of this moment. Doors are barriers and places of ingress and egress. Doors are solid yet permeable. Doors have locks to close them tight and hinges that allow them to swing freely. Doors shut out and hold in. They exclude and contain. All this reality is also symbolized in this celebration. The rite is an encounter with the reality contained within the doors: the manifold presence of Christ, in gathered assembly, proclaimed Word, priestly minister, eucharistic species (See SC 7; Paul VI's encyclical *Mysterium Fidei*, 34–45). The door is the way that those gathered leave to love and serve the Lord as met in the hungry and thirsty, the sick and imprisoned (see Matt 25).

Sign the Inquirers with the Cross

This second major element of the action of the rite has two major foci: touch and the sign of the cross. The minister touches each inquirer, at least on their forehead, but also, optionally, on each of their senses. When one enters Christ, Christ's Body, the Church, one does so completely and bodily. No aspect of one's person is left out. The forehead is prominent, a place that everyone can see. The early Christians thought of this signing as a kind of branding, like a slave would be branded as the property of a master, or a soldier would be branded as sign of service to the emperor. Christians were branded as belonging to Christ (see Tertullian). Also signed are the other senses: ears, eyes, lips, breast, shoulders, hands, feet. It is not just what one thinks that is bound to Christ, but all that one senses, experiences, feels, does. This ceremony speaks of complete adherence to Christ.

The second focus of this action is the sign of the cross. When the senses are touched, it is with the sign of the cross. This sign is a fundamental way to speak of Christ. In the earliest days of the Church, it may have been the first letter of Christ's name, the Greek letter *chi*, X. Hence, one was marked with Christ's name, meaning that one was joined to Christ. Later, in the Middle Ages, the symbol became associated with Christ's death. Here the emphasis is Pauline: we have been crucified with Christ so that we might be raised with him (Rom 6:3-11; Gal 2:20). The touching of all the senses with the cross speaks of the totality with which we enter Christ: total self-gift to the point of dying and rising. This step of entering the Order of Catechumens in not one lightly taken!

Enter the Church

After gathering at the door and receiving the sign of the cross on their senses, the catechumens (for that is what they now are after the ceremony at the door) finally cross the threshold of the church. The door that had kept them out and marked their status as outsiders now becomes the way to inclusion and participation. All move to take their places in the church in order to hear the Word of God. They enter to encounter Christ in his Word.

Hear the Word Proclaimed

We will explore the various Scripture passages in the second part of the book. Here we will briefly examine the dynamics of the proclamation of the Word. This is a verbal experience, but it is instructive to look at the actions that are part of the ritual.

Rite of Becoming a Catechumen—Liturgy of the Word (nn. 61–67)

Reading I: Genesis 12:1-4a

Responsorial psalm: Psalm 33

Verse before the gospel

Gospel: John 1:35-42

Homily

Intercessions for the catechumens

Prayer over the catechumens

There is a threefold dynamic to the Liturgy of the Word, this particular one or any Liturgy of the Word. First, a reader proclaims the Word to the assembly. God speaks to his people. Second, the assembly listens to the Word proclaimed and reflects on it in silence. Third, the assembly responds in the song of the psalm and in prayer to what it has heard.

Are Dismissed

These new catechumens are no longer who they had been. They are now signed by Christ's cross and have begun the process of ongoing encounter with Christ in his Word. But they are not yet full members of Christ. For that reason, they do not remain when the community celebrates the Eucharist. Rather, they go out and continue their study and their living under the guidance of their catechists and sponsors. In time they will be ready for the fullness of membership in Christ.

Significance of the Rite

Like all rituals in the Catholic Church, the Acceptance into the Order of Catechumens takes place *in medias res*. The inquirers have already begun to cooperate with God's grace in their life before they make their first contact with the parish. They have already had some experience of Christ that has attracted them to the community, whether that contact was someone already a member, or God's Word, or the movement of the Spirit within them. Contact with the Church and membership in Christ do not begin in the ceremony. Rather, what has already begun is ratified and intensified. The relationship reaches a new and now formal and external level. Now they have changed from being inquirers, those on the outside seeking to understand what is inside, to catechumens, those who are instructed.

To celebrate their acceptance as catechumens, inquirers must have made some progress: they must know enough about Christ and the Christian community to want to start the process. They must see that their lives are more and more in conformity with Christian standards and values. They must want to change, to conform themselves to Christ and be members of his Body, the Church. They must have begun a prayer life. They must know some members of the community. In other words, their inquiry and their contact with the Gospel must have an effect on them and the way they lead their lives.

Then the gathering at the door, being signed with the cross, entering the church, and hearing the Word can be seen, not as something they have never done before, but as naming and then deepening what has already begun.

Excursus: The Rites during the Period of the Catechumenate

The period of the catechumenate is key for the growing life of faith. The RCIA lays out four types of catechesis—or instruction, formation—that must mark the period (75):

- learning in gradual and complete instruction the teachings and norms of the Church, grounded in the Scriptures and leading toward a deeper participation in the mystery of salvation in Christ
- starting to live the Christian way of life in the midst of the community of believers
- participating in liturgical rites aimed to help the catechumens in their learning and life

- living out the implications of what they are learning, living, celebrating, and praying in acts of charity and in witnessing to their
faith in everyday life

In this section, we will explore the rites that are designed to help the
catechumens in the process of their instruction: blessings and exorcisms.
Again, we are interested in the overall shape of the celebrations and the
symbolic, nonverbal expression that makes up the ritual. The RCIA
gives the following as a basic outline for a celebration during the period
of the catechumenate:

Period of the Catechumenate—Celebration of the Word (nn. 81–89)

Song

Readings and responsorial psalms

Homily

Concluding rites

[Minor exorcism or anointing]

Blessing

When Is It Celebrated?

These celebrations of the Word can be celebrated whenever the catechumens gather. They can be part of every catechetical session and they
can be part of gatherings that take place on Sunday, after the Liturgy
of the Word, when the catechumens are dismissed from the Sunday
assembly. These celebrations play an important part in the ongoing fa-
miliarization of the catechumens with God's Word, and especially with
God's Word as a reality that is proclaimed. Here we have a reminder that
the Word of God is not primarily words studied in a book but rather
a living conversation that takes place in community, demanding to be
heard, reflected upon, and responded to.

Where Is It Celebrated?

These celebrations of the Word are celebrated wherever the catechumens gather: in homes, in the rectory, in the catechumenon of the church
(the space set aside for ongoing catechesis within the church building).

Who Are the Actors?

The chief actors are the catechumens, the catechists, and the sponsors, that is, all who are present for the catechumenal sessions. The leadership of the liturgy would normally be taken by the priest or deacon present, or by the catechist. There might also be a cantor to lead the responsorial psalm and the opening song. These liturgies would also follow the principle articulated in the Constitution on the Sacred Liturgy that ministers do everything but only those things associated with their ministry. Hence the leaders lead and the cantors sing.

What Do They Do?

There are three major components to these celebrations of the Word. First, there is the proclamation of the Word. This shares in the comments we made above about the role of the Word in the life of catechumens, and in fact of all Christians.

Second, there is the imposition of hands. This takes two forms. During the minor exorcism and during the blessing, the priest, deacon, or catechist extends hands over the catechumens while saying the prayer. For minor exorcisms, the catechumens kneel, a sign of their ongoing conversion and willingness to submit to the power of God rather than the power of the world. After the blessing, a second form of imposition of hands takes place: the presider places his hands on the head of each of the catechumens as a sign of the invocation of God's power and the Holy Spirit.

The gesture of imposing hands, either extended over a group or placed on an individual's head, is full of meaning. When touch is involved, there is a certain intimacy to the gesture. It shares a world with parents soothing a fevered brow or calming an overactive or distraught child. It is similar to the hand on a shoulder giving impetus to an action or handing over a responsibility. In the next section, when we explore the verbal dimensions of the sacrament of baptism, we will see how the prayers of blessing and prayers of exorcism give specificity to the inchoate emotional content of the laying on of hands.

When the imposition of hands is general, the gesture seems to have two possible meanings. It can be an invocation, a calling down on those gathered, usually of a power or force greater than them, such as the Holy Spirit. It can also be seen as a ritual embrace of the whole group within the family of believers gathered. The interpretation depends on the broadness of the gesture and the size of the group gathered. The smaller the group, the more intimate the nature of the gesture; the larger the group, the broader the gesture.

The anointing of the catechumens is a rich symbol. Part of its meaning is contained in the words that are spoken, first when the oil is blessed and then when the oil is applied. We will simply reflect here for a moment on the significance of applying oil, leaving the further interpretation to the next section of the book. Oil is a fruit of the earth, cultivated from olive trees, gathered, crushed, often filtered, and then used for a variety of purposes. It can burn to give light, function as a soap to lift off grime and dirt, soothe wounds and burns, and help tone an athlete for competition or help in the rubdown afterward. Mixed with aromas it can serve as a perfume. It is a food, helping to cook and to dress various things to eat. The natural product of the olive tree is one of the most common and most symbolic elements used in the liturgy of the Church: anointing catechumens, anointing the sick, anointing the newly baptized, anointing those to be confirmed, anointing priests' hands and bishops' heads, anointing altars and the walls of new churches. It speaks of healing, cleansing, and consecrating, depending on the kind of oil used.

In this particular ceremony, as a rite within the catechetical sessions and the Liturgy of the Word that is part of it, the anointing speaks of the slow process of cleansing motives, of strengthening for the competition being fought between the values of the Gospel and the values espoused by the world. The use of oil invokes the sense of touch again, as at the signing with the cross at the rite of becoming a catechumen. The catechumen is anointed by a priest or deacon on the breast, the place of the heart, where strength resides (symbolically), or on the hands, the instruments of action, where mind and body come together to accomplish the desires of the person. The anointing is celebrated when it is deemed "beneficial or desirable" (98).

We will discuss the further implications of this anointing in the next section, but only touch briefly on the nonverbal symbolization here.

Significance of the Rite

This rite celebrated throughout the catechumenate provides a context for what is happening. The four types of catechesis laid out in RCIA 75 are summarized and symbolized in this celebration. The proclamation, hearing, and responding to the Word of God ritualizes all the learning taking place in the various catechetical sessions, whether during the week or on Sunday. The prayers enable the catechumen to develop a vocabulary for calling on God for help in adversity and in thanksgiving for God's love and presence. The homily helps the catechumen apply the Word of God to life, in prayer and action. The minor exorcisms, blessings, and anointing symbolize the struggle to put what is learned into practice.

The Rite of Election

Overall Shape: Elected for Baptism (A First Reading)

The Rite of Election is the second major step in the process of becoming a Christian. It takes place at another key moment of discernment, when the catechumen is ready to begin final preparation for entrance into the Christian community. The RCIA again offers criteria to help make sure that the catechumen has reached this point of readiness.

> Before the rite of election is celebrated, the catechumens are expected to have undergone a conversion in mind and in action and to have developed a sufficient acquaintance with Christian teaching as well as a spirit of faith and charity. With deliberate will and an enlightened faith they must have the intention to receive the sacraments of the Church, a resolve they will express publicly in the actual celebration of the rite (120).

The basic structure of the Rite of Election or Enrollment of Names is simply a formalizing of the call the catechumens are receiving to plunge deeper into the relationship with Christ in the Church. It is a call that they feel internally, but it is also a call that comes from the community of believers. Christ called his followers. They responded to the call they heard. The Rite of Election is part of the call. Fittingly, it normally takes place on the First Sunday of Lent, the season of discipline and conversion for Christians. Here is the outline:

Rite of Election or Enrollment of Names (nn. 129–37)

Liturgy of the Word

Homily

Presentation of the catechumens

Affirmation by the godparents [and the assembly]

Invitation and enrollment of names

Act of admission or election

Intercessions for the elect

Prayer over the elect

Dismissal of the elect

[*Liturgy of the Eucharist*]

A Second Reading

When Is It Celebrated? First Sunday of Lent

One of the changes mandated by the bishops at the Second Vatican Council was that the season of Lent should have a twofold character instead of the rather single-minded emphasis on personal penance that had characterized it in the years previous. They directed that the season be marked both by baptismal and penitential themes, with the aim of celebrating Easter with minds and hearts renewed. Both the sacraments of baptism and penance are about conversion, the process of turning the direction of our lives to God in Christ with the Holy Spirit. It makes sense, then, that the season of Lent be the final intense period of preparation for the celebration of the sacraments of initiation. The First Sunday of Lent ushers in the period and sets the tone for all that follows.

Where Is It Celebrated? The Cathedral Church of the Diocese

The usual place for the celebration of the Rite of Election is the diocesan cathedral, the head church of the local community of believers. This is the bishop's own church and the site for the most important liturgies, especially ordinations and key moments in the life of the local Church community. The name "cathedral" comes from the fact that central to the design of the building is the bishop's chair (in Latin, *cathedra*) where he presides over the liturgies held in the cathedral and, symbolically, over the life of the diocese.

That the Rite of Election normally takes place in the cathedral is a reminder that there are few things more important to the life of the community than the calling of new members. Growth is the most important sign of life for any organism and the Body of Christ is no different. The Rite of Election is a chance for the bishop to underline this importance and hold it forth for the whole community of believers in the local community.

Who Are the Actors?

Once again the primary focus of this rite is the people involved. It calls people by name and gives this action a formal ratification by entering the names in a book. This rite has diocesan import, and so the bishop presides.

Catechumens

The catechumens are now close to the end of their period of preparation. Those responsible for their formation have determined that they are ready for the final stages of the process. During the ceremony they progress from being catechumens to being elect. They are called by name and take on a new role in the community.

Godparents

In this rite we meet godparents for the first time. They can be the same persons as the sponsors but usually are not. The godparent accompanies the elect throughout the scrutinies celebrated during the season of Lent and at the celebration of the sacraments at the Easter Vigil. Godparents are chosen by the catechumens (sponsors can be, but can also be chosen by the ministers of the parish): "It is a very ancient custom of the Church that adults are not admitted to baptism without godparents, members of the Christian community who will assist the candidates at least in the final preparation for baptism and after baptism will help them persevere in the faith and in their lives as Christians" (Christian Initiation: General Introduction [CIGI] 8). This role is crucial and begins to take on particular import from this celebration on.

The Faithful

Since the elect are becoming members of a particular community of faith, it is important that members of that community be present at the various celebrations. The rite makes provision for those gathered to give their affirmation to the process and to stake a claim in the ongoing formation of the new members.

Other Ministers

The role of the bishop was discussed above when we spoke about the cathedral as the site of the celebration of the Rite of Election. Others involved can be readers, cantors, representatives of the various parishes who present the catechumens to the bishop, and those who help with the enrollment of names.

What Do They Do?

The basic rite is very simple. Those who are ready are called by name and have their names written in the Book of the Elect.

Called by Name, Called by the Bishop

The calling takes place in two steps. First of all, the names of the catechumens are called out one by one. (There are some provisions for adapting this if the numbers are very large, but it is clear that at some point, either at this ceremony in the cathedral or at the home parish previously, the individual names of the catechumens are to be called out loud.) When their names are called, they gather before the bishop with their godparents. By this action it is clear that they are called out from among the others gathered for some special notice. They are accompanied by some who are already full members of the community.

The bishop engages the godparents and possibly the rest of the assembly in dialogue ascertaining ritually that the candidates are ready for this next step.

Finally, the bishop, acting on behalf of the whole Church, calls these catechumens to enroll their names. The call comes to each person individually but also through the Church.

Write Names in a Book

The second main action of the Rite of Election is the writing of the names in the Book of the Elect. Usually, the parish has its own book. If there are many catechumens, sometimes the names have already been written and the books are simply presented to the bishop at this time.

Clearly, though, the rite sees the enrolling of names as pivotal in the celebration. It gives the naming a sense of permanence. The names are not just called to vanish in the air but are now inscribed in a book for permanent remembrance. This is a major step in the process.

Significance of the Rite

The basic meaning of this rite is contained in its name: Rite of Election or Enrollment of Names. The catechumens have progressed far enough in their Christian life, in learning doctrine, in the ability to pray, in immersion in liturgy, in living the mission of Christ, that their interior call is ratified by the whole community. The bishop declares that, given the testimony of those who know them, God elects them—chooses them—for final preparation. Their commitment has been judged sufficient for these newly elect to be entrusted with the most important documents of Christian life: the Creed and the Lord's Prayer. They are ready for a final, intense push in their formation, ready for the scrutinies.

Excursus: The Rites during the Period of Enlightenment

The season of Lent is marked by special liturgical celebrations for the elect. They undergo three major public scrutinies, when they are aided by the whole assembly in their movement from a life rooted in the world to a life rooted in Christ. They receive the Creed and the Lord's Prayer, the statements that summarized belief and spirituality for a follower of Jesus, from the community of believers. Finally, on Holy Saturday morning, they are anointed with the oil of catechumens and participate in the ceremony called the Ephphetha, an Aramaic word used by Jesus when he healed a man who was deaf and had a speech impediment.

Scrutinies

The scrutinies take place during the parish Mass on the Third, Fourth, and Fifth Sundays of Lent. They all follow the same structure.

Order of the Scrutinies (nn. 150–56)

Liturgy of the Word

Readings (of the Third, Fourth, and Fifth Sundays of Lent, Year A of the Lectionary)

Homily

Invitation to prayer (the elect kneel or bow their heads)

Intercessions for the elect (godparents place their right hands on the elects' shoulders)

Exorcism (in two parts, with an imposition of hands)

Dismissal of the elect

Liturgy of the Eucharist

Structurally, the main intent of the scrutinies is to sustain the elect in their final prayerful preparation for the celebration of the sacraments of initiation at the Easter Vigil. The "exorcism" is a prayer that prays for the elect to be loosed from the forces of sin and division and joined more closely to Christ. The specific themes of the prayers are taken from the readings and will be studied in the second section.

The first noticeable gesture is that the elect kneel for the intercessions and prayer. This is a gesture that speaks of their submission to the power of the Lord in helping them rid their lives of forces other than that of God. Kneeling is a type of bow and indicates humility. It is a form of acceptance of the prayers of the community and a recognition of need. At the same time, the godparents place their right hands on the shoulders of the elect. They are not alone as they undergo this experience of weakness and need. The whole Christian community, in the person of the godparents, accompanies the elect in their journey.

The gesture of the imposition of hands is used again in this rite. We find first an individual imposition of hands on each of the elect done by the presider (the Latin text specifies that this imposition be done in silence) and then a general imposition of hands done by the presider over all the elect during the prayer. Again, there is a sense of invocation of the Holy Spirit and the desire to pour God's mercy and grace on these elect, to gather them into the community of believers.

Presentations

Two key Christian texts are presented to the elect. During the third week of Lent the elect receive the Creed and during the fifth week the

Lord's Prayer. These summarize what a Christian believes and how a Christian prays.

Order of the Presentations

Presentation of the Creed (nn. 157–63)

Liturgy of the Word

Readings

Homily

Presentation of the Creed (Apostles' or Nicene)

Prayer over the elect

Dismissal of the elect

Presentation of the Lord's Prayer (nn. 178–84)

Liturgy of the Word

Readings

Gospel reading (Lord's Prayer)

Homily

Prayer over the elect

Dismissal of the elect

Ritually, two things seem important. First, there is no provision that any sort of written document be handed to the elect. Both the presentation of the Creed and the presentation of the Lord's Prayer are conceived as oral actions, involving speaking and listening, rather than the conveyance of a document, like the giving of a deed. This seems to highlight the interpersonal character of the exchange rather than its formality.

Second, there is a general imposition of hands during the prayer over the elect, sharing the same meaning that we have seen above.

Holy Saturday Morning: Recitation of the Creed and the Ephphetha

On Holy Saturday morning there is an opportunity for a final set of preparations, a final morning retreat prior to the celebration later in the night. The rite unfolds this way:

Holy Saturday Preparatory Rites (nn. 193–205)

Song

Greeting

Reading of the Word of God

Homily

Ephphetha

Prayer before the recitation of the Creed

Recitation of the Creed

Concluding rites

Ritually, this celebration is a way to mark the day as a special one and to give the elect a chance to gather one last time to reflect on what they are about to undertake. In the Ephphetha, the celebrant touches the ears and the lips of the elect, following the actions of Jesus. This forms an *inclusio* with the Rite of Becoming a Catechumen, a final signing of the senses that have played so important a role in this process of coming to Christ: hearing his Word and sharing it with others. It also is a preparation for the hearing and eating and drinking that will take place later that night.

The recitation of the Creed is a rehearsal for the formal recitation that will take place immediately prior to baptism during the night vigil.

The blessing at the conclusion makes provision, as one has now come to expect, for the imposition of hands over the elect. This constant invocation of God's power over the elect is an ongoing reminder that we are in need of God's presence and grace to make progress in the Christian life.

The Celebration of Baptism

*Overall Shape (A First Reading): Light, Word, Initiation
(Baptism and Confirmation), Eucharist, Sent Forth (Mystagogy)*

The liturgy of the Easter Vigil is probably the most complicated liturgy celebrated in parish churches during the year. It is a rich juxtaposition of symbols. Here is the general outline:

Easter Vigil (nn. 218–43)

Ceremony of light

Blessing of the new fire

Lighting of the paschal candle

Procession into church

Singing of the Easter proclamation

Liturgy of the Word

Three to seven readings from the Old Testament, each with responsorial psalm, silence, and a prayer

New Testament reading

Gospel acclamation (singing of the Easter "Alleluia")

Gospel

Homily

Celebration of the sacraments of initiation

Celebration of baptism

Presentation of the candidates

Litany of Saints

Prayer over the Water

Profession of faith

• Renunciation of sin

• Profession of faith

Baptism

Explanatory rites

• Clothing with a baptismal garment

• Presentation of a lighted candle

Celebration of confirmation

Invitation

Laying on of hands

Anointing with chrism

Renewal of the baptismal promises (at the Easter Vigil)

Liturgy of the Eucharist

What we note about the overall structure is that it summarizes the process of initiation. The ceremony of light ritualizes the dynamic of God's revelation coming to those gathered and the response of those who have seen God's light.

The Liturgy of the Word this night gathers together all salvation history and situates the assembly within the overarching trajectory of God's plan for his creatures. The dynamics of proclamation, response, silence, and prayer give a taste of much of the catechumenal experience: attentiveness to God's Word and our response in both word and prayer (and eventually action).

That ritualization of the catechumenate continues in the celebration of baptism. The procession to the font with the singing of the Litany of the Saints reminds us that we are not acting alone and that the community that has an investment in this act is not simply the one gathered. It involves the whole local Church (diocese) through the presence of those called by the bishop (the elect) and the bishop's delegate (the presiding priest). The prayer over the water takes up the themes of the readings and reminds us that God is acting now as he has done in the past. The renunciation of sin and profession of faith ritualize the process of conversion that has been taking place throughout the catechumenate, especially in the period of purification and enlightenment. It is the whole purpose of Lent. The central action is the immersion of the elect in water while invoking the triune name of God. The explanatory rites spell out some of the further meaning of the rite: new clothes, a lighted candle. The celebration of confirmation seals the action in the Holy Spirit. The whole community renews its own baptism with the profession of faith and the sprinkling with the baptismal water. Then all the newly baptized join the rest of the community of believers for the first time in the eucharistic banquet. The sacrifice it represents calls to mind that baptism is a dying with Christ in order to rise with him in glory. The table is the culmination of the whole process: from door, to Word, to font (understood as both womb and tomb), to altar/table, a journey of conversion that leads ultimately to Christ.

When Is It Celebrated? The Easter Vigil

The celebration of the Easter Vigil is to take place during the night between Holy Saturday and Easter Sunday, after fall of dark and before sunrise. It is a vigil, a protracted time in prayer for watching and waiting.

It reminds the community of the story of the wise and foolish virgins who were called to watch for the coming of the master (Matt 25:1-13). We too receive that call to watch and wait. The whole community gathers in this nighttime experience of remembering and praying.

Where Is It Celebrated? Parish Church (Out of Doors, Ambo, Font, Altar)

This liturgy has several spatial focal points. It begins outside around a large fire. It moves to the body of the church and the ambo (the lectern) for the Liturgy of the Word. The baptismal font serves as the center for the next part of the liturgy. The Vigil finds its culmination when the community gathers around the altar to receive the nourishment of the Body and Blood of the risen Lord.

Who Celebrates?

The Faithful

The Easter Vigil is the most important liturgical celebration of the whole year. The faithful join together to renew their participation in the dying and rising of Christ. The local community of believers does not exhaust the reality of the Church, of course. They represent here and now the whole Church gathered in the dark throughout the world to remember and experience the reality of Christ's dying and rising.

Elect

The elect are the primary subjects of the action. After months, perhaps years, of preparation, they now go through the final actions of transition from outside to inside, a transition that began at the doors of the church when they were admitted to the Order of Catechumens. Tonight they experience fire and water as the means by which they join Christ.

Godparents

The godparents accompanied the elect through the scrutinies and presentations. Now they support them through the final moments of their journey. They stand by them and finally welcome them into the fellowship of believers, walking at their side and sharing the eucharistic banquet with them.

Celebrant

The celebrant leads the whole community in its entrance into the mystery of God's plan for us in Christ. Blessing the fire, lighting the candle, listening to God's Word and unfolding its import for those gathered, bringing new members into the Body of Christ by water and chrism, presiding at the Lord's table—this series of ritual actions, led by the priest, in the power of the Holy Spirit, helps mold the community more and more into conformity with Christ.

Other Ministers (Readers, Cantors, Gift Bearers, Acolytes, Full Complement of Ministers)

This night is when the whole complement of parish ministers is visible: deacons, acolytes, readers, cantors, choir, ushers, greeters, and on and on. The complexity of the ritual demands many hands to make the work light. It requires the full diversity of ministry to reveal the richness of Christ's Body and to approximate the variety of needs served by the Church.

What Do They Do?

Light a Fire (Outside)

The community gathers around a blazing fire. The presider blesses the fire, prepares and lights the Easter candle, and inaugurates the procession into church with incense. The deacon leads the procession with the paschal candle. Three times he proclaims, "Christ our light!" All light their individual candles once in their places in church. The deacon, bathed in the light of the candles, sings praise to God for the gift of true light.

Hear the Word Proclaimed (Salvation history; Ambo)

The presider introduces the tour of salvation history. Readers and cantors lay out the main stories that shape our present. The readings and psalms (as we will see later) orient us to the font. The presider places the whole narrative within the context of prayer. The ambo, the place for proclaiming the Word, is the focal point of this section of the celebration.

Rite of Baptism (Font)

In the light of Christ and in the context of the stories of our forebears in the faith, we embark on the journey to union with God in Christ. It is so transforming a journey that it must be told in a variety of ways, with a variety of gestures and symbols.

Litany of Saints (procession to font). The assembly of believers gathers at the font. The movement from the place of hearing the Word to the place of baptism is done in solidarity with the whole Church, living and dead—the communion of saints. The litany invokes the names of those who have gone before, and its very structure (names called out by cantors, petition returned by the whole assembly) embodies a sense of community. This corporate movement and corporate prayer sets the context for the act of calling new members into the body of believers.

Blessing of water (touch, candle). When everyone has arrived at the font, the presider invites those present to pray over the water. He then embarks on a rehearsal of the events of salvation history that have just been proclaimed in the Liturgy of the Word. Here, however, they are not simply story, but living events now present. Historic water and present water merge to become the matrix for this act of new birth. At the moment of the invocation of the Holy Spirit upon the water, the presider can touch the water or plunge the Easter candle into it. The touch embodies the power and action of the Spirit. Plunging the candle intensifies this action, hinting at the fertility of the water through God's potent penetration. The assembly ratifies this prayer and action with its "Amen."

Profession of faith. This profession has two parts, both done in dialogue form. The first is the renunciation of sin, the second the profession of faith. In the ancient tradition (e.g., as described in the Mystagogical Catecheses), the renunciation was ritualized in several ways. The candidates would face the west and darkness and remove their old clothes. They would spit in that direction and renounce "the devil and all his works and all his pomps." Then they would turn toward the light, the east, and profess their faith and immediately be baptized in the very act of professing.

The current ritual eliminates the stripping off of the old and the physical gestures of renunciation (the spitting and the turning from the west's darkness to the light of the rising sun). Nevertheless, the dialogical character is maintained. This question and answer format is a clear reminder that this is a process of entry into a community. The one not yet a member must assure those already members that they know and understand the key requisites of belonging.

Baptism (immersing or pouring). The ritual gives two options for baptizing: immersion or infusion (pouring). Immersion means that the candidate goes into the water and has the water poured over him or her. Sometimes baptism is done by submersion, when the candidate goes completely under the water, though this is not as common. Infusion occurs when the candidates stay out of the water and simply have water poured over them, usually on their head.[31]

Baptism is performed by the minister and is not self-administered. One is brought into a community by those already members; one does not simply insert oneself into it.

This baptism is a threefold action with three immersions or three infusions. On one level this triple action gives the ceremony great dignity and solemnity. Theologically, it is interpreted in an trinitarian way and recognizes that baptism involves the newly baptized in the rich life of Father, Son, and Holy Spirit.

Explanatory rites. A rich array of rituals accompanies the water baptism. These actions express other dimensions of the process of joining Christ. Each has rich human overtones and a substantial scriptural background that give them layers of meaning.

• Possible anointing with chrism on the crown of the head

If confirmation is not celebrated (though it normally would be), the newly baptized are anointed with chrism on the crown of the head. Chrism, a blend of olive oil with perfume (usually balsam), is in human terms a cosmetic, designed to make someone attractive to another. The use of this perfume after stripping out of old clothes and washing in water speaks of personal preparation for meeting someone important.

That the anointing is on the crown of the head carries the symbolism further. Such grooming allows the scent to remain on the air. It marks the one perfumed as somehow set apart from others not so groomed. In biblical terms it speaks of consecration such as was done to priests, prophets, and kings. The person becomes an anointed one, sharing the life of "the Christ," the anointed one of God.

• White garment

The next task after bathing and grooming is to get dressed again. But the old clothes are no longer right. Only a new set of clothes will do. Hence, the newly baptized person dons a white garment, symbolizing newness and cleanness. Since it is anticipated that the newly baptized will be caught up in the excitement of the moment, the godparents help them into their new outfit. This help also reminds all involved that this new clothing is a uniform, the identifying garb of the Christian community, which longtime members now share with the newcomers.

• Lighted candle

The godparents continue their service to the newly baptized by presenting a candle lighted from the Easter candle, handed them by the presider. The candle serves several functions. It speaks of the festivity of the moment. As an object made up of wick, wax, and flame, it is dangerous and finite—it will only burn as long as there is fuel, yet in that time it can burn and harm. It also provides light, and light of a particular kind, warm and yellow, creating shadow yet also giving sharp definition to all it illumines. Since the candle is lighted from the Easter candle, it continues the fire that began the ceremony and unites the newly baptized holding it not only with the whole community that has gathered but also with Christ whose light it shares.

Confirmation

A significant change from the previous tradition enters the celebration at this point. The reformed Rite of Christian Initiation of Adults calls for the celebration of confirmation as a normal part of the process. That in itself is not new. The novelty is that the rite calls for doing it even when the bishop is not present; in the Western part of the Church, that is new. The Eastern Churches have had that custom for centuries, but the West had decided to celebrate confirmation only when the bishop was present. Now the decision is to keep the rites themselves intact: baptism, confirmation, and First Eucharist are the complete initiation of someone who enters the Body and the life of Christ. The bishop is present through the chrism consecrated by him at the chrism Mass. The rite is associated with baptism since it is to take place wherever the baptism does (n. 231).

Imposition of hands with prayer. Once again in confirmation we find the imposition of hands. The gesture is specifically linked to the invocation of the Holy Spirit upon the newly baptized. The New Testament and early tradition linked this gesture with the conferring of the gift of the Holy Spirit.

Anointing with chrism on forehead. This is a very different anointing from the one done on the crown of the head. Anointing on the crown invokes the image of oil poured over the head and dripping into the beard of Aaron (see Ps 133:2)—almost an immersion in oil. Anointing on the forehead presents the image of a branding, designating someone as specially set apart, tattooed, almost, with Christ. While the presider uses the oil to mark the forehead with the sign of the cross, the godparent stands behind the newly baptized with right hand on his or her shoulder. This gesture of support and solidarity reminds us that insiders (the godparents) are bringing the outsiders (the ones being confirmed) inside.

Sign of peace. The rite of confirmation ends with the sharing of the sign of peace. This is another gesture that has changed in the reform. During the Middle Ages, due to a theology of confirmation that saw it as creating a "soldier of Christ," the bishop would tap the newly confirmed on the cheek.[32] Now we return to the original gesture of the sign of peace,[33] a welcoming of the newly baptized and confirmed person into the community of faith.

Renewal of Baptismal Promises and Sprinkling with Baptismal Water for All

The revised rites of the Easter Vigil provide for the possibility of all those gathered to renew their own baptismal promises at this point. The presider leads them in the renunciation of sin and the profession of faith, the same promises made moments before by the newly initiated. Then the newly consecrated waters are used to bless the assembly. It is a gesture that concretizes the experience for all those who have participated.

Liturgy of the Eucharist (At the Altar)

The celebration of the Liturgy of the Eucharist is the culmination of all that has gone before. In fact, the whole point of the celebration has been to incorporate these new members into the eucharistic assembly of Christ's Body. For the first time the neophytes (those newly enlightened in baptism) participate in the prayer of the faithful.

Preparation of the altar and gifts. Some of the neophytes at least help to bring forward the gifts of bread and wine that will be used for the Eucharist.

Eucharistic prayer. For the first time they can join the whole community in the eucharistic prayer and experience it as their prayer, led on their behalf by the presider.

Communion rite. Communion under both the species of bread and of wine serves as the "climax of their initiation and center of the whole Christian life" (RCIA 243). This communion in the Body and Blood of Christ is the start of a life of communion with Christ, both in- and outside the liturgy.

Concluding rite. The neophytes are sent forth to love and serve the Lord (see Matt 25:31-46), to take up the life they have been preparing for.

Significance of the Rite

The celebration of baptism is the culmination of a lengthy, complex process. All that has come before is gathered up and rehearsed once more. The light of Christ, which had entered the life of the believer at some point, perhaps only as a small ray of insight or hope, has blazed forth in the night to banish darkness. The Word of God, revealing the depth and richness of God's plan for his people down through the centuries and millennia, has been proclaimed and revealed as also being God's Word and plan for us. Those new to the faith revealed their struggle by rejecting sin and professing faith. They were washed from sin, died to their old life and rose to life in Christ. They were clothed in Christ and received the charge to keep the flame of faith alive. The presence of the Holy Spirit in their lives was revealed by chrism and a welcome into the temple of the Spirit. They prayed as part of the priestly people, placed themselves on the altar with the gifts of bread and wine, and shared in Christ's Body and Blood fully in their First Holy Communion. They are sent into the world to continue their encounter with Christ in the hungry, thirsty, sick, and imprisoned.

Excursus: The Period of Mystagogy and the Demands of Christian Living

All that we have described to this point is simply the preparation and the start. The whole point of this process is to become a member of Christ's Body so as to live as Christ taught us: to love God and to love our neighbor as ourselves (see Matt 22:34-40; Luke 10:25-37).

The neophytes have some idea of what this life entails. They have studied and prayed for months and have begun to take on the form of

Christ. But with the celebration of the sacraments of initiation, they enter a new phase of life in Christ. The Order of Christian Initiation envisions a period of time in which the community remains particularly attentive to the new members to help them in their transition, and perhaps to help them if their initial enthusiasm starts to flag in the face of the daunting realities of living Christ in the world.

The particular shape of this period of mystagogy (the unfolding of the meaning of the mysteries that were celebrated at the Easter Vigil) includes the following:

- neophytes and faithful growing together
- meditation on the Gospel
- sharing in the Eucharist
- doing works of charity (RCIA 244)

In other words, they begin the daily routine of life in Christ. These tasks have as their goal the deepening of what has begun in the rites. The life in Christ is shared by old-timers and newly baptized together. Meditation on the Gospel allows the story of Christ to become more and more, not just the story of Christ from long ago, but also the story of the neophyte and the Christian community. The sharing in the Eucharist allows the neophyte to share in the experience of the disciples on the road to Emmaus: to feel the burning in their heart as they hear the word of Christ proclaimed and to recognize him in the breaking of the bread (Luke 24:13-35). Doing works of charity lives out another aspect of Christ's presence in their lives, namely, the presence in the poor and disadvantaged: "Lord, when was it that we saw you hungry and gave you food? . . . Truly I tell you, just as you did it to one of the least of these who are members of my family, you did it to me" (Matt 25:31-46, esp. vv. 37, 40).

The Sundays of the Easter season are designated as particularly appropriate for allowing the mystagogy to unfold in a formal way (RCIA 247). There should be a celebration that brings the period to a close (RCIA 249), and it is appropriate to celebrate the anniversary of baptism (RCIA 250). These markers, however, should not obscure the fact that in a sense the mystagogy never ends: The baptized never cease to uncover the fullness of the life that they have entered. It is a lifetime journey of discovery of the presence of Christ in their life and in the world.

Conclusion

In this chapter we have explored the shape of adult initiation. It is a complex and manifold shape. First there is the overall shape of the experience. Someone not yet a member of the community comes to faith and by a series of steps comes into communion with Christ in the Catholic Church. These steps take someone from the world outside the doors of the church to the altar and then back to the world, but now they are transformed and able to see the world as Christ's.

Within this overall shape, there is the shape of the individual celebrations: the Rite of Becoming a Catechumen, the blessings and exorcisms, the Rite of election, the scrutinies, the presentations, and the rite of celebrating the sacraments of initiation. Each of these celebrations enables the person coming to faith to take the next step in the process of coming to Christ: walking through the door, being placed in the protection of the cross, gaining strength for the journey, being chosen for baptism, baring the psyche for transformation, receiving the basic tools of the faith, and being welcomed to Christ and Christ's Body. This is a great journey, one that never ends.

Notes, Chapter One

[1] For example, see G. R. Beasley-Murray, *Baptism in the New Testament* (Grand Rapids, MI: Eerdmans, 1962); R. Schnakenburg, *Baptism in the Thought of St. Paul* (Oxford: Blackwell, 1964); Reginald H. Fuller, "Christian Initiation in the New Testament," in *Made, Not Born: New Perspectives on Christian Initiation and the Catechumenate*, Notre Dame Liturgical Studies (Notre Dame, IN: University of Notre Dame Press, 1976), 7–31; Adela Yarbro Collins, "The Origin of Christian Baptism," *Studia Liturgica* 19 (1989): 28–46, reprinted in Maxwell E. Johnson, *Living Water, Sealing Spirit: Readings on Christian Initiation* (Collegeville, MN: Liturgical Press, A Pueblo Book, 1995), 35–57; Gordon Lathrop, "Baptism in the New Testament and Its Cultural Settings," in *Worship and Culture in Dialogue: Reports of International Consultations, Cartigny, Switzerland, 1993, Hong Kong, 1994*, ed. S. Anita Stauffer (Geneva: Lutheran World Federation, 1994), 17–38; Kilian McDonnell and George

T. Montague, *Christian Initiation and Baptism in the Holy Spirit: Evidence from the First Eight Centuries* (Collegeville, MN: Liturgical Press, A Michael Glazier Book, 1991); Kilian McDonnell, *The Baptism of Jesus in the Jordan: The Trinitarian and Cosmic Order of Salvation* (Collegeville, MN: Liturgical Press, A Michael Glazier Book, 1996); Bryan D. Spinks, *Early and Medieval Rituals and Theologies of Baptism: From the New Testament to the Council of Trent* (Burlington, VT: Ashgate, 2006), 3–13. See the bibliography in Maxwell E. Johnson, *The Rites of Christian Initiation: Their Evolution and Interpretation*, Alcuin Club Collection 76 (Collegeville, MN: Liturgical Press, A Pueblo Book, 1999), 394–95. Johnson's revised edition (Collegeville, MN: Liturgical Press, A Pueblo Book, 2007) does not contain a separate bibliography, but consult his bibliography in the notes on pp. 1–40. There is a substantial bibliography in Bruno Kleinheyer, *Sakramentliche Feiern I: Die Feier der Eingliederung in die Kirche*, Gottesdienst der Kirche, Handbuch der Liturgiewissenschaft 7.1, ed. Hans Bernhard Meyer et al. (Regensburg: Pustet, 1989), 23–35. See also the treatment of Paul Turner, *Ages of Initiation: The First Two Christian Millennia* (Collegeville, MN: Liturgical Press, 2000), 1–3, and the corresponding sources and bibliography on the accompanying CD-ROM; Paul Turner, *The Hallelujah Highway: A History of the Catechumenate* (Chicago: Liturgy Training Publications, 2000), 3–13, 175.

[2] See Aidan Kavanagh, *The Shape of Baptism: The Rite of Christian Initiation*, vol. 1, Studies in the Reformed Rites of the Catholic Church (Collegeville, MN: Liturgical Press, A Pueblo Book, 1978), 16–23.

[3] For an overview of this period, see Robert Cabié, "The Origins of Christian Initiation (to the Middle of the Second Century)," in *The Sacraments*, vol. 3, *The Church at Prayer*, ed. A. G. Martimort (Collegeville, MN: Liturgical Press, 1988), 13–16; Kleinheyer, *Sakramentliche Feiern*, 35–56; Adrien Nocent, "Christian Initiation During the First Four Centuries," in *Sacraments and Sacramentals*, vol. 4, Handbook of Liturgical Studies, ed. Anscar J. Chupungco (Collegeville, MN: Liturgical Press, A Pueblo Book, 2000), 5–29; and Turner, *Ages*, 4–6, with the accompanying sources and commentary on CD-ROM.

[4] A handy compilation of patristic sources on baptism is Thomas M. Finn, *Early Christian Baptism and the Catechumenate: West and East Syria*, vol. 5, Message of the Fathers of the Church (Collegeville, MN: Liturgical Press, A Michael Glazier Book, 1992); and *Early Christian Baptism and the Catechumenate: Italy, North Africa, and Egypt*, vol. 6, Message of the Fathers of the Church (Collegeville, MN: Liturgical Press, A Michael Glazier Book, 1992). We will cite the books in this way: Finn, MFC + volume number, page number. The *Didache* can be found in Finn, MFC 5, 32–36. For some commentary, see Johnson, *Rites* (2007), 43–47; Kavanagh, *Shape*, 37–40; Turner, *Highway*, 14–16; Spinks, *Early and Medieval*, 14–16.

[5] Finn, MFC 6, 36–41. See especially I Apology 61 and 65. For commentary see Johnson, *Rites* (2007), 49–55; Kavanagh, *Shape*, 42–45; Turner, *Highway*, 17–21; Spinks, *Early and Medieval*, 25–28.

[6] Finn, MFC 6, 115–28, especially chapters 9 and 19. For commentary see Johnson, *Rites* (2007), 83–90; and Turner, *Highway*, 26–30; Spinks, *Early and Medieval*, 31–32.

[7] The original studies to recognize the "Egyptian Church Order" as the *Apostolic Tradition* of Hippolytus were those of Eduard Schwartz, *Über die pseudoapostolischen*

Kirchenordnungen, Schriften der wissenschaftlichen Gesellschaft in Strassburg 6 (Strassburg, 1910); and R. H. Connolly, *The So-Called Egyptian Church Order and Derived Documents*, Texts and Studies 8.4 (Cambridge, 1916). Bernard Botte, *La Tradition apostolique de Saint Hippolyte: Essai de reconstitution*, 5th ed., Liturgiewissenschaftliche Quellen und Forschungen 39 (Münster: Aschendorff, 1989) offers a substantial interpretive essay and an attempt to reconstruct the original text. Marcel Metzger, in three recent articles, "Nouvelles perspectives pour la prétendue Tradition apostolique," *Ecclesia Orans* 5 (1988): 241–59; Metzger, "Enquêtes autour de la prétendue Tradition apostolique," *Ecclesia Orans* 9 (1992): 7–36; and Metzger, "A propos des règlements écclesiastiques et de la prétendue Tradition apostolique," *Revue des sciences religieuses* 66 (1992): 249–61, raises some questions about naming a specific author for a document like the *Apostolic Tradition*, which is clearly compiled from a number of sources. Paul Bradshaw, in "Ancient Church Orders: A Continuing Enigma," in *The Search for the Origins of Christian Worship: Sources and Methods for the Study of Early Liturgy*, 2nd ed. (New York: Oxford University Press, 1992, 2002), 73–97, esp. 80–83; and "Redating the *Apostolic Tradition*: Some Preliminary Steps," in *Rule of Prayer, Rule of Faith: Essays in Honor of Aidan Kavanagh, O.S.B.*, ed. Nathan Mitchell and John F. Baldovin (Collegeville, MN: Liturgical Press, A Pueblo Book, 1996), 3–17, brings the questions of Metzger with several of his own to an English-speaking audience. See the arguments contained in Paul F. Bradshaw, Maxwell E. Johnson, and L. Edward Phillips, *The Apostolic Tradition: A Commentary*, ed. Harold W. Attridge (Minneapolis: Fortress, 2002), esp. 1–17. Alistair Stewart-Sykes, however, continues to affirm the authorship of Hippolytus of Rome: Hippolytus, *On the Apostolic Tradition: An English Version with Introduction and Commentary* by Alistair Stewart-Sykes, Popular Patristics Series 22 (Crestwood, NY: St. Vladimir's Seminary Press, 2001).

The question of authorship is crucial to ascertain the date and place of composition and especially of influence. If Hippolytus cannot be the author (or the compiler and editor), then the early third-century date and the Roman context cannot be presumed.

[8] Finn, MFC 6, 43–51. See commentaries in Johnson, *Rites* (2007), 96–110; Kavanagh, *Shape*, 54–64; Charles Whitaker, "Baptism," in *Essays on Hippolytus*, ed. Geoffrey J. Cuming, Grove Liturgical Study 15 (Bramcote, Nottinghamshire: Grove Books, 1978), 52–60; Turner, *Highway*, 36–43; Spinks, *Early and Medieval*, 28–31.

[9] Finn, MFC 5, 111–206. For commentary see Kavanagh, *Shape*, 40–42; Gabriele Winkler, "The Original Meaning of the Prebaptismal Anointing and Its Implications," *Worship* 52 (1978): 24–45, reprinted in Johnson, *Living Water, Sealing Spirit*, 58–81; Johnson, *Rites* (2007), 55–63, 144–48; Spinks, *Early and Medieval*, 19–25, 71–80.

[10] The classic treatment of this period is J. D. C. Fisher, *Christian Initiation: Baptism in the Medieval West*, Alcuin Club Collection 47 (London: SPCK, 1965; repr. Chicago: Hillenbrand Books, 2007). See also Nathan D. Mitchell, "Dissolution of the Rite of Christian Initiation," in *Made, Not Born*, 50–82; Johnson, *Rites* (2007), 115–307; Kleinheyer, *Sakramentliche Feiern*, 57–136; Nocent, "Christian Initiation," 49–63; Cabié, "The Origins," 17–77; Turner, *Ages*, 7–33, and the accompanying

sources and commentary on the CD-ROM; Turner, *Highway*, 49–123; Kavanagh, *Shape*, 64–70; Spinks, *Early and Medieval*, 109–58.

[11] For some background, see Edward Yarnold, *The Awe Inspiring Rites of Initiation: The Origins of the R.C.I.A.*, 2nd ed. (Collegeville, MN: Liturgical Press, 1971, 1994). See also William Harmless, *Augustine and the Catechumenate* (Collegeville, MN: Liturgical Press, A Pueblo Book, 1995), esp. 79–106.

[12] Text of John the Deacon in E. C. Whitaker, *Documents of the Baptismal Liturgy*, rev. and exp. ed. by Maxwell E. Johnson (Collegeville, MN: Liturgical Press, Pueblo, 1960, 1970, 2003), 208–12; hereafter cited as Whitaker/Johnson. The *Old Gelasian Sacramentary* is a blend of Roman and Gallican materials. The Roman strata are as old as the year 550, though the manuscript itself was copied in the monastery of Chelles around 750. For background on the sacramentary, see Cyrille Vogel, *Medieval Liturgy: An Introduction to the Sources*, rev. and trans. William G. Storey and Niels Krogh Rasmussen (Washington, DC: Pastoral Press, 1986), 64–70; and Eric Palazzo, *A History of the Liturgical Books: From the Beginning to the Thirteenth Century*, trans. Madeleine Beaumont (Collegeville, MN: Liturgical Press, A Pueblo Book, 1998), 42–46. The text can be found in Whitaker/Johnson, *Documents*, 212–43.

[13] The letter of John to Senarius includes an anointing of the ears and nostrils in a ceremony that seems to block the ears and nostrils against everything except that which is holy. The ceremony in the *Old Gelasian Sacramentary* is related but different, with a citation of the gospel passage that makes reference to the healing of the deaf and mute person.

[14] Background in Vogel, *Medieval Liturgy*, 164–66, and Palazzo, *A History*, 175–85. While the material seems to date from around 700, the manuscripts are from the ninth century. Text in Whitaker/Johnson, *Documents*, 244–51.

[15] See *Enchiridion on Faith, Hope, and Love*, CCL 46 (1959), 72–79; English translation and commentary in Finn, MFC 6, 148–54. See the commentary in Mark Searle, "Infant Baptism Reconsidered," in Johnson, *Living Water, Sealing Spirit*, 373–75; Johnson, *Rites* (2007), 185–98.

[16] For example, Walafrid Strabo (+ 849), *De ecclesiasticarum rerum exordiis et incrementis*, c. 27, in J.-Ch. Didier, *Faut-il baptiser les enfants? La réponse de la tradition* (Paris, 1967), 239–40, cited by Searle, 375.

[17] See Mario Righetti, "L'Ordo Baptismi' del Rituale Romano. 1. La sua formazione," in *Manuale di storia liturgica*, vol. 4, *I sacramenti - i sacramentali* (Milan: Ancora, 1959), 139–40. The earliest known example of this unified ritual is *Incipit ordo ad infirmum caticuminum faciendum siue baptizandum*, in the eighth-century *Gellone Sacramentary*; background in Vogel, *Medieval Liturgy*, 70–78; Palazzo, *A History*, 46–48; text in *Liber Sacramentorum Gellonensis*, ed. A. Dumas, CCL 159 (Turnhout: Brepols, 1981), 339–47.

[18] See Paul Turner, *Highway*, 118–34, and the bibliography on 177–78; Johnson, *Rites* (2007), 309–73, esp. 362–69; Spinks, *Early and Medieval*, 134–56. There is a good history of the development of the Ritual in Manlio Sodi and Juan Javier Flores Arcas, eds., *Rituale Romanum: Editio Princeps (1614)*, Monumenta Liturgica Concilii Tridentini 5 (Vatican City: Libreria Editrice Vaticana, 2004), ix–lxxvi; for Castellani, see xxxiv–xxxvi; for Santori, see xxxvii–xlii.

[19] See Johnson, *Rites* (2007), 315–53; Kleinheyer, *Sakramentliche Feiern I*, 136–49. We will be treating the theology of baptism in more detail in chapters 5 and 6. See the overview by Susan Wood, *One Baptism: Ecumenical Dimensions of the Doctrine of Baptism* (Collegeville, MN: Liturgical Press, A Michael Glazier Book, 2009), 44–82.

[20] Apostolic Constitution *Apostolicae sedi*, 18 June 1614, in *Rituale Romanum: Editio Princeps (1614)*, ed. Manlio Sodi and Juan Javier Flores Arcas, Monumenta Liturgica Concilii Tridentini 5 (Vatican City: Libreria Editrice Vaticana, 2004), 3–6.

[21] *Rituale Romanum (1614)*, "De Sacramamento Baptismi rite administrando," nn. 19–209, pp. 13–47; introductory rubrics, nn. 19–65, pp. 13–20; "Ordo baptismi parvulorum," nn. 66–97, pp. 21–26; "De baptismo adultorum," nn. 98–186, pp. 27–44; the last pages deal with the rite of baptism by a bishop, the blessing of the font outside the Easter Vigil, and Pentecost, nn. 187–203, pp. 44–47. See the English/Latin edition (1925 Latin text) translated and edited by Philip T. Weller, *The Roman Ritual: In Latin and English with Rubrics and Planechant Notation*, vol. 1, *The Sacraments and Processions* (Milwaukee: Bruce, 1950), 20–137: introductory rubrics, 20–37; baptism of children, 36–57; baptism of adults, 56–137. The last edition of the *Rituale Romanum* prior to the reforms of the Second Vatican Council can be found in *Rituale Romanum: Editio typica (1952)*, edited by Manlio Sodi and Alessandro Toniolo, Monumenta Liturgica Piana 2 (Vatican City: Libreria Editrice Vaticana, 2008): "De sacramento baptismi," nn. 19–333, pp. 13–113; introductory rubrics, nn. 19–89, pp. 13–25; "Ordo baptismi parvulorum," nn. 90–142, pp. 25–39; "Ordo baptismi adultorum," nn. 143–223, pp. 39–70. The last part of the 1952 baptismal ritual is filled out with an order for supplying rites when a child is baptized in an emergency (nn. 224–253, pp. 71–81); supplying omitted rites for adults (nn. 254–312, pp. 81–106); the bishop's ritual (nn. 313–17, pp. 106–7); the blessing of the font (nn. 318–28, pp. 107–11); and a short form for blessing the water (nn. 329–33, pp. 112–13).

[22] "Ordo Baptismi adultorum in varios gradus distribuitur, per quos catechumeni, progrediente instructione, usque ad Baptismum perducuntur" (*AAS* 34 [1962]: 310–38).

[23] See Righetti, "L' 'Ordo Baptismi,'" 135–38; Kavanagh, *Shape*, 86–97; Paul F. X. Covino, "The Postconciliar Infant Baptism Debate in the American Catholic Church," in Johnson, *Living Water, Sealing Spirit*, 327–49.

[24] Text in *Enchiridion Documentorum Instaurationis Liturgicae I (1963–1973)*, ed. Reiner Kaczynski (Turin: Marietti, 1976), 2–27, chap. 1, 3–12. The constitution was approved on 4 December 1963, with 2,147 bishops voting "placet" and four voting "non placet." The English translation is in *Documents on the Liturgy, 1963–1979: Conciliar, Papal, and Curial Texts* (Collegeville, MN: Liturgical Press, 1982), 4–27, chap. 1, 5–13. Some commentaries are: Joseph Andreas Jungmann, "Constitution on the Sacred Liturgy," in *Commentary on the Documents of Vatican II*, vol. I, ed. Herbert Vorgrimler (New York: Herder and Herder, 1967), 1–87; Frederick R. McManus, *Sacramental Liturgy* (New York: Herder and Herder, 1967); J. D. Crichton, *The Church's Worship: Considerations on the Liturgical Constitution of the Second Vatican Council* (New York: Sheed and Ward, 1966); *The Commentary on the Constitution and on the Instruction on the Sacred Liturgy*, ed. A. Bugnini and C. Braga (New York:

Benziger Brothers, 1965); *The Liturgy of Vatican II: A Symposium in Two Volumes*, ed. William Baraúna and Jovian Lang (Chicago: Franciscan Herald Press, 1966); *Costituzione liturgica "Sacrosanctum Concilium": Studi*, Biblioteca Ephemerides Liturgicae, Subsidia 38, ed. The Congregation for Divine Worship (Rome: CLV Edizioni Liturgiche, 1986).

[25] See Peter Fink, "Three Languages of Christian Sacrament," in *Worship: Praying the Sacraments* (Washington, DC: Pastoral Press, 1991), 29–44, here 29.

[26] See the commentaries of Jungmann, "Constitution," 49–51; Ignatius Oñatibia, "Baptism," in Bugnini, *Commentary on the Constitution*, 167–73; Crichton, *The Church's Worship*, 170–72; McManus, *Sacramental Liturgy*, 121–33.

[27] Paul VI, Motu proprio *Sacram Liturgiam*, on putting into effect some prescriptions of the Constitution on the Liturgy, 25 January 1964, in DOL, n. 20, 84–87.

[28] See the details in A. Bugnini, *The Reform of the Liturgy, 1948–1975* (Collegeville, MN: Liturgical Press, 1990), 584–91.

[29] The Latin *editio typica* is *Ordo Initiationis Christianae Adultorum* (Vatican City: Typis Polyglottis Vaticanis, 1972; rev. ed. 1974). A most convenient source in English is *Rite of Christian Initiation of Adults*, in *The Rites of the Catholic Church*, vol. 1 (Collegeville, MN: Liturgical Press, A Pueblo Book, 1990), 15–356. We will be using this edition, but citing only the paragraph numbers.

[30] See Turner, *Highway*, 156–70; Johnson, *Rites* (2007), 381–401; Bugnini, *The Reform of the Liturgy*, 584–97; Kleinheyer, *Sakramentliche Feiern*, 246–66; Thomas Morris, *The RCIA: Transforming the Church: A Resource for Pastoral Implementation*, rev. ed. (New York: Paulist, 1997); *Christian Initiation of Adults: A Commentary*, Study Text 10, rev. ed. (Washington, DC: USCC, 1988).

[31] A fourth method of baptism is aspersion, when water is sprinkled on the candidate. This method is usually not considered sufficient except in extreme circumstances. All four methods are described by S. Anita Stauffer, *On Baptismal Fonts: Ancient and Modern*, Alcuin/GROW Liturgical Study 29/30 (Bramcote, Nottinghamshire: Grove Books, 1994), 9–10.

[32] This is first found in the thirteenth-century pontifical compiled by William Durand, bishop of Mende. Text is in Michel Andrieu, *Le Pontifical au Moyen-Age, Tome III: Le Pontifical de Guillaume Durand*, Studi e Testi 88 (Vatican City: Biblioteca Apostolica Vaticana, 1940), 333–34. For background on this pontifical see Vogel, *Medieval Liturgy*, 253–55; Palazzo, *A History*, 207–9.

[33] The sign of peace was originally called the *osculum pacis*, the kiss of peace. The long journey from a kiss of peace to an *alapa* (slap) to today's exchange of a handshake, is worthy of exploration.

Chapter Two

The Shape of Children's Baptism

M ost baptisms celebrated today in North America are celebrated for children not yet two years old. This chapter will
describe the ceremony for the baptism of children. It is similar
to that of the baptism of adults. The mental and emotional capacity of
the child receiving baptism, however, is different. While it is clear in the
initiation of adults that those baptized make a life choice for themselves,
the baptism of a child includes roles for parents and godparents not envisioned in the adult rite. We will see that baptism expresses a different
theology when children rather than adults celebrate the ceremony.

Introduction: Some Historical Background

*The Baptism of Children in Scripture
and the Early Church to AD 650*[1]

The New Testament makes no direct reference to the baptism of infants. We do find references to the baptism of households: of Cornelius
(his "relatives and close friends" were gathered [Acts 10:24], the Holy
Spirit "fell upon all who heard the word" [10:44], so Peter "ordered them
to be baptized" [10:48]); of Lydia (Acts 16:14-15); and of the jailer
of Ephesus (Acts 16:19-34). Paul mentions that he had baptized the
household of Stephanas (1 Cor 1:16). In Acts, Luke's interest, of course,

is in the growth of the Church "in Jerusalem, in all Judea and Samaria, and to the ends of the earth" (Acts 1:8), not specifically in the topic of the baptism of infants.

The first to refer to the baptism of infants seems to be Tertullian in North Africa (+ 220), who is not in favor of baptizing them: "let them come when they are growing up, when they are of an age to be instructed."[2] Tertullian's student, Cyprian of Carthage (+ 258?), perhaps in the midst of violent persecution, takes a much different tack, urging parents not to wait even the customary eight days to have their children baptized.[3] Origen (+ 254?), in Alexandria, Egypt, also accepted the traditional character of the baptism of children: "The church has received from the apostles the custom of administering baptism even to infants, for those who have been entrusted with the secrets of the divine mysteries knew very well that all are tainted with the stain of original sin, which must be washed off by water and the spirit."[4] The *Apostolic Tradition* (ca. 220?) makes provision for infants who cannot speak for themselves to be baptized before adults.[5] Commentators such as John the Deacon, writing in Rome about 500, deal with a situation in which both adults and children are baptized.[6]

As the quotation from Origen suggests, the baptism of infants became the springboard for a theology of original sin—why else baptize infants unless they needed forgiveness? Augustine later used this argument in his controversy with the Pelagians.[7]

By the end of the patristic period (around the year 650), the baptism of infants had become standard practice. The Roman liturgical books assumed that those baptized were infants.[8] In mission areas, the initial baptisms were of adults and whole families (e.g., the baptism of Clovis and the Franks around 496). Subsequently, infants were baptized soon after birth, the practice that would prevail for the whole Church throughout the Middle Ages until the time of the Reformation and beyond.

From the Middle Ages to the Second Vatican Council (1962–65)[9]

The Middle Ages saw the gradual development of the celebration of Christian initiation into several separate ritual moments: baptism of infants, confirmation of children (any time from the first years to about age ten, though some were confirmed later or not at all), and a first reception of Communion (from the time of baptism to about the age of ten or twelve or even fourteen). The connection between Easter and baptism, so important in the North Africa of Tertullian and Augustine and the

Rome of Leo the Great and the deacon John, was severed because of fears induced by a high infant mortality rate coupled with a strong doctrine of original sin. This concern can be seen in the decision to condense the celebration into a single ceremony and to use a ritual designed for those on their deathbed.[10] Since the children cannot speak for themselves, godparents speak their parts. What follows is an outline of the medieval rite in its final shape as found in the 1614 *Rituale Romanum*.

Order of Baptism (1614)

At the door of the church

The priest vests in a purple stole

Questioning of the child, with godparent answering

Exsufflation (breathing) three times in the face of the child

Sign of the cross on the forehead and over the heart of the child

Prayer

Imposition of hand with prayer

Blessing and imposition of salt into the mouth of the child

Three prayers of exorcism

Sign of the cross on the forehead of the child

Imposition of hand with prayer

Placing of the edge of the stole over the child, leading all into the church and to the font, while reciting the Creed and the Lord's Prayer

Outside the baptistery door

Exorcism

Touching of the ears and nostrils of the child with saliva and the formula "Ephpheta"

Renunciation of Satan in dialogue with the godparent

Anointing with the oil of catechumens on the breast and between the shoulders

[Within the baptistery?]

The priest changes to a white stole

Profession of faith

Question regarding the will to be baptized

Baptism (child held by godparents) with formula and three infusions of water in the sign of the cross

Anointing with chrism on the crown of the head with a formula

Pax tibi ("Peace to you")

Presentation of the white garment (using a white linen cloth in place of an actual garment)

Presentation of a lighted candle

Dismissal

As we noted in the previous chapter, the original rite dating from the eighth century is intended for a catechumen in danger of death. The priest directly addresses the infant as if it could respond, but the responses are given by the godparents. It is the rite for adults abridged for celebration in a single ceremony.

The Reforms of the Second Vatican Council and the New Rite (1969)[11]

The ceremony just outlined formed the ritual context that the fathers of the Second Vatican Council addressed in the Constitution on the Sacred Liturgy. After laying out general principles of the reform of the liturgy in the first chapter, including theological, pastoral, and juridical norms, they discussed baptism in chapter 3, which focuses on the sacraments and sacramentals. The baptism of infants is the focus of articles 67–70. The bishops at the council decreed that the Rite of Baptism for Children should make clear that infants are being baptized: they cannot speak for themselves (67). The 1614 ritual, as we saw above, directly addressed the child as if it could respond—the responses were performed by the godparents, answering on its behalf.

The reformed rite should take into account circumstances in which large numbers of children are baptized in a single ceremony (68). This paragraph highlights especially the needs of mission countries, where sometimes hundreds of children could be baptized in a single ceremony. The new rite should take this circumstance into account, abbreviating some rites and texts in the light of the pastoral situation.

When children are baptized outside of church because of special circumstances, the ceremony for bringing them into church should clearly show that these children have already "entered the church" (69). For instance, if the child was baptized in the hospital or at home because of fears for its life, there should be a formal bringing of the child to church. The custom had been simply to "supply the ceremonies" that had been omitted because of the emergency. But this approach did not take into account that the child had been baptized. To treat the child as if it were not yet baptized was contrary to the reality. A new rite should make clear exactly what is happening when this pastoral circumstance occurs.

Outside of the Easter season, the water should be freshly blessed for each celebration (70). The former custom was to keep the Easter water all year long. During the summer months and into the fall and winter, because chrism had been added to the water as part of the blessing, the water would often become moldy and take on an unpleasant scent. This particular decision was based on both pastoral and theological objectives: to allow for healthy water and to highlight the paschal character of baptism by repeating the blessing in each celebration.

One of the study groups of the Consilium for the implementation of the Constitution on the Sacred Liturgy worked on the Rite of Baptism for Children while it also dealt with the rite for adults. The members considered the adult rite to be the basis for other forms of celebration. The group addressed the children's rite beginning in 1964 and prepared the final draft in late 1968. Pope Paul VI approved it, and the document was published on May 15, 1969. The English translation came out soon thereafter. Changes clarifying the understanding of original sin were incorporated in an emended version that appeared in 1973.[12]

Structure of the Rite of Baptism for Children (1969)

The Rite of Baptism for Children (RBC) takes place soon after the child has been born and when the parents have been suitably prepared (RBC 5.1):

> Before the celebration of the sacrament, it is of great importance that parents, moved by their own faith, or with the help of friends or other members of the community, should prepare to take part in the rite with understanding. They should be provided with suitable means such as books, letters addressed to them, and catechisms designed for families. The pastor should make it his duty to visit them or see that they are visited; he should try to gather a group of families together

and prepare them for the coming celebration by pastoral counsel and common prayer.

In this preparation of the parents, we find highlighted one of the major differences from the 1614 rite: the parents must prepare, since the child is baptized into the faith of the Church, which is also their faith.

As we explore the Rite of Baptism for Children together, the reader will find it handy to have a copy of the ritual with which to follow our discussion.[13]

When Is It Celebrated?

The baptism of children is celebrated soon after the birth of the child. The introduction lays out several criteria (8). When the child is in danger of death, the baptism should take place as soon as possible. Either before or after the birth of the child, the parents should receive preparation for the celebration. The introduction calls for the baptism to take place in the "first weeks" after birth, but no longer retains the previous stipulation of "within eight days" of the 1917 Code of Canon Law. Another key concern is that the mother of the child be present at the celebration. When baptism was celebrated in the first days after birth, the mother often could not be present, and the godmother took her place. The introduction makes clear that the mother's presence is crucial to the celebration.

Baptism should be celebrated in a way that highlights its paschal character. The Easter Vigil or any Sunday is a most appropriate time, since on those days the Church commemorates the resurrection of the Lord. On occasion, baptism should also be celebrated at Sunday Mass so that the whole community can take part in the joy of the new member and experience the "necessary relationship between baptism and eucharist" (9). On a practical level, if there are adults celebrating their initiation at the Easter Vigil, it might be advantageous not to celebrate the baptism of children at the same time. The two rituals are different enough from each other that confusion for both celebrant and the faithful might ensue.

Where Does the Celebration Take Place?

The normal place to celebrate the baptism of children is in the parish church of the family. Each parish church should have a baptismal font.

Only if the child is in danger of death should baptism take place some-where other than in the parish church (10–13).

Overall Shape: From outside the Church to the Altar (A First Reading)

The celebration of the Rite of Baptism for Children is a journey, from the door of the church, to the ambo where God's Word is proclaimed, to the font, to the altar. Here is a schematic outline of the basic rite for several children (RBC 32–71):

Reception of the Children (At the Door of the Church)

Liturgy of the Word (gathered at the ambo)
> Readings and homily
> Intercessions (prayer of the faithful)
> Prayer of exorcism and anointing before baptism

Celebration of the sacrament (at the baptismal font)
> Blessing and invocation of God over baptismal water
> Renunciation of sin and profession of faith
> Baptism
> Explanatory rites
>> Anointing after baptism
>> Clothing with white garment
>> Lighted candle
>> Ephphetha or prayer over ears and mouth

Conclusion of the rite (at the altar)
> Lord's Prayer
> Blessing

What emerges clearly from this brief overview of the ritual is its fun-damental shape as a journey: into the church, to the Word, to the font, to the altar. In this it summarizes the life path of a Christian: to be a faithful disciple, to follow Christ where he leads. We will explore the implications of this journey further.

Second Reading

An outline of a ceremony does not exhaust its meaning. Now we will explore the actions of the Rite of Baptism for Children as we did the ceremony for adults in chapter one.

Who Are the Actors?

Children

The main focus of the action is the children who are to be baptized. What age are these children? Infants from the first days after birth until they arrive at catechetical age, about six or seven years old. Once they reach catechetical age, they celebrate using the adaptations contained in the Rite of Christian Initiation of Adults.[14]

The RBC anticipates that the child can do and say nothing for itself. It is carried to the church, to the ambo, to the font, to the altar. The actions are directed to the child. The verbal elements, with rare exceptions, are directed to the parents, godparents, and the assembly of the faithful.

Parents

The parents are a second main focus of the RBC (see RBC 5). They carry the child, answer questions on their child's behalf at the door, receive instruction about their responsibilities, hear the Word, reject sin and profess faith, carry the child to the font and altar, and make a commitment for the child until it is old enough to live the faith on its own.

Godparents

The godparents' role is to support the parents. They must be fully initiated active members of the Catholic Church (i.e., baptized, confirmed, and regularly receiving Holy Communion). To have one godparent is required, though there can be a godmother and a godfather. Both must be baptized and confirmed Catholics. A non-Catholic baptized person may serve as a Christian witness to the baptism, but in that case there must be a Catholic godparent also.

The godparents make the same promises as the parents, acting on behalf of the whole community of believers. They offer their prayers and support to the child and its parents. They do not normally carry the child as they did in the former rite, since the mother is present. They no longer speak in the place of the child. In fact no one speaks in place of the child. Parents and godparents speak for themselves; the child is addressed, but no response is expected (see CIGI 10; RBC 6).

The Faithful

Those gathered for the baptism will include the family, friends, and neighbors of the child. The RBC also anticipates that others will be present, representing the parish community and the whole People of God. Their responsibilities begin before the baptism and continue after, in providing the prayerful and faith-filled environment needed by the child and its parents to survive in a world distorted by darkness and sin. In the ceremony itself, the gathered assembly walks in procession, adds its voice to prayer, in a particular way adds its assent to the profession of faith, goes to the font and altar, and joins in the prayers as appropriate (see RBC 4).

Celebrant

The ordinary minister is a priest or deacon. If a catechist presides, there is a special order found in chapter 4 (RBC 132–56). The priest has a special responsibility to ensure that the parents are prepared to undertake responsibility for their child's growth in the faith. He leads the celebration, preaches the Word, leads the prayers and profession of faith, performs the baptism, blesses those present (see CIGI 11–15; RBC 7).

Other Ministers

The same varieties of ministers are needed as in other liturgical celebrations. First would be a reader, who proclaims the Word. A cantor leads the group in the psalm between the readings and could also lead the music during the processions and in the acclamations that accompany certain actions. Acolytes or servers carry the needed books and liturgical objects. Sacristans and environment ministers ensure that the church has been properly prepared for the celebration.

When Do They Do It?

The medieval tradition of baptizing children as soon as possible after birth still helps shape the current ritual. Other factors, however, should also be taken into account. First of all, the health of the child must be considered. If there are any physical problems, the child should be baptized without delay. Another consideration, not a part of the tradition before, is the health of the mother. She should be present at her child's baptism. According to another criterion, the parents should celebrate only when they are properly prepared and have the requisite level of understanding of the faith and of their responsibilities to their child (8).

Baptism has a paschal character. Therefore, either the Easter Vigil or a Sunday is the best time for celebrating. What is more, Sunday baptisms can take place at Mass "so that the entire community may be present and the necessary relationship between baptism and eucharist may be clearly seen" (9). As Tertullian pointed out in the third century, however, "every day is a Lord's day: any hour, any season, is suitable for baptism. If there is a difference of solemnity, it makes no difference to the grace."[15]

Where Do They Do It?

Since the primary meaning of baptism is entering the paschal mystery of Christ and entering the Christian community that is Christ's Body, the normal place for celebration is the parish church. Only in cases of emergency should baptisms occur in private homes or hospitals. Every parish church should have a prominent baptismal font where the baptism in water takes place.

What Do They Do?

Gather at the Door (nn. 32–41)

All that we said about doors in chapter one applies here as well, with this difference: the one to be baptized does not come to the door to ask entrance but is brought to the door, usually carried in the arms of mother or father. The action at the door is more complex. The parents and godparents, already baptized, bring their child to the church to be admitted. The warm arms of embrace speak of love and protection. The bringing to the church broadens the horizon of the child beyond family and neighborhood to the Church and the world. The child has already lived in multiple environments: hospital, home, extended family, neighborhood. The child's life, already God's gift, is now inserted into a new web of relationships that promise not just life but life everlasting—in Christ's Body, the Church.

Three events take place at the door:

- Parents and celebrant engage in a question-and-answer dialogue, naming the child and stating what they want for their child: faith, baptism, life in Christ.
- The parents and godparents are instructed about their duties.
- The child is signed with the cross by the celebrant and parents and godparents.

The rite begins with conversation, a simple exchange between the celebrant and those gathered, especially the parents. This dialogue is an act of community participation. The child receives its name now in a Christian context. Naming is one of the tasks that God gave the first man and woman (see Gen 2). Naming permits identification and allows for relationship. Once someone has a name, we can enter into their frame of reference by calling them by that name. Knowing someone's name implies some stake in that person's life and the possibility of entering into relationship with him or her. The Scriptures also tell of those who receive new names when they enter relationship with God: Abram and Sarai become Abraham and Sarah (Gen 17:1-22); Simon becomes Peter (Matt 16:13-20). The call to discipleship requires that a name be called and that someone answer.

The instruction given by the priest to those present is one of the novelties of the reformed rite. Previously, the ceremony was one that was adapted from the baptism of adults. The child was addressed directly, and the sponsors answered on its behalf. The bishops at Vatican II asked that the rite be revised to take into account that children are being baptized and that parents and godparents take the responsibility to raise the child in the faith. The short instruction directed to the parents and godparents ritualizes this concern.

The rite at the door concludes with the celebrant, the parents, and the godparents signing the child's forehead with the cross. Sometimes others present also sign the child. This gesture reveals all we mentioned in chapter one, especially emphasizing that the child is marked with the most dramatic image of Christ's love: his total self-giving on the cross where he revealed his love for the Father and the world. The child now bears the brand-mark of the name of Christ, the X (the Greek letter *chi*, the first letter of Christ's name) that claims ownership of a new member of the Body of Christ. The sign of the cross is both a welcome and a challenge. It welcomes the child into the community of believers. It challenges those charged with the child's upbringing to arm the child with the faith and patience that will be needed to follow Christ unreservedly.

Process to the Church for the Liturgy of the Word (nn. 42–43)

The assembly now moves into the body of the church. They make their way to the place where they can hear God's Word. The movement into the body of the church constitutes the gathered assembly into a community of hearers. The simple act of entering and finding a place establishes a community. The journey now begun has several stages and, in fact, does not end.

Listen to God's Word (nn. 44–46)

Now the Word is proclaimed. The addition of a Liturgy of the Word was one of the new elements of the 1969 reform of the Rite of Baptism for Children. The Word of God is directed to the parents, the godparents, and the family to deepen their appreciation of the great gift and great responsibility that God has given them. We will explore this dynamic of God's Word more in part 2.

The rubrics make provision for the children to be removed to a separate place (n. 14). Unless the children would prevent others from hearing the Word because of crying or other distractions, however, it seems better that they remain with the group. Some say that this part of the ceremony is superfluous, that the children cannot understand what is happening. In fact, parents constantly do and say things to and for their children that cannot now be understood. Parents talk to them and read to them. Mother and father establish the context into which the child will grow. This same human dynamic is at play in the Liturgy of the Word. The children hear the stories of faith, of Jesus blessing the little children, and begin the process of becoming part of the story themselves. At the same time, parents and godparents become more conformed to the Christian message as they hear the Word of God proclaimed to them in their specific roles on behalf of their children.

Pray and Invoke the Saints (nn. 47–49)

We will deal with the prayer texts in the next part of our consideration, but it is sufficient here to note that praying with children is a normal part of raising a child. The naming of the saints, in particular, recalls the list of people that children pray for when they go to bed ("God bless Mommy and Daddy and Grandma and Grandpa . . ."). Here the dynamic is reversed, asking that the saints add their prayers to ours. The names of the child's patron saints are specifically identified as important to include.

To have a patron in heaven and realize the extent of the communion of saints lies at the heart of this moment.

Anoint the Child's Breast with Oil of Catechumens (nn. 51–52)

This anointing raises other associations than does the anointing of catechumens who are adults. There the images are more of an athlete preparing for competition. Here other dimensions of the image come to the fore. The oil can be medicinal, soothing rough skin. It can guard against the effects of a rough-and-tumble world. The oil can be cleansing, helping to flush away the buildup of dirt. It can simply be a sign of love and care, allowing touch to communicate presence. For many parents, moments like this with their child become moments of amazement at the fragile gift of life that has been placed in their care. The accompanying text places the action of anointing within the context of protecting the child from the devil and forces of original sin. (This is a reminder that nonverbal gestures and symbols need to have words clarify their use and meaning.) All these gestures and symbols combine in the act of anointing the child on the breast with the oil of catechumens.

The rite makes provision to impose hands instead of anointing. This sign of invocation of the Holy Spirit and of blessing conveys God's power and the community's blessing to the child.

Process to the Baptistery (n. 53)

This second procession reminds the assembly that it can never really become comfortable. Hearing God's stories forces us to respond. The journey continues to a variety of way stations. The ceremony keeps us on the move. Gathering at the waters raises images of the People of Israel at the Red Sea (Exod 14), and having their thirst quenched at the waters of Meribah (Exod 17:1-7), or later, crossing the Jordan (Josh 3:7-17), or the journey of Naaman the Syrian to the Jordan seeking to have his leprosy cured (2 Kgs 5). All those journeys are recalled in this one.

Bless Water (nn. 54–55)

The blessing of water confronts us with one of the most important symbols that we possess. The prayer can be the one used at the Easter Vigil or another provided in the rite. Here we point out simply that the celebrant in the prayer highlights the presence and use of water, touches it and sets it apart for this holy use.

Renounce Sin and Profess Faith (nn. 56–59)

This section of the ritual has been redone in the light of the role of the parents and godparents. Once again, they are reminded of their responsibilities toward their child. They engage in dialogue with the celebrant to reject sin and profess their faith. At the end, the whole assembly gives its "Amen" to what has occurred, reminding all present that this act of professing faith is one of entering a community of believers, not something done alone or even simply within a family. All members of the Christian community have a stake in this child's future.

Baptize the Child in Water (With Three Immersions or Pourings)

The varieties of ways that water is part of our life were detailed in chapter 1. Once again, though, we reflect on the different implications of the symbol when the main subject is a child. Water requires vigilance and attention. The child loves to splash but has to be watched. The water delights and cleanses. The meaning that we saw in chapter 1 (the initiation of adults) is present but is here mediated by adults on behalf of the child.

The child is bathed three times in water. This can be by immersion (for instance, sitting the child in water and pouring water over it, rather than submersion of the infant) or by pouring water over the child's head without immersing the child in the water. During the bathing the child is held by mother or father. This reveals the utmost joy and the deepest seriousness of what is occurring: life in a community committed to Christ's Body, the Spirit's temple, God's own people. To receive the child lovingly in an ample towel and dry him or her, as might be done so often at home, highlights both the ordinariness and the uniqueness of God's presence and action in our lives (nn. 60–61).

Anoint the Crown of the Child's Head with Chrism (n. 62)

We saw that in the initiation of adults the anointing of the crown of the head with chrism is usually omitted. The celebration of confirmation with its anointing of the forehead with chrism is proposed as taking its place.

Within the context of baptizing a child the anointing with chrism has its own unique context, which the words used during it direct and specify. Here we focus on the multiple senses that the symbol and gesture provide. The scent of chrism on the crown of the child's head calls to mind the scents that parents apply to their child as part of their care and love. We do not anoint governors or presidents, but we do lavish scent upon our children.

The soft spot in the head of a child requires gentleness and reminds us of the still-developing life and future of the child. The chrism reminds us that the future involves us in Christ's roles as priest, prophet, and king.

Clothe the Child in a White Garment (n. 63)

Dressing a child is different from an adult dressing him- or herself. Once again, the rite is changed from the adult rite of initiation, because it is a child who is baptized. With the baptismal garment, families often focus on family traditions, the handing on of a piece of clothing from one generation to the next. The custom of simply placing a white piece of cloth over the child, even if it was made or decorated by members of the parish, pales in comparison to the significance of a family's own baptismal garment. The few minutes it takes to dress a child in a venerable gown is worth the extra effort to allow the family to feel a part of a generational tradition. When there is no such family tradition, the rubric encourages the family to prepare its own baptismal garment. Perhaps the garment provided by the parish may help create a new tradition.

Present the Parents and Godparents with a Candle Lighted from the Paschal Candle (n. 64)

To present parents and godparents with a candle on behalf of the child has so many overtones: light, warmth, joy, revelation, but also heat and burning. The large paschal candle flickers over the whole celebration at the font. The human associations of candles and flamers are various: they may raise memories of Olympic flames passed from hand to hand through country after country, then burning as a beacon of the assembly and teamwork. They could remind us of eternal flames, like that at Arlington National Cemetery, burning in memory of lost loved ones and unnamed heroes. This baptismal candle is a beacon of hope for a new life now enlightened by Christ and surrounded by love of family and friends. The rite suggests that the father or godfather might light the candle from the paschal candle.

Touch the Child's Ears and Mouth (nn. 65–66)

Parents marvel at the learning curve of their children. Each day brings new experiences and new growth. The child's senses are the means by which that learning takes place. The celebrant touches these organs of sensory input to remind parents that God is learned, Christ is heard, and the Spirit is drunk in, as is knowledge. The text begs that these pathways be opened, suggesting that without this opening they are blocked. We will explore this more in part 2.

Process to the Altar (n. 67)

Of course, every party includes food. The baptism will end with family and friends gathering to eat and drink in celebration of the great event: birth and new birth. The move to the altar is a prelude to the child's future eating and drinking that will take place from this sacred table, the altar of the Lord's sacrifice, here at church. Though the Latin tradition does not celebrate confirmation or offer Communion until the child has reached the age of discretion, the ceremony takes us to the altar to remind us what the future holds: confirmation in the Spirit and communion in the Body and Blood of the Lord (see CIGI 1–2).

Pray the Lord's Prayer (nn. 68–69)

The quintessential meal prayer is the Our Father, when we say, "Give us this day our daily bread." Gathered around the altar, sign of Christ's total self-gift, we join our voices in a common prayer. A family that is bound even closer than by ties of kinship together professes a common faith and rootedness in God as "Our Father."

Bless the Parents and All Present (nn. 70–71)

The tasks of parenthood are great. The rite ends with hands extended over mother, then father, then all. This new member of our community is entrusted to our care, and we are strengthened to take on the duties. Finally, we are dismissed to take up the tasks of being Church outside the church building in the liturgy of the world.

The final rubric of the rite recalls that, in some places, the final act of baptism is a procession to the Marian shrine where the child is placed under the protection of Mary and the Holy Family.

Conclusions

Some Issues from History

The baptism of children grew from the rite for adults. The specific needs of children, so very different from those of adults, led to the abandonment of some forms inherited from the adult rite. The components that seemed particularly not adapted to children's needs were the long catecheses, the elaborate scrutinies, and the handing over of the Creed and the Lord's Prayer. What also seemed not adapted to children was elaborating the ritual over a longer period of time and then celebrating the actual baptism once a year at the Easter Vigil. The decision emerged, over the centuries, to utilize the rite for a catechumen in danger of death. That ceremony contained the essentials of the various celebrations and could be used whenever necessary for the celebration with children. In fact, it seemed that children were in constant danger of death in that world. Mortality rates were very high in late antiquity and the early Middle Ages. The possibility that the child would be restricted to a life outside of heaven seemed to make waiting for Easter foolish and fool-hardy. The inability of the children to speak for themselves had already been solved by having the godparents take on that role on their behalf. In cultures where children had no rights until they came of age, the use of proxies to speak for them was common. This cultural form was ap-plied to baptism.

Issues Arising from the Shape of the Celebration

The Rite of Baptism for Children as it is celebrated today makes clear that in baptism one begins a journey that starts outside the church and culminates at the altar. The journey involves a community; the hearing of God's revelation and responding to it; engaging in a conflict with the forces of evil; being washed, anointed, clothed, and enlightened. It finds its ritual fulfillment at the altar, the centerpiece of Christian life and celebration, from which believers are constantly nourished by Christ's own Body and Blood. It is from the altar that they are sent forth.

Issues Arising from the People Celebrating Baptism

This form of baptism is celebrated for children. For the first time the Church has developed a ritual aimed at those who cannot speak for themselves. A question then emerges: in whose faith does this baptism occur? One need not have full use of reason to receive this sacrament. The child's participation in a family and a community that will take re-sponsibility for the faith life of the child is enough for the child to enter the Christian family. Baptism is not something earned nor is it about knowing and articulating propositions of the faith. It is about member-ship in a community of faith in which we find various levels of maturity.

Second, the role of parents and godparents fills out this understanding. The life of baptism is not only about the salvation of an individual but also about the mutual relationships that exist in a community of believers. The child only grows and develops because parents and others concerned for the child's welfare act constantly on his or her behalf. That same reality emerges in baptism. The ritual reveals the dependence of the child and the responsibility of the parents and, through the godparents, of the whole community to see to the raising of the child in faith. The action, directed at the child, is also directed to the whole community, which must commit itself on the child's behalf to prayer and example of the Christian life. The parents especially emerge as the primary caregivers of the child, the first educators, the first believers.

Issues that Emerge from the Symbols Used

Most of the symbols are the same as those in adult baptism. Two, however, change somewhat in the rite of baptizing a child.

The first change involves anointing of the child on the crown of the head with chrism. This action is usually omitted when an adult is baptized. The decision in the reform of the rite was that, since the adult would ordinarily receive confirmation with the anointing of the forehead, a second anointing would be confusing. Anointing on the crown of the head, especially of a young infant, is an action that requires care and tenderness. Yet the text associated with the anointing invokes Christ as priest, prophet, and king, images of strength and determined activity. Even a young child shares in the mission of Christ, revealing that the mission is one accomplished by grace, not by human power.

A second change from the adult rite is the placement of the Ephphetha ceremony, when the priest touches the ears and tongue of the person. In the adult ceremony, this rite takes place on Holy Saturday morning (although it can be anticipated during the rites of the catechumenate: see RCIA 104–5). It is a call to be opened and likewise a removal of barriers to openness. The one to be baptized is to be opened to the missionary call of baptism. Barriers to the return of the Creed are removed. The ceremony is celebrated with a clear eye on the Vigil to follow that evening.

In the baptism of children, however, the rite comes after baptism, just before the procession to the altar. What it seems to emphasize is the removal of barriers to hearing of and speaking about what has happened. The newly baptized child will learn these realities as it grows and develops as a follower of Jesus.

Adults are catechized before baptism; children are catechized after baptism. Nevertheless, both must continue in a lifelong process of growing into the full stature of Christ.

Issues Arising from the Time of Baptism

The baptism of children can take place at the Easter Vigil but more normally takes place on Sunday, the weekly commemoration of the Lord's resurrection. This choice of time makes clear the paschal character of baptism: dying and rising with Christ.

Another possibility is that baptism can be celebrated at Sunday Mass with the whole congregation. This especially highlights the communal dimension of baptism, that the whole community of faith has responsibility for raising this child in the faith. The rite also cautions that this not be done too often lest the community tire of it. Some parishes have discovered that good catechesis helps the community to revel in this new life of faith in their midst and so they always celebrate baptism at Mass. Others never give their people the experience for fear of—what? Too long a celebration, too noisy a time, not wanting to challenge the notion that baptism is something private to a single family? None of these reasons seem sufficient to keep a parish from ever enjoying the experience of baptism at Mass.

Notes, Chapter Two

[1] The scriptural data have been subjected to intense scrutiny in the recent past. Particularly pertinent are Oscar Cullman, *Baptism in the New Testament* (London: SCM, 1950); Joachim Jeremias, *Infant Baptism in the First Four Centuries*, tr. David Cairas (Philadelphia: Westminster, 1962); Kurt Aland, *Did the Early Church Baptize Infants?* trans. G. R. Beasley-Murray (Philadelphia: Westminster, 1963); G. R. Beasley-Murray, *Baptism in the New Testament* (New York: Macmillan, 1962); Joachim Jeremias, *The Origins of Infant Baptism : A Further Study in Reply to Kurt Aland*, trans. Dorothea M. Barton (Naperville, IL: Alec R. Allenson, 1963); *Baptism, the New Testament and the Church: Historical and Contemporary Studies in Honour of R.E.O. White*, ed. Stanley E. Porter and Anthony R. Cross (Sheffield, England: Sheffield Academic Press, 1999), see esp. the bibliographical essay on 33–39. See the bibliography in Johnson, *Rites* (1999), 401–2, and the bibliography here in chap. 1, note 1.

² *De baptismo* 18; text in Finn, MFC 6, 127.

³ Letter 74; see the discussion in Finn, MFC 6, 15 and 130.

⁴ *Commentary on Romans* 5:9; see the commentary in Finn, MFC 6, 15.

⁵ Chapter 21; text in Finn, MFC 6, 49.

⁶ After describing a number of customs for celebrating baptism in Rome, John says: "I must say plainly and at once, in case I seem to have overlooked the point, that all these things are done even to infants, who by reason of their youth understand nothing. And by this you may know that when they are presented by their parents or others, it is necessary that their salvation should come through other people's profession, since their damnation came by another's fault" (John the Deacon, *Epistula ad Senarium* 7, ed. Andre Wilmart, in *Analecta Reginensia*, Studi e Testi 59 [Vatican City, 1933], 170–79, here 175. English translation in Whitaker/Johnson, *Documents*, 211).

⁷ *Enchiridion on Faith, Hope, and Love,* CCL 48–50; text in Finn, MFC 6, 153–54.

⁸ See the *Gelasian Sacramentary, Liber sacramentorum romanae aeclesiae ordinis anni circuli (Sacramentarium Gelasianum),* Rerum Ecclesiasticarum Documenta, Series Maior, Fontes IV, 3rd ed., ed. Leo Cunibert Mohlberg (Rome: Herder, 1960, 1981), Liber I, 26–65; text in Whitaker/Johnson, *Documents*, 213–37; background on the *Gelasian Sacramentary* in Vogel, *Medieval Liturgy*, 64–70; Palazzo, *A History*, 42–46. See also Ordo Romanus XI, in *Les Ordines Romani du Haut Moyen-Age,* vol. 2, *Spicilegium Sacrum Lovaniense,* Études et documents 23 (Louvain: Spicilegium Sacrum Lovaniense, 1948), 417–47; text in Whitaker/Johnson, *Documents*, 244–51; background on Ordo Romanus XI in Vogel, *Medieval Liturgy*, 164–66; Palazzo, *A History*, 175–85.

⁹ Basic sources include J. D. C. Fisher, *Christian Initiation: Baptism in the Medieval West,* ACC 47 (London: SPCK, 1965; repr. Chicago: Hillenbrand Books, 2007); Fisher, *Christian Initiation: The Reformation Period,* ACC 51 (London: SPCK, 1970; repr. Chicago: Hillenbrand Books, 2007); see the bibliography in chapter 1, note 10.

¹⁰ See chapter 1, note 17, for the reference to Righetti, "L'Ordo Baptismi.'"

¹¹ See Cabié, "The Origins," 84–96; Kleinheyer, *Sakramentliche Feiern,* 149–90; Nocent, "Christian Initiation in the Roman Church from the Fifth Century to Vatican II," in Chupungco, *Sacraments and Sacramentals,* 64–65, 74–79; Turner, *Ages,* 45–48 and accompanying documentation; Bugnini, *The Reform of the Liturgy,* 598–612; Mark Searle, *Christening: The Making of Christians* (Collegeville, MN: Liturgical Press, 1980), 20–104; Timothy Fitzgerald, *Infant Baptism: A Parish Celebration* (Chicago: Liturgy Training, 1994), 23–66.

¹² See the details in Bugnini, *Reform,* 598–602.

¹³ *The Rites,* 361–466.

¹⁴ Part 2, section 1: Christian Initiation of Children Who Have Reached Catechetical Age, nn. 252–330.

¹⁵ *De baptismo* 19, in Whitaker/Johnson, *Documents*, 10–11.

Part Two

The Words of Baptism

In this second part of our treatment of the sacrament of baptism, we move from the physical objects, the movements, the gestures, the sights, the sounds, and the smells of the celebration of baptism, to the words that determine the meaning of the actions. Symbols and gestures by themselves can throw off meanings in many directions. When a word is spoken ("With this ring I thee wed"), the gesture and symbol take on more specific (though not a single) significance. In these two chapters, the stories, songs, and prayers that accompany the movements and gestures of baptism will find their particular place in unfolding the meaning of the action. In chapter 3, we will explore the words of Scripture that are proclaimed during the various celebrations of the Rite of Christian Initiation of Adults and the Rite of Baptism for Children. The prayers and other verbal elements of the rituals will form the focus of chapter 4.

Chapter Three

The Scriptural Readings in Baptism

Introduction

The Second Vatican Council gave special importance to the role of Sacred Scripture in the celebration of the sacraments. Perhaps the most important reason for emphasizing the role and importance of the words of the Bible is that when they are proclaimed in the liturgy they are Christ speaking to us. The underlying conviction of the tradition is expressed thus: "He is present in his word, since it is he himself who speaks when the holy Scriptures are read in the Church" (SC 7).[1] The Word proclaimed is not simply the reading of a text from the past. It is not conveying mere information about what happened once upon a time. Rather, the Word that is proclaimed is understood to be Christ speaking to us today. This speaking is not just any speaking, not just the physical act of vibrating vocal cords and eardrums responding in sympathy. Not bare facts and not physical sound, but interpersonal communication is taking place. Speaker and hearer enter into a relationship. Personal presence is offered by the speaker and anticipates reception by the hearers in the interchange.

The Passover Haggadah expresses a similar conviction that the hearers of the account of the history of salvation participate in the event of communication. When the story of the first Passover is read during the Seder, those hearing the Word are the ones being led from slavery to freedom.

> In every generation let each man look on himself as if *he* came forth
> from Egypt. As it is said: "And thou shalt tell thy son in that day, saying:
> It is because of that which the Lord did for me when I came forth out
> of Egypt" [Exod. 13:8]. It was not only our fathers that the Holy One,
> blessed be he, redeemed, but us as well did he redeem along with them.
> As it is said: "And He brought us out from thence, that He might bring
> us in, to give us the land which He swore unto our fathers" [Deut. 6:23].
>
> Therefore we are bound to thank, praise, laud, glorify, exalt, honor,
> bless, extol, and adore Him who performed all these miracles for our
> fathers and for us. He has brought us forth from slavery to freedom,
> from sorrow to joy, from mourning to holiday, from darkness to great
> light, and from bondage to redemption. Let us then recite before him
> a new song: Hallelujah.[2]

The same dynamic holds true for Christians as they hear the words of
Scripture during the celebration of the liturgy. The Word proclaimed is
telling us not just what happened in history but also what is happening
here and now.

Since Sacred Scripture is God's own Word spoken in our midst, it is
the foundation of all our worship:

> Sacred Scripture is of the greatest importance in the celebration of the
> liturgy. For it is from Scripture that the readings are given and explained
> in the homily and that psalms are sung; the prayers, collects, and litur-
> gical songs are scriptural in their inspiration; it is from the Scripture
> that actions and signs derive their meaning. Thus to achieve the reform,
> progress, and adaptation of the liturgy, it is essential to promote that
> warm and living love for Scripture to which the venerable tradition of
> both Eastern and Western rites gives testimony. (SC 24)

It is of the nature of the liturgy to include words—in fact, God's words,
and our response in dialogue with them:

> Although the liturgy is above all things the worship of the divine
> majesty, it likewise contains rich instruction for the faithful. For in the
> liturgy God is speaking to His people and Christ is still proclaiming
> his Gospel. And the people are responding to God both by song and
> prayer. (SC 33)

The fathers of the council recognized that reading from Scripture is an
essential part of the liturgy. It is not simply a preparation or a detachable
prelude. It is of the essence of all that is happening:

That the intimate connection between words and rites may stand out in the liturgy:

(1) In sacred celebrations there is to be more reading from holy Scripture and it is to be more varied and apposite.

(2) Because the spoken word is part of the liturgical service, the best place for it, consistent with the nature of the rite, is to be indicated even in the rubrics; the ministry of preaching is to be fulfilled with exactitude and fidelity. Preaching should draw its content mainly from scriptural and liturgical sources, being a proclamation of God's wonderful works in the history of salvation, the mystery of Christ, ever present and active within us, especially in the celebration of the liturgy. (SC 35)

In the chapter on "The Most Sacred Mystery of the Eucharist," the council fathers made a number of statements about the use of Scripture that have had a bearing on the celebration of the other sacraments.

The treasures of the Bible are to be opened up more lavishly, so that a richer share in God's word may be provided for the faithful. (SC 51)

This is a specific affirmation about how the Scriptures should become a more ample part of the celebration of Mass. There is no equivalent in chapter 3 on "The Other Sacraments and the Sacramentals," but, combined with the comments in SC 35, the intent is clear that each of the sacraments, including baptism, should have "more lavish" reading of the Word of God. In fact, the celebration of baptism had no reading of Scripture as part of the ceremony in the ritual in use before Vatican II.

A further statement on the Eucharist bears consideration in relationship to the other sacraments:

The two parts that, in a certain sense, go to make up the Mass, namely, the liturgy of the word and the liturgy of the eucharistic, are so closely connected with each other that they form but one single act of worship. (SC 56)

The reading of Scripture at Mass is not optional or secondary. It is a constitutive element of eucharistic worship itself. By analogy, it would seem that this is also the case for the reading of the Scriptures in other sacraments. The reading of God's Word is not normally a component that can be dispensed with when baptism is celebrated.

The Reading of the Word of God
in the Rite of Christian Initiation of Adults

Even a casual reading of the order for adult initiation reveals a preeminent role for the reading of Scripture. It is a key element in each stage and each step of the process.

The Period of Evangelization and Precatechumenate

The name of this period, "evangelization[3] and precatechumenate," gives a hint of how important God's Word is. "It is a time of evangelization: faithfully and constantly the living God is proclaimed and Jesus Christ whom he has sent for the salvation of all. Thus those who are not yet Christians, their hearts opened by the Holy Spirit, may believe and be freely converted to the Lord and commit themselves sincerely to him" (RCIA 36). Several points are worth noting. God's Word is self-revelation. The Word is trinitarian, for Christ is proclaimed too, and the Holy Spirit makes ready the hearts of people. God initiates the communication and acts within the hearers so they can take in the Word and respond to it. The Word begins in God and ends in God, and the hearing and responding are due to God's presence and grace in the individual and community. The results of this interaction of God's Word in the life of a person are belief, conversion, and commitment.

"During this period, priests and deacons, catechists and other laypersons are to give the candidates a suitable explanation of the Gospel" (RCIA 38). This first explanation of the Gospel involves interactions with members of the Christian community in prayer and activity, and not just words. This whole interaction, in fact, is part of the evangelization taking place.

What this "suitable explanation" should help engender in inquirers is suggested by paragraph 42:

- the beginning of the spiritual life
- the fundamentals of Christian teaching
- evidence of first faith
- initial conversion
- intention to change one's life and enter into relationship with God in Christ

- first stirrings of repentance
- a beginning prayer life
- experience of the company of other Christians, both ordained and lay

This understanding of evangelization implies a theology of God's Word. It is first of all God's own Word. In that Word, God reveals himself. The book of Genesis portrays a God who creates by his Word: "Then God said, 'Let there be light'; and there was light" (Gen 1:3). God does not create and then vanish from the place of his creation. He enters into relationship with the human beings and all that he has created. For example, as soon as God has created the man and the woman, he begins to speak with them (Gen 1:28-30; 2:16-17; 3:8-19). These stories set the stage for unfolding the relationship between God and his human creation, a relationship marked by love, sin, and the promise of redemption.

The story moves into even more explicit forms of communication with the stories of the patriarchs and other heroes of the faith: of Noah; of Abraham, Isaac, and Jacob; of Joseph; and, finally, of Moses. The prophets continue the message of God to his people, calling them time and again to return to fidelity. God's special care and concern are revealed by his establishment of a covenant, a relationship that implies a mutual set of obligations imposed on all the involved parties.[4]

When we reflect on how God reveals himself, several points emerge. God communicates with words, that is, the Uncreated One "speaks" in created form, in the sounds and tonalities of human vocal cords and thought patterns. Clearly, God wants his creatures to hear and understand. The communication takes place principally in the form of narrative. Even law codes are embedded in the context of the story of God giving the law to his people. God is a character in a story that occurs at a given time and place, within history (the Timeless One found within time).

Research on how "word" (in Hebrew, *dabar*) functions in the Bible has revealed that the Jewish people understood "word" not as an abstract concept about communication, but as a powerful act that accomplishes what it says. Recent linguistic and anthropological studies put this insight into analogous terms, such as "performative language": words make things happen; e.g., when I say, "I do," I enter into marriage with my beloved who also says, "I do."[5]

The Word of God in the period of evangelization and precatechumenate performs this kind of powerful change in the lives of those who are seeking God.

Rite of Acceptance into the Order of Catechumens[6]

We have already explored the ritual and nonverbal context of the Word in this celebration: the gathering outside the church, a verbal accepting of the Gospel, and the signing of the candidates with the cross at least on the forehead but also on other senses and parts of the body. Then at the invitation of the celebrant the catechumens and the others present enter the church in procession to participate in the Liturgy of the Word.

Another context of this celebration is the specific structure of celebrating the Word. The reader proclaims the scriptural passage to the assembly. A period of silence invites the hearers to heed the promptings of the Holy Spirit to hear and receive the Word. The cantor leads those gathered in the responsorial psalm, God's Word becoming their words in reaction to what has been heard. The pattern of the first reading repeats itself with the second reading. The gospel is followed by the homily, which further unfolds what has occurred, both in action and in word. These divine elements are then gathered into prayer and offered to God. The pattern of the reading is: proclamation → silent acceptance → verbal response → finally, prayer.[7]

The readings recommended include Genesis 12:1-4a, the beginning of the story of Abraham. God calls Abram (not yet renamed Abraham) from his homeland and sends him to a new country. This highlights the experience of the new catechumens. They are being called from what is familiar and safe to an engagement with a new set of possibilities. God is calling them to a new land.

The responsorial psalm is Psalm 33:4-5, 12-13, 18-19, 20 and 22. The responsorial verse can be either, "Happy the people the Lord has chosen to be his own," or "Lord, let your mercy be on us, as we place our trust in you." Each refrain summarizes the sense of the psalm and its use in this rite. The new catechumens have been called, just as Abram was called. The relationship is initiated: God shows mercy to those responding to his call, and those called trust in the Lord.

The recommended gospel is John 1:35-42. John the Baptist identifies Jesus as the Lamb of God, and two of his disciples follow Jesus. One of them, Andrew, finds his brother Peter, and tells him, "We have found the Messiah." This story captures the incipient experience of the catechumens who have begun a relationship with the One who changes lives. They are called to risk familiar relationships to begin one that is exciting with possibilities but also fraught with the unknown.[8]

The Proclamation of the Word
during the Period of the Catechumenate

Formation in the Word of God is an integral part of the period of the catechumenate.[9] Paragraph 75 of the RCIA outlines the content of this period: four classic aspects of Christian life that the catechumen is entering. A suitable *catechesis* is supported by celebrations of the Word. They begin to share the Christian *journey of life*. Catechumens should *celebrate* the Word in the liturgy. Finally, having learned the faith in catechetical and liturgical environments and having begun to learn Christian living from the example of members of the Christian community, catechumens are called to *proclaim in words and deeds* the Gospel they have heard. The combination of catechesis, Christian living, liturgical celebration, and active evangelization, all of which involve God's Word, grounds the move toward conversion and faith—the key outcomes for someone coming to Christ.

Celebrations of the Word

These celebrations of the Word during the period of the catechumenate take place in three contexts. One is a public Celebration of the Word especially for catechumens. A second context is the community's regular Sunday worship, as they reflect on the Word of God as it is systematically proclaimed in the liturgical year. The third context is in conjunction with catechetical sessions.

The main purpose for the celebrations of the Word is given in paragraph 82: to implant teachings in the heart of the catechumens; to instruct them in the ways of prayer; to explain the fundamentally symbolic character of Christian time and celebration; and to enable their eventual participation with the whole community of faith in Sunday worship. There are some interesting presuppositions embodied in these stated purposes: that the appeal of Scripture is to the heart and imagination as well as to the mind, that the Celebration of the Word is always related to prayer, that Word is an essential component of the symbolic structure of liturgy, and that a goal of proclaiming the Word is to participate in the Christian community.

The format of the celebration outside Mass is very similar to the Liturgy of the Word within Mass: a song, a reading followed by a sung responsorial psalm, a homily, and some prayer to conclude the celebration (85–89). When done in conjunction with a catechetical session, it helps set a prayerful context (84). On Sundays, the dismissal from the assembly usually leads to a meeting to reflect upon that Word that was just heard (83, 89 with its note).[10]

The use of the scriptural Word in the period of the catechumenate is extensive. It could encompass the whole of the Sunday lectionary if a catechumen continues to reflect and pray for three years: "The duration of the catechumenate will depend on the grace of God and on various circumstances. . . . The time spent in the catechumenate should be long enough—several years if necessary—for the conversion and faith of the catechumens to become strong" (76).

It would seem that the Rite of Christian Initiation of Adults is anticipating that virtually every meeting of catechumens would be accompanied by the Word. There would be meetings on Sunday for the deeper study of the Word, and meetings during the week for study in the context of the Celebration of the Word. In some parish communities, the weekday meetings are more catechetical, and the Sunday readings focus more on faith development and liturgy. Both Sunday and weekday gatherings can be times for fostering the life of Christian community and apostolic work.[11]

The rite anticipates that the celebrations of the Word will permeate the whole process of catechesis: "During the period of the catechumenate there should be celebrations of the Word of God that accord with the liturgical seasons and that contribute to the instruction of the catechumens and the needs of the community" (81).

The Celebration of the Word in the Rite of Election or Enrollment of Names[12]

This celebration normally occurs on (or around) the First Sunday of Lent and is led by the bishop of the diocese or his delegate. In this celebration, catechumens enter the final stage of their preparation for baptism. This rite occurs when catechumens have experienced a conversion of mind and action, are sufficiently acquainted with Christian teaching, and have developed a spirit of faith and charity (120). With this celebration those approaching baptism are now called "elect" (chosen) or "competentes" (co-petitioners) or "illuminandi" (those to be enlightened).

As we saw in part 1, the ritual elements of this celebration are minimal. The catechumens are presented and affirmed by their sponsors and by the gathered faithful. Their names are enrolled, the bishop admits them among the elect, and he extends his hands over them in prayer.

The readings normally are those of the First Sunday of Lent.[13] The gospel is always that of the temptation of Christ, in one of the Synoptic versions.

Year A[14]

Genesis 2:7-9; 3:1-7 (The creation of our first parents, and sin.)

Psalm 51:3-4, 5-6, 12-13, 17 (Be merciful, O Lord, for we have sinned.)

Romans 5:12-19 or 5:12, 17-19 (Where sin increased, there grace increased all the more.)

Verse before the gospel: Matthew 4:4b (One does not live on bread alone, / but on every word that comes forth from the mouth of God.)

Matthew 4:1-11 (Jesus fasted for forty days and forty nights and was tempted.)

Year B

Genesis 9:8-15 (God's covenant with Noah when he was delivered from the flood.)

Psalm 24:4-5, 6-7, 8-9 (Your ways, O Lord, are love and truth to those who keep your covenant.)

1 Peter 3:18-22 (The water of the flood prefigured baptism, which saves you now.)

Verse as in Year A
Mark 1:12-15 (Jesus was tempted by Satan, and the angels ministered to him.)

Year C

Deuteronomy 26:4-10 (The confession of faith of the chosen people.)

Psalm 91:1-2, 10-11, 12-13, 14-15 (Be with me, Lord, when I am in trouble.)

Romans 10:8-13 (The confession of faith of all believers in Christ.)

Verse as in Year A
Luke 4:1-13 (Jesus was led by the Spirit into the desert and was tempted.)

Commentary[15]

The plan of the readings of the First Sunday of Lent falls within the overall organization of the Lenten Lectionary. The account of the temptation from each of the Synoptic Gospels continues the traditional use of the account on Lent's first Sunday. The introduction to the Lectionary describes it thus:

> The Old Testament readings are about the history of salvation, which is one of the themes proper to the catechesis of Lent. The series of texts for each Year presents the main elements of salvation history from its beginning until the promise of the New Covenant.
>
> The readings from the Letters of the Apostles have been selected to fit the Gospel and the Old Testament readings and, to the extent possible, to provide a connection between them (n. 97).[16]

The narrative of the temptation of Christ occurs in each Synoptic Gospel after Christ's baptism and is the prelude to the inauguration of his public ministry. Each evangelist gives the story a distinctive tone. Mark's version is the shortest. Matthew and Luke both recount that there are three temptations, though the order of the temptations is different according to the unique plan of the particular gospel.

The readings of Year A tell the story of creation and the introduction of sin into the world by our first parents, Adam and Eve. The fruit of the tree seduces them to choose themselves and their hunger over God's fabulous generosity shown forth in the garden. They are tempted by the serpent and succumb. It is a story that resonates with human experience in every age. Paul introduces us to the parallel between Christ and Adam (later tradition will extend this reflection to Mary and Eve). The choice of Adam leads to sin, the choice of Christ to salvation for all. What was broken by the revolt of the early pair is made whole by the actions of Christ. The gospel story according to Matthew shows us Christ hungry after forty days of fasting in the desert, but able to resist the blandishments of the tempter. The culminating temptation reveals the only one worthy of worship: God alone.

In Year B, the primary image is that of Noah and the flood. God destroys the sin of the world through a flood and then makes a covenant with Noah, symbolized by the rainbow, never more to act so catastrophically. First Peter makes the connection between the image of the flood and baptism. Here we see a usual way the liturgy (and the writers of the early Church) make connections: by typology. They were convinced that all true events and persons are intimately connected. Everything in the

Old Testament prefigures what is coming in the New, in Christ Jesus.[17] The story of Christ's temptation in Mark's gospel takes place in the wilderness, like the world after the devastation of the flood. He is not alone but surrounded by the beasts (like those on the ark?) and receives the ministry of angels. Then he immediately begins his ministry proclaiming the Gospel. Year B is the only year that contains the beginning of the public ministry. The role of proclamation of the Word of God as part of the process of conversion is here made explicit.

The theme of a public, even liturgical, professing of faith is clear in the readings of Year C. The public profession of faith given in Deuteronomy that names the core identity of the Chosen People is paralleled in the profession that we find in Paul's Letter to the Romans. Paul attaches the promise of salvation to the professing of faith in proclaiming that Jesus is Lord. The object of faith has changed: from the narrative of God's fidelity to the proclamation of Christ as fulfillment of God's plan. Luke has transposed the second and third temptations from the order in Matthew. He brings the temptations to culmination at the temple in Jerusalem where Jesus is revealed as God's Elect. Only Luke tells us that the devil will return in the last hours in Jerusalem to offer a final temptation. Jerusalem is the goal of Jesus' journey throughout the gospel; it is the place where he suffers, dies, is buried, and rises again. It is the place from which the Gospel will be proclaimed to the whole world.

The Rite of Election, using these readings, inaugurates the final, intense preparation for baptism by confronting the community with the reality of sin but also showing us that in Christ sin is overcome and that he joins us in our struggle.

The Celebration of the Word during the Period of Purification and Enlightenment

The key celebrations during the period of purification and enlightenment are the scrutinies and the presentations. The scrutinies take place on the Third, Fourth, and Fifth Sundays of Lent. They are the final preparation for baptism and confront the elect with all in their lives that is not yet in conformity with Christ. The readings of Year A are used and form the basis of the prayers of the rites. The gospels especially shape the prayers.

In contrast, the presentations are usually celebrated during the week. The elect are formally presented with the Creed and the Lord's Prayer, two texts that the baptized use constantly in their public life of prayer.

The Celebration of the Word in the Scrutinies

The scrutinies are a crucial part of the final stage of preparation before the celebration of the sacraments of initiation at the Easter Vigil. They flow out of the readings appointed for the Third, Fourth, and Fifth Sundays of Lent, especially the gospels. The nonverbal aspects take place immediately after the homily. The elect are called before the faithful who are gathered. They are asked to bow their heads or to kneel, and all pray for them during a period of silence. Then intercessions are offered on their behalf. The priest concludes with a complex prayer of exorcism: a prayer directed to the Father, an imposition of hands in silence, and finally a second prayer to Christ while extending his hands over the elect. The same ritual pattern is followed for each of the three scrutinies. What changes are the prayers, which are based on the readings of the Sunday. We will examine the prayer texts in the next chapter.

3rd Sunday of Lent, Year A

Exodus 17:3-7 (Give us water, so that we may drink.)

Psalm 95:1-2, 6-7, 8-9 (If today you hear his voice, harden not your hearts.)

Romans 5:1-2, 5-8 (The love of God has been poured into our hearts through the Holy Spirit that has been given to us.)

Verse: John 4:42, 15 (Lord, you are truly the Savior of the world; / give me living water, that I may never thirst again.)

John 4:5-42 (The water that I shall give will become a spring of eternal life.)

4th Sunday of Lent, Year A

1 Samuel 16:1b, 6-7, 10-13a (David is anointed as king of Israel.)

Psalm 23:1-3a, 3b-4, 5, 6 (The Lord is my shepherd; there is nothing I shall want.)

Ephesians 5:8-14 (Arise from the dead, and Christ will give you light.)

Verse: John 8:12 (I am the light of the world, says the Lord; / whoever follows me will have the light of life.)

John 9:1-41 (The man who was blind went off and washed himself and came back able to see.)

5th Sunday of Lent, Year A

Ezekiel 37:12-14 (I will put my spirit in you that you may live.)

Psalm 130:1-2, 3-4, 5-6, 7-8 (With the Lord there is mercy and fullness of redemption.)

Romans 8:8-11 (The Spirit of the One who raised Jesus from the dead dwells in you.)

Verse: John 11:25a, 26 (I am the resurrection and the life, says the Lord; / whoever believes in me will never die.)

John 11:1-45 (I am the resurrection and the life.)

Commentary.[18] The three scrutinies use the familiar figures from John's gospel, the Samaritan woman at the well, the man born blind, and Lazarus, to provide a point of entry for understanding what is unfolding for the elect during Lent and what the liturgical rite of the scrutinies is celebrating.

John's gospel has its own dynamics and properties that make it appropriate for use in these rites preparing for the celebration of baptism. In each story, Jesus enters into dialogue with key people and by a series of spiral conversations leads them through familiar territory into an ever more profound understanding of who God is, how God is operating, and how their own life is changing because God is working in them.[19]

The Samaritan woman meets Jesus and is led by a conversation that proceeds incrementally from alienation to belonging. She rejoins life with her fellow townspeople, and enters into relationship with Jesus. Water serves as the symbolic catalyst of her journey. What has been dry and lifeless now becomes fertile and fresh because of the presence of the Lord.

The man born blind receives his sight, but not just physical sight. His encounter with Jesus allows him to move from the darkness to light. While he is the one who is the object of Jesus' attentions, pointed conversations occur between the man who was born blind and the leaders who are looking to trip him up and find fault with Jesus. The irony is that the one who was blind now sees and those whose eyes have never been blind cannot see.

Lazarus never speaks in the gospel story. The conversation takes place between Jesus and the sisters of Lazarus. The topic is life, both physical and eternal. Jesus leads Mary and Martha to reflect on the gift of life and what prevents them from embracing the gift of eternal life.

These three gospel passages have been chosen to illuminate the path that the elect are taking as they approach baptism: water leading them into relationship with Christ and the community, sight that allows them to see beyond the common to the graced, and life that overcomes physical death. This is the same path that the faithful follow in their own journey of faith in life and during Lent. In the next chapter we will see how the scrutiny prayers expand these themes.

The Celebration of the Word in the Presentations

The Creed and the Lord's Prayer are building blocks for the life of faith. They organize one's life as a believer, and they are both part of the celebration of every Sunday Mass. They are presented to the elect during Lent, and the Creed is handed back by them on the morning of Holy Saturday in anticipation of the baptismal profession of faith with the community that night at the Easter Vigil. The Lord's Prayer is handed back during the celebration of the Easter Vigil. Here are the readings and a commentary for these two moments:

The presentation of the Creed (Third Week of Lent):[20]

> Deuteronomy 6:1-7 (Listen, Israel: You shall love the Lord your God with all your heart.)
>
> Psalm 19:8, 9, 10, 11 (Lord, you have the words of everlasting life.)
>
> Romans 10:8-13 (The confession of faith of the elect.) or 1 Corinthians 15:1-8a (The Gospel will save you only if you keep believing what I preached to you.)
>
> Verse: John 3:16 (God loved the world so much, he gave us his only Son, that all who believe in him might have eternal life.)
>
> Matthew 16:13-18 (On this rock I will build my Church.) or John 12:44-50 (I, the light, have come into the world, so that whoever believes in me need not remain in the dark any more.)

These readings combine accounts of professing faith (e.g., Deut 6) with assurances of how faith is a sure foundation of our life (e.g., Matt 16).

The presentation of the Lord's Prayer (Fifth Week of Lent):

> Hosea 11:1b, 3-4, 8c-9 (I have led you with cords of love.)
>
> Psalm 23:1-3a, 3b-4, 5, 6 (The Lord is my shepherd; there is nothing I shall want.) or Psalm 103:1-2, 8 and 10, 11-12, 13 and 18 (As a father is kind to his children, so kind is the Lord to those who fear him.)

Romans 8:14-17, 26-27 (You have received the Spirit that makes you God's children and in that Spirit we cry out, "Abba, Father!") or Galatians 4:4-7 (God has sent the Spirit of his Son into our hearts: the Spirit that cries, "Abba, Father!")

Verse: Romans 8:15 (You have received the Spirit which makes us God's children, and in that Spirit we call God our Father.)

Matthew 6:9-13 (The presentation of the Lord's Prayer.)

These readings highlight the relationship of faith that creates a bond of love between us and God, who is called Father, Abba. The intimate relationship that Jesus has with his Father is here revealed as one that we also share.[21]

The Celebration of the Word in the Preparation Rites on Holy Saturday[22]

The elect are asked to spend Holy Saturday as a day of reflection. They gather with some members of the community in prayer as a preparation for the Vigil they will celebrate that night (RCIA 185). After a song and greeting, a reading or perhaps several follow, interspersed with psalms or hymns in between. The optional Ephphetha rite includes the celebrant touching the ears and lips of the elect. The reciting of the Creed includes the elect coming before those assembled to give back the version of the Creed they had received at the presentation. The ritual elements with their readings include:

Recitation of the Creed. Matthew 16:13-17 (You are Christ, the Son of the living God.) or John 6:35, 63-71 (To whom shall we go? You have the words of eternal life.)

Here we have examples of those who profess their faith in Christ. It is life-giving, for he is the Way, the Truth, and the Life. The journey of the catechumens has been simultaneously with him and to him. The elect find encouragement for their own profession of faith.

Ephphetha rite. Mark 7:31-37 (Ephphetha, that is, be opened.)

Mark's account of Jesus exorcising and healing the deaf man provides a context for a recognition of closeness of the elect to Christ and their need for him. The elect (and all Christians) need to be freed from the powers of evil and opened to the workings of faith and to Christ himself. This account prepares the elect for the renunciation of sin and for the immersion in Christ in baptism.

These readings help to unfold the significance of the rites by highlighting the relationship that the rites imply: our faith is in Christ Jesus, who opens us to his Word and his love.

The Celebration of the Word in the Sacraments of Initiation (Easter Vigil)

As we saw above, the Easter Vigil unfolds in four parts. The first part is the ceremony of light, with the blessing of the new fire, the procession with the Easter Candle, and the singing of the Exsultet in its light. The second is the Liturgy of the Word. The third is the celebration of baptism and confirmation, and the fourth and final part of the celebration is the Eucharist. The readings[23]:

1. Genesis 1:1–2:2 or 1:1, 26-31 (God looked at everything he had made, and he found it very good.)
   Psalm 104 (Lord, send out your Spirit, and renew the face of the earth.) or Psalm 33 (The earth is full of the goodness of the Lord.)
2. Genesis 22:1-18 or 22:1-2, 9a, 10-13, 15-18 (The sacrifice of Abraham, our father in faith.)
   Psalm 16 (You are my inheritance, O Lord.)
3. Exodus 14:15–15:1 (The Israelites marched on dry land through the midst of the sea.)
   Exodus 15 (Let us sing to the Lord; he has covered himself in glory.)
4. Isaiah 54:5-14 (With enduring love, the Lord your redeemer takes pity on you.)
   Psalm 30 (I will praise you, Lord, for you have rescued me.)
5. Isaiah 55:1-11 (Come to me that you may have life. I will renew with you an everlasting covenant.)
   Isaiah 12 (You will draw water joyfully from the springs of salvation.)
6. Baruch 3:9-15, 32–4:4 (Walk toward the splendor of the Lord.)
   Psalm 19 (Lord, you have the words of everlasting life.)
7. Ezekiel 36:16-17a, 18-28 (I shall sprinkle clean water upon you and I shall give you a new heart.)
   Psalm 42 (Like a deer that longs for running streams, my soul longs for you, my God.) or Isaiah 12 (You will draw water joyfully from the springs of salvation.) or Psalm 51 (Create a clean heart in me, O God.)

Romans 6:3-11 (Christ, raised from the dead, dies no more.)

Verse (Alleluia, alleluia, alleluia.)

Year A	Year B	Year C
Matthew 28:1-10 (He has been raised from the dead and is going before you to Galilee.)	Mark 16:1-7 (Jesus of Nazareth, the crucified, has been raised.)	Luke 24:1-12 (Why do you seek the Living One among the dead?)

Commentary[24]

The readings of the Easter Vigil recapitulate the history of salvation into which the elect are about to be baptized. God's plan, begun in creation and carried out in history, fleshed out by the prophets and reflected upon in the Wisdom literature, made manifest in the life, death, and resurrection of Christ Jesus, now takes on a new embodiment in the elect who, after months and perhaps even years of preparation, will now be washed in the fountain of new life. These readings raise up the examples of those who have gone before and fill those present with the conviction that God continues to act in our midst as he did so powerfully in the events here recounted.

In terms of the elect who are gathered, the readings sum up the whole process that they have followed from the period of evangelization and precatechumenate, through the period of the catechumenate, and up to the period of purification and enlightenment. The Liturgy of the Word during the Easter Vigil presents a panorama of the key figures (Abraham and Isaac, Moses and the people of Israel) and of key themes (creation, redemption, life, splendor, rescue, cleansing, refreshment, and ultimately new life in Christ). The alternation of narrative and silence, the voices of celebrant and assembly in prayer and song, combine to draw the elect into the very story they are hearing. The Spirit that fills the Word also fills their hearts and gives them the capacity to recognize the varied stories as but a single tale and also as their own.

The Readings of the Period of Postbaptismal Catechesis or Mystagogy

During this final period, which leads into the day-to-day living of life in Christ in the Church, the newly baptized receive help in making the transition into this new communal existence. This period allows for a deeper appropriation of the gospel they have heard and the opportunity to enter ever more deeply into the life of the sacraments. The sacraments lead to a deepened understanding of Scripture and more regular contact with the faithful. This slow process is inaugurated in the Sunday Masses for the neophytes, that is, the Sundays of Easter. The readings of Year A are particularly apt for this process (RCIA 244–47).

Second Sunday of Easter[25]

Acts 2:42-47 (All who believed were together and had all things in common.)

Psalm 118 (Give thanks to the Lord for he is good, his love is everlasting.)

1 Peter 1:3-9 (God has given us new birth to a living hope through the resurrection of Jesus Christ from the dead.)

Verse: John 20:29 (You believe in me, Thomas, because you have seen me, says the Lord; / blessed are they who have not seen me, but still believe!)

John 20:19-31 (Eight days later Jesus came and stood in their midst.)

Third Sunday of Easter

Acts 2:14, 22-23 (It was impossible for Jesus to be held by death.)

Psalm 16 (Lord, you will show us the path of life.)

1 Peter 1:17-21 (You were saved with the precious Blood of Christ, as with that of a spotless, unblemished lamb.)

Verse: Luke 24:32 (Lord Jesus, open the Scriptures to us; / make our hearts burn while you speak to us.)

Luke 24:13-35 (They recognized Jesus in the breaking of bread.)

Fourth Sunday of Easter

Acts 2:14a, 36-41 (God has made Jesus both Lord and Christ.)

Psalm 23 (The Lord is my shepherd; there is nothing I shall want.)

1 Peter 2:20b-25 (You have returned to the shepherd and guardian of your souls.)

Verse: John 10:14 (I am the good shepherd, says the Lord; / I know my sheep, and mine know me.)

John 10:1-10 (I am the gate for the sheep.)

Fifth Sunday of Easter

Acts 6:1-7 (They chose seven men filled with the Spirit.)

Psalm 33 (Lord, let your mercy be on us, as we place our trust in you.)

1 Peter 2:4-9 (You are a chosen race, a royal priesthood.)

Verse: John 14:6 (I am the way, the truth, and the life, says the Lord; / no one comes to the Father, except through me.)

John 14:1-12 (I am the way and the truth and the life.)

Sixth Sunday of Easter

Acts 8:5-8, 14-17 (Peter and John laid hands on them, and they received the Holy Spirit.)

Psalm 66 (Let all the earth cry out to God with joy.)

1 Peter 3:15-18 (Put to death in the flesh, Christ was raised to life in the spirit.)

Verse: John 14:23 (Whoever loves me will keep my word, says the Lord, / and my Father will love him and we will come to him.)

John 14:15-21 (I will ask the Father and he will give you another Advocate.)

Ascension [can take the place of the Seventh Sunday of Easter]

Acts 1:1-11 (As the apostles were looking on, Jesus was lifted up.)

Psalm 47 (God mounts his throne to shouts of joy: a blare of trumpets for the Lord.)

Ephesians 1:17-23 (God seated Jesus at his right hand in the heavens.)

Verse: Matthew 28:19a, 20b (Go and teach all nations, says the Lord; / I am with you always, until the end of the world.)

Matthew 28:16-20 (All power in heaven and on earth has been given to me.)

Seventh Sunday of Easter

Acts 1:12-14 (All these devoted themselves with one accord to prayer.)

Psalm 27 (I believe that I shall see the good things of the Lord in the land of the living.)

1 Peter 4:13-16 (If you are insulted for the name of Christ, blessed are you.)

Verse: John 14:18 (I will not leave you orphans, says the Lord. / I will come back to you, and your hearts will rejoice.)

John 17:1-11a (Father, glorify your Son.)

Vigil of Pentecost

(One of the four Old Testament readings can be chosen, or all four can be read to form a vigil analogous to the Easter Vigil.)[26]

1. Genesis 11:1-9 (It was called Babel because there the Lord confused the speech of all the world.)
   Psalm 33 (Blessed the people the Lord has chosen to be his own.)
2. Exodus 19:3-8a, 16-20b (The Lord came down upon Mount Sinai before all the people.)
   Daniel 3 (Glory and praise forever!) or Psalm 19 (Lord, you have the words of eternal life.)
3. Ezekiel 37:1-14 (Dry bones of Israel, I will bring spirit into you, that you may come to life.)
   Psalm 107 (Give thanks to the Lord; his love is everlasting.)
4. Joel 3:1-5 (I will pour out my spirit upon the servants and handmaids.)

Psalm 104 (Lord, send out your Spirit, and renew the face of the earth.)

Romans 8:22-27 (The Spirit intercedes with inexpressible groanings.)

Alleluia verse (Come, Holy Spirit, fill the hearts of the faithful / and kindle in them the fire of your love.)

John 7:37-39 (Rivers of living water will flow.)

Pentecost

Acts 2:1-11 (They were all filled with the Holy Spirit and began to speak.)

Psalm 104 (Lord, send out your Spirit, and renew the face of the earth.)

1 Corinthians 12:3b-7, 12-13 (In one Spirit we were all baptized into one body.)

Verse (Come, Holy Spirit, fill the hearts of your faithful / and kindle in them the fire of your love.)

John 20:19-23 (As the Father sent me, so I send you: Receive the Holy Spirit.)

Commentary[27]

The mosaic of readings during the Easter Season serves as a slow unfolding of various dimensions of life in the Church. The neophytes have been to the mountaintop during the Easter Vigil. But now begins the slow process of entering into the mainstream of life in the Church. Naturally, they are enthusiastic (literally, filled with God). But now that enthusiasm must be marshaled to support the long haul of life in Christ and in the Church. For most, this life is more a marathon during which neophytes (and all Christians) must pace themselves rather than a sprint that requires an all-out effort from the start.

The Acts of the Apostles is an apt book to reflect on. Here we find ample evidence of the Spirit at work in the early community but also a recognition that the gifts of the Spirit must be organized for the good of the whole body. The First Letter of St. Peter, possibly written as a baptismal sermon, introduces those who hear it to the life of the Body of Christ, the temple of the Spirit, that must continue to grow and develop. The gospel accounts invite the neophytes and their brothers and sisters in the faith to contemplate life in Christ: this life was transformed by the forces of death, and now Christ leads the faithful, new and old, as a Good Shepherd, and calls them to be united always in the Holy Spirit, the Paraclete.

The readings provide a context in which the neophytes and the members of the community who welcome them continue the journey of conversion that they have begun. By continuing to learn the elements of the faith, joining in the life of the community, praying together in the liturgy, and doing apostolic works, they slowly but surely deepen their life as followers of Christ.

The journey that those coming to faith in Christ make is always interpreted by the Word of God. From the time of their initial recognition of the Lord at work to their final ritual engagement as members of his body at work in the world, God's own Word permeates the process. Finally, the persons are called to retell their personal stories as also Christ's story in the Spirit.

The Reading of the Word of God in the Rite of Baptism for Children

To bring out the paschal character of baptism, it is recommended that the sacrament be celebrated during the Easter Vigil or on Sunday, when the Church commemorates the Lord's resurrection. On Sunday, baptism may be celebrated even during Mass, so that the entire community may be present and the necessary relationship between baptism and eucharist may be clearly seen, but this should not be done too often. (RBC 9)

Baptism at Mass

When the baptism of children is celebrated during Sunday Mass, the readings are usually those of the Sunday. All that was said above about the role of the Lectionary in the RCIA is pertinent for the baptism of children. In this rite, however, the hearers of the scriptural readings are not those to be baptized but rather the parents of the child to be baptized. The child is being baptized in the faith of the Church and in the faith of the parents and godparents. Their faith needs nourishment to provide the context for their child's growth into the community of believers.

Since every Sunday is a celebration of the paschal mystery of Christ's dying and rising, every Sunday's readings provide a particular context for understanding how the paschal mystery takes shape in daily lives of the faithful.

Baptism outside Mass

When baptism takes place outside of Mass, particular readings are suggested for use during the celebration.

One or two passages from the gospels can be read. These four readings are mentioned within the description of the celebration:

John 3:1-6	The meeting with Nicodemus.
Matthew 28:18-20	The apostles are sent to preach the Gospel and to baptize.
Mark 1:9-11	The baptism of Jesus.
Mark 10:13-16	Let the little children come to me.

Chapter 7 of the rite offers further selections. In addition, other passages, "which better meet the wishes or needs of the parents," can be chosen (44).

The other readings include:

Old Testament

Exodus 17:3-7	Water from the rock.

Ezekiel 36:24-28   Clean water, a new heart, a renewed spirit.
Ezekiel 47:1-9, 12   The water of salvation.

New Testament

Romans 6:3-5   Baptism: a sharing in Christ's death
                         and resurrection.
Romans 8:28-32   We have become more perfectly like God's
                         own Son.
1 Corinthians   Baptized in one Spirit to form one body.
12:12-13
Galatians 3:26-28   Now that you have been baptized you have put
                         on Christ.
Ephesians 4:1-6   One Lord, one faith, one baptism.
1 Peter 2:4-5, 9-10   A chosen race, a royal priesthood.

Responsorial psalm

Psalm 23   The Lord is my shepherd; there is nothing I
                         shall want.
Psalm 27   The Lord is my light and my salvation.
Psalm 34   Come to him and receive his light!

Gospel

Matthew 22:35-40   The first and most important commandment.
Matthew 28:18-20   Christ sends his apostles to teach and baptize.
Mark 1:9-11   The baptism of Jesus.
Mark 10:13-16   Jesus loves children.
Mark 12:28b-34   Love God with all your heart.
John 3:1-6   The meeting with Nicodemus.
John 4:5-14   Jesus speaks with the Samaritan woman.
John 6:44-47   Eternal life through belief in Jesus.
John 7:37b-39a   Streams of living water.
John 9:1-7   Jesus heals a blind man who believes in him.
John 15:1-11   Union with Christ, the true vine.
John 19:31-35   The death of Christ, the witness of John the
                         apostle.

These readings form a rich collection of themes and plots that help
the parents, godparents, family members, and others of the faithful to ex-

perience Christ's presence in this ritual event. The readings from the Old Testament reveal God at work in water. Water gives life and is cleansing. The New Testament readings turn to Christ. His followers have become one with Christ in his dying and rising. Just as this child has donned a new baptismal garment, so the faithful are clothed in Christ. They are no longer isolated by the sin of the world but have become joined to one another in Christ. In the Church we form but a single priesthood for the worship of God, as Christ has taught us. The psalms exult in images of refreshment and light. Christ in the gospels heals body and soul. He offers teaching that changes relationships to their very core. He embraces children and challenges his followers to behave in the same way. He offers those on the fringes of society a place with him and with a community of believers.

Out of the riches listed above only one or two readings will ring out in the celebration. The implication is that those present are called to return often to hear God's Word and enter into the richness of the vision of life in Christ that is offered in baptism to their child and to them.

Summary and Conclusion

In this chapter we began by reflecting on how Christ is really present to us in his Word. Far from being stories from a long-ago, distant country, the Word of God proclaimed in the liturgy is a living narrative. In the faithful reading of the Word, those who hear come to recognize that the narratives of their own lives are caught up in the story of God's presence and action in their midst. The God of history is the God of the present.

The stories of God acting both through water and in Christ shape the liturgical use of water, oil, and light and reveal their meaning in the light of the paschal mystery. Water is life-giving—the kind of life revealed in the readings. Oils both tone muscles and perfume skins—muscles tested in battles of biblical dimensions and scented skin marking those belonging to the one in whose image they are sealed. Light breaks the dark—revealing the one who has been waiting all along.

In the next chapter, we explore words of prayer, rooted in Scripture and paired with rites and symbols even more directly.

Notes, Chapter Three

[1] The theme of the manifold presence of Christ is one developed in the midst of the twentieth-century liturgical movement. For an exposition of the documents and a commentary see Michael G. Witczak, "The Manifold Presence of Christ in the Liturgy," *Theological Studies* 59 (1998): 680–702.

[2] *The Passover Haggadah*, ed. Nahum Glatzer (New York: Schocken, 1953, 1989), 59–61. See *The Mishnah*, Tractate Pesahim 10.5, trans. Herbert Danby (Oxford: Oxford University Press, 1933), 150–51.

[3] "Evangelization" comes from the Latin word *evangelium*, in turn from the Greek *euangelion*, meaning "good news." The gospel (from "god" and "spel," Old English for "good news") tells of God's plan of salvation for all peoples through Jesus Christ, in the Holy Spirit. See William G. Thompson and Gerard S. Sloyan, *The Collegeville Pastoral Dictionary of Biblical Theology*, ed. Carroll Stuhlmueller (Collegeville, MN: Liturgical Press, 1996), s.v. "Good News/Gospel."

[4] See Lucien Deiss, *God's Word and God's People* (Collegeville, MN: Liturgical Press, 1976).

[5] See George S. Worgul, *From Magic to Metaphor: A Validation of the Christian Sacraments* (New York: Paulist, 1980); David N. Power, *Sacrament: The Language of God's Gift* (New York: Crossroad, 1999). See Louis-Marie Chauvet, *The Sacraments: The Word of God at the Mercy of the Body* (Collegeville, MN: Liturgical Press, A Pueblo Book, 2001); Kathleen Cannon, *New Dictionary of Sacramental Worship* (*NDSW*), ed. Peter E. Fink (Collegeville, MN: Liturgical Press, A Michael Glazier Book, 1990), s.v. "Word, Theology of the"; Irene Nowell, William Thompson, and Gerard Sloyan, *The Collegeville Pastoral Dictionary of Biblical Theology*, ed. Carroll Stuhlmueller (Collegeville, MN: Liturgical Press, 1996), s.v. "Word."

[6] See Kathleen Hughes, "Acceptance into the Order of Catechumens," in *Celebrating the Rites of Adult Initiation: Pastoral Reflections*, ed. Victoria M. Tufano (Chicago: Liturgy Training Publications, 1992), 1–13, esp. 10; Richard N. Fragomeni, "Acceptance into the Order of Catechumens," in *Commentaries on the Rite of Christian Initiation of Adults*, ed. James A. Wilde (Chicago: Liturgy Training Publications, 1988), 5–13; Morris, *The RCIA*, 100–115.

[7] See Michael Downey, *NDSW*, s.v. "Silence, Liturgical Role of"; Lawrence Cunningham, "Silence," in *The Catholic Experience* (New York: Crossroad, 1985), 64–87. Pope John Paul II speaks of it this way: "the liturgical proclamation of the word of God . . . is . . . a dialogue between God and his people, a dialogue in which the wonders of salvation are proclaimed and the demands of the covenant are continually restated. On their part, the People of God are drawn to respond to this dialogue of love by giving thanks and praise, also by demonstrating their fidelity to the task of continual conversion," in his apostolic letter *Dies Domini*, On Keeping the Lord's Day Holy, 31 May 1998, n. 41; see *The Liturgy Documents: A Parish Resource*, vol. 2, ed. David A. Lysik (Chicago: Liturgy Training Publications, 1999), 26.

⁸ See the commentary in Pamela E. Jackson, *Journeybread for the Shadowlands: The Readings of the Rites of the Catechumenate, RCIA* (Collegeville, MN: Liturgical Press, 1993), 13–24.

⁹ See *Before and after Baptism: The Work of Teachers and Catechists*, ed. James A. Wilde (Chicago: Liturgy Training Publications, 1988), esp. James B. Dunning, "Prebaptismal and Postbaptismal Catechesis for Adults," 53–65.

¹⁰ See *Before and after Baptism*, esp. Gerard S. Sloyan, "Forming Catechumens through the Lectionary," 27–37; and Catherine Dooley, "The Lectionary as Sourcebook of Catechesis in the Catechumenate," 39–51. See also James B. Dunning, *Echoing God's Word: Formation for Catechists and Homilists in a Catechumenal Church* (Arlington, VA: North American Forum on the Catechumenate, 1993), esp. 96–148.

¹¹ See, e.g., Morris, *The RCIA*, 116–49. See also *Journey to the Fullness of Life: A Report on the Implementation of the Rite of Christian Initiation of Adults in the United States* (Washington, DC: United States Catholic Conference, 2000), esp. 20.

¹² See Allan Bouley, "Election or Enrollment of Names," in Wilde, *Commentaries*, 25–33.

¹³ RCIA 128 makes provision for other readings to be chosen, particularly when the Rite of Election must be celebrated on some other day for pastoral reasons.

¹⁴ All the parenthetical explanations are from the *Lectionary for Mass*, vol. 1 (Collegeville, MN: Liturgical Press, 1998).

¹⁵ Lectionary for Mass: Introduction, n. 97, in *The Liturgy Documents*, vol. 1, 4th ed. (Chicago: Liturgy Training Publications, 2004), 145. See Normand Bonneau's commentary on the lectionary, *The Sunday Lectionary: Ritual Word, Paschal Shape* (Collegeville, MN: Liturgical Press, 1998), 96–107. See the commentary in Morris, *The RCIA*, 150–65. See Rita Ferrone, *On the Rite of Election*, Forum Essays, Number 3 (Chicago: Liturgy Training Publications, 1994), esp. 29–30, 37–58. See also Jackson, *Journeybread*, 25–72. A good commentary from a historical-critical perspective is Dianne Bergant, with Richard Fragomeni, *Preaching the New Lectionary, Year A* (Collegeville, MN: Liturgical Press, 2001), 86–92; *Year B* (1999), 93–99; *Year C* (2000), 92–98. See also the commentaries (from a liturgical point of view) of Adrien Nocent, *The Liturgical Year*, vol. 2 (Collegeville, MN: Liturgical Press, 1977), 69–77, 131–42, 161–64; and Adolf Adam, *The Key to Faith: Meditations on the Liturgical Year* (Collegeville, MN: Liturgical Press, 1998), 47–51.

¹⁶ Lectionary for Mass: Introduction, in *The Liturgy Documents*, vol. 1, 145.

¹⁷ See Enrico Mazza, *Mystagogy: A Theology of Liturgy in the Patristic Age* (Collegeville, MN: Liturgical Press, Pueblo, 1989); David N. Power, *The Word of the Lord: Liturgy's Use of Scripture* (Maryknoll, NY: Orbis, 2001).

¹⁸ See Jackson, *Journeybread*, 73–87, 103–19, 121–40. See also the commentaries by Bergant and Fragomeni (see note 15 above for *Year A*), 97–114; by Adam (note 15 above), 54–64; by Nocent (note 15 above), 92–130. In addition, consult Robert D. Duggan, "Coming to Know Jesus the Christ: The First Scrutiny," in Wilde, *Commentaries*, 43–51; Duggan, "God Towers over Evil: The Second Scrutiny," Wilde, *Commentaries*, 53–59; Mark Searle, "For the Glory of God: The Third Scrutiny," in Wilde, *Commentaries*, 61–71; Mark R. Francis, "To Worship God in Spirit and in Truth," in Tufano, *Celebrating*, 63–71; Jan Michael Joncas, "I Once Was Blind and

Now I See: Second Scrutiny," in Tufano, *Celebrating*, 83–91; Rita Ferrone, "Lazarus, Come Out! Third Scrutiny," in Tufano, *Celebrating*, 105–13.

[19] See Raymond Brown, *The Gospel According to John (I–XII)*, The Anchor Bible 29 (Garden City, NY: Doubleday, 1966), 164–98, 369–82, 420–37. See also Francis J. Moloney, *The Gospel of John*, Sacra Pagina 4 (Collegeville, MN: Liturgical Press, A Michael Glazier Book, 1998), 113–64, 289–312, 322–46.

[20] The parenthetical explanations of the readings for all the following rites are from *The Rite of Christian Initiation of Adults* at the paragraph numbers indicated.

[21] See Jackson, *Journeybread*, 89–101, 141–63; Morris, *The RCIA*, 176–80.

[22] See Jackson, *Journeybread*, 165–71; Morris, *The RCIA*, 192–94.

[23] The parenthetical explanations of these readings are from the *Lectionary for Mass*, vol. 1 (Collegeville, MN: Liturgical Press, 1998).

[24] Lectionary for Mass: Introduction, n. 99, *The Liturgy Documents*, vol. 1, 146; Bonneau, *The Sunday Lectionary*, 63–68. See the commentaries in Bergant and Fragomeni, *Year A*, 136–49; *Year B*, 147–60; *Year C*, 144–57. See the liturgical commentaries in Nocent, *The Liturgical Year*, 3:113–29; Adam, *The Key to Faith*, 77–80.

[25] The parenthetical explanations for the Sundays of Easter and Pentecost are from the *Lectionary for Mass*, vol. 1 (Collegeville, MN: Liturgical Press, 1998). "Allelluia" may be used as the psalm response throughout the season of Easter.

[26] The 2008 emendation of the Third Typical Edition of the *Missale Romanum* lays out how the Vigil of Pentecost should be celebrated. *Missale Romanum: Supplementum excerptum ex editione typica tertia emendata* (Vatican City: Libreria Editrice Vaticana, 2008), 2–5. See also the Bishops' Committee on Divine Worship, "Celebrating the Extended Vigil of Pentecost," *Newsletter* 45 (April 2009): 16.

[27] See "Lectionary for Mass: Introduction," n. 100, *The Liturgy Documents*, vol. 1, 146–47; Bonneau, *The Sunday Lectionary*, 79–93. See Morris, *The RCIA*, 210–23. See also Bergant and Fragomeni, *Year A*, 152–205; Nocent, *The Liturgical Year*, 3: 159–67, 176–82, 189–90, 198–200, 205–12, 217–20, 227–30, 236–38, 244–55; Adam, *The Key to Faith*, 81–96.

Chapter Four

The Words of Prayer at Baptism

Introduction

We have been reflecting on the role of words in the celebration of baptism. The previous chapter explored the words of Scripture. The stories and images of the Old Testament and the descriptions and theological reflections of the New Testament focus the meaning of the celebration of baptism. The dynamics of proclaiming God's Word within a liturgical assembly provided the foundation for understanding the specific readings within the various celebrations.

This chapter studies the biblical Word transformed into prayer and the subsequent extended role of the Word in celebration. Liturgical prayers draw on scriptural images and phrases to articulate the presence of God, his actions in our midst, and our attitudes and response to his presence and action among us.

First, we will give an overview of the structure of prayer and its inherent dynamic. Then we will look at specific prayers from the various rites of the celebration of the baptism of adults and children. There are other verbal forms such as instructions and performative words, including the formula of baptism itself, that we will also consider.

How We Pray Liturgically

Prayer, of course, is a vast topic. It expresses the relationship between God and ourselves. There are as many forms of prayer as there are persons praying. Prayer can be formal or informal, verbal or nonverbal, long or short, offered at home or at church or anyplace else. Our consideration is directed to the prayers that are contained in the official liturgy of baptism, the Rite of Christian Initiation of Adults and the Rite of Baptism for Children.[1]

When we think of our prayers during liturgy, we immediately realize that a particular pattern emerges in the way that we pray. This first section will explore the pattern of our prayer.

The Structure of Prayer

Manuals of liturgy distinguish between "major euchology" and "minor euchology." Major euchology includes the great prayers of a liturgical act. Examples would be the eucharistic prayer at Mass, the prayer of consecration at an ordination, or the nuptial blessing at a marriage. For the celebration of baptism, the major prayer is the blessing of baptismal water. Minor euchology includes shorter prayers that are used at various times and places in the course of a celebration. At Mass, this would refer to the opening prayer or collect, the prayer over the gifts, and the prayer after communion. At baptisms, this would include exorcisms and blessings during the catechumenate or in the Rite of Baptism for Children. Major euchology differs from minor euchology in length and density of thought and imagery.[2]

Every prayer has a structure. Some structures are more elaborate while others are simpler. Prayers have a place within larger ritual structures and also have their own internal structure. Understanding these various interrelationships can help in understanding the specific meaning of the prayer in its larger context and in itself.[3]

Structure I: The Process of Prayer

The first structure we will describe is the "ideal type" of a liturgical prayer, in particular the form called the collect. The ideal type is the basic structure that underlies most prayers. Not every prayer always follows the ideal type exactly, but the ideal type allows a template against which we can see how a given prayer is put together. This type is called the "collect" in part because it "collects" the prayers of all who are present into the prayer of the celebrant.

In the ideal type, the celebrant[4] first invites everyone to pray. All present then spend a short time in silent prayer. The celebrant then proclaims the prayer aloud, and at its end all present say "Amen," a Hebrew word meaning "so be it," which affirms the prayer that has been spoken.

Invitation by the celebrant. The formal experience of prayer begins when the celebrant calls everyone to that act. It can be as simple as the phrase "Let us pray." The invitation can also be more elaborate, reminding those present of various motives for prayer. At other times the invitation can be implicit. In all circumstances, this moment identifies the action in which the community will be engaging: prayer.

Silent reflection. The rubric provides a moment for all to spend in silent prayer. The role of silence was discussed above in some detail. Here we simply recall that the invitation to pray should engage all those present in praying: this whole community of believers and not only the celebrant should spend some time in prayer.

We will note as we study various concrete prayers that silence is sometimes replaced by something else. Sometimes the community prays on its own behalf in petitions, saying after each one, "Lord, hear our prayer," for example. The Litany of the Saints directs the faithful to say "Pray for us" after each saint's name is invoked. At other times, the invitation initiates an action, perhaps a sort of "prayer in act."

Body of the prayer. After all have spent some time in silent prayer, the celebrant collects these silent prayers into the words the ritual gives him to say. These words are rarely extemporized. Rather, they are derived from the Church's long history of prayer, whether verbatim from an ancient source or composed from several modern sources.[5]

Response/ratification by the people. As the prayer concludes with a typical formula, the people make the prayer their own by saying "Amen." This indicates that the prayer says what the person had prayed in silence after the invitation (at least ideally).

Structure II: The Body of the Prayer

The overall structure of the prayer given above forms the context for the spoken prayers that the faithful offer during each liturgy. There is always, at least implicitly, an invitation, a time for interior silent prayer, a traditional text spoken by the celebrant, and ratification by those present. It is characteristic of both major and minor euchology.

Within that general structure, the prayer led by the celebrant aloud also has a structure. It is addressed to God, acknowledging certain divine characteristics. The celebrant asks God to do certain things on behalf of the community and the world and concludes by offering praise to the triune God. A handy way of keeping track of this structure is You, Who, Do, Through. We will explain this mnemonic more thoroughly below.

Invocation. We address God by name (You). This seemingly simple fact of "calling someone by name" hides the wonder that the all-powerful Creator of the world and everything in it chooses to be in relationship with his creatures. We can call upon God who answers us. We do not talk about God; we talk directly to God.

Relative predicate. After calling upon God in prayer, we recognize that this is a God who has acted and continues to act in our midst. This recognition is usually set in the form of a relative clause (Who). This is a God who has certain qualities and characteristics. The prayer tradition is rich in its memory of and attributes for God.

Petition. The personal God who has acted toward us in particular ways in the past is now asked to act in the present, either on our behalf or on behalf of others for whom we may be praying (Do). What God is asked to do usually flows from the specific name of God invoked and the particular activity or quality of God mentioned earlier in the prayer. The diversity of what we ask for in prayer is immense. This part of the prayer often asks that we be granted the ability to act in a Godlike way now and in the future.

Doxology. The prayer usually concludes with a trinitarian flourish. We praise God for being who he is. The prayer is mediated through Christ our Lord, God's Son, and offered in unity with the Holy Spirit, who is the active presence of God in the world (Through).[6] Christian prayer always ends with a reminder that we all are projected into the future (for ever and ever).

Structure III: A Theological Structural Approach

As these two brief structural analyses have shown, our prayer tradition is rich and somewhat complex, with structures within structures. But what emerges from even a cursory examination of the treasury of the Church's prayer is the priority of two characteristics: remembering and petitioning.[7]

Anamnesis (memorial). Our faith is rooted in history. When God created the heavens and the earth (Gen 1), he also inaugurated time. All the books of the Bible, including the Hebrew Bible, the Apocrypha/Deutero-canonical Books, and the New Testament, emerge from this sense of the unfolding of God's relationship with his people in time. For Christians, that time culminates in the incarnation of the Word in the person of Jesus Christ. *Anamnesis* is the Greek word for "remembrance" and is used in the account of the Last Supper as reported by Paul in 1 Corinthians 11:23-24 and in Luke 22:19, "Do this in remembrance of me."

Prayer that emerges from this radical historical sensibility is conscious of what has gone before. Jewish and Christian prayer typically names what God has done in the past. The Scriptures abound with prayers of this sort. The prayer in Nehemiah 8–9 at the rededication of the people to the covenant is typical. God is remembered as creator and redeemer. Christian prayer, following Christ's command to "do this in memory of me" (1 Cor 11:24), sees Christ as the fulcrum of this remembering.

This role of remembering as part of prayer is most obvious in the major euchology of eucharistic prayers, prayers of ordination, and the like. It is found, but in lapidary style, in the minor euchology like collects and is sometimes subsumed into the simple naming of God, for instance, in many prayers over the gifts or prayers after communion.

Memorial as a theme of theology has emerged only recently, as scholars began using the prayers of the tradition as a source of theological reflection. It has proved to be especially enriching to eucharistic theology, and we will see that it has a great deal to contribute to the theology of baptism.[8]

All that we do is rooted in what God has first done. We begin our prayers by remembering some aspect of that divine activity. A key element here is God's act of establishing a covenant with his people. That covenant is not simply a contractual arrangement, an establishment of some sort of quid pro quo, but rather is a bond similar to marital fidelity (see, e.g., the book of the prophet Hosea). It is not about business but rather about love. The memorial part of a prayer rehearses the story of this relationship over time. Longer prayers do this at greater length. Perhaps the most complete articulation is found in Eucharistic Prayer IV, based on an earlier prayer from the Eastern tradition.[9]

A study of the prayers of the tradition reveals that the anamnesis, the memorial, the remembrance, is not simply a personal, subjective, psychological calling to mind of something that once happened for the sake of nostalgia or creating a historical chronology. Rather, the kind of memorial done in a prayer is public (the whole community is doing it, and the memory itself is of a public event); it is objective (not subjective or dependent on someone's own personal recollection); it is dynamic (not passive—it leads to some further action); and it is forward-looking (not nostalgic).

Prayers do not just remember. They move from remembering what God has done to asking God to do something here and now.

Epiclesis (invocation/petition). The point of the remembering is achieved in the epiclesis or invocation/petition. We remember what God has done as a prelude for asking God to continue to act in a similar way in our midst here and now. We ask that he be faithful to himself and to his covenant. Ultimately, we ask him to continue the work accomplished by his Son Jesus Christ through the working of the Holy Spirit.[10] *Epiclesis* is the Greek word for "invocation." In theology, it often refers to the invocation of the Holy Spirit.

The prayer tradition makes clear that we are not dealing with the God of the deists. They conceive of God as the great watchmaker in the sky who started the world (wound it up) and then lets it tick on with no further interaction. Our God, the God of Jesus Christ, is the one who has acted out of covenant love for his creatures and now continues to do so through the action of the Holy Spirit. The major euchology almost always mentions the work of the Spirit explicitly. The minor euchology most often does not.

The Holy Spirit is the dynamic force that moves us from the past (what God has done) to the present and future (what God is doing and will do). Any result of the prayer occurs because of the presence and action of the Holy Spirit. In fact, in the silence that precedes the prayer (see structure 1 above), it is the Spirit who moves us to prayer initially. Prayer begins and ends in the Holy Spirit.

The Theology Inherent in the Structure

This first section of the chapter has laid out the basic structure of prayer that we find in the celebration of the liturgy, any liturgy, in the Catholic Church. Whenever we pray, the theology and the dynamics inherent in liturgical prayer are also present. As we will see in part 2 of this chapter, this general theology will be specified within the context of celebrating baptism.

Remembering and Asking

We are creatures and are contingent. We come from God and are set into a particular time and place. We remember the story of how God first created the world and how he has interacted with it since. We ponder the men and women with whom God entered into a loving relationship and the ups and downs of those stories of love. Our remembrance situates us in that history. In the light of God's action in the past, we now have the confidence to ask God to be faithful to those actions and to the covenant that he formed with Abraham, Isaac, and Jacob and renewed in a definitive way in the Word made flesh who died and rose again for our salvation. Our remembering and asking are rooted in a particular sense of who God is and who we are.

Mediation

Every prayer reminds us that all is done "through Christ our Lord." Jesus Christ, the second person of the Trinity became human, proclaimed the Good News of the kingdom of God, healed the sick and forgave sinners, gathered disciples and taught them, and suffered, died, and was buried. And he rose again. This creedal formulation, repeated every Sunday and at every baptism, reminds us that the uncreated God always acts in a mediated way in creation. His Son is the highest manifestation of that mediation, combining in his person full humanity and full divinity. No one can speak God's love to humans more effectively than he. No one can convey human love to God more effectively than he. For this reason, all prayer is "through Christ our Lord" who knows us better than we know ourselves.

Ordering

Our prayer in the liturgy is always ordered. The community of believers gathers and its actions are organized with certain persons taking particular roles: decorators, sacristans, ushers, readers, servers, ministers of Communion, cantors, psalmists, deacons, priests, and others too numerous to mention all work together. Their prayer and worship is called to order and led by the celebrant, assisted by others. All pray, but one person articulates the prayer. All are part of the one Church, but one person connects the particular community to the larger body of believers. There are many members but only one head, whether it be of a parish, a diocese, or the whole Church throughout the world.

Trinity

Every prayer is inherently trinitarian. In general, prayer is addressed to the Father, through the Son, in the Holy Spirit. There are variations on this pattern, but the fundamental orientation of prayer following this pattern helps us to keep the richness of the divine life always before us.

Silence and Affirmation

Prayer is an articulation of God's presence and action in our midst. It is led by the celebrant who orders the community and connects it to the local bishop and to the Church universal. But prayer is also the activity of each person present. That action takes place both in silence and in words. The silence is the prerequisite for prayer. It is in silence that each person opens up to the work of the Spirit, becomes aware of needs personal and communal, offers up gifts and needs. And each person ratifies the words of the tradition spoken by the celebrant with the spoken "Amen." Silence and word are indispensable building blocks for the prayer of the Church.[11]

Temporal Axis (Remembering the Past, Asking for Today, Awaiting the Kingdom)

Every prayer inserts us into the vast arc of history. We pray out of a past that has shaped us. We pray out of a present sense of gratitude and need for who we are and what we and our world need now. We pray with the realization that all is oriented toward a final consummation in God's kingdom where he will be all in all. Every prayer brings us from a remote past to a distant future within a present that embraces all who exist.[12]

Action and Qualities (We Do Something, We Become Something)

Every prayer has the capacity to change us. By remembering what God has done and then asking God to act that way here and now, we open ourselves to God's working in and on us. We ask for strength to act, or for healing, or for the blessings of God on those in need. We ask that particular virtues be strengthened in us. Each petition has the capacity to alter us and the fabric of our lives. Every prayer is an act of trust that God will continue to be our foundation in the changes that we request.[13]

The Prayers of Baptism in the RCIA

The Rite of Christian Initiation of Adults and the Rite of Baptism for Children contain more prayers than we can comment on in the space available. We will focus on some key texts and hope to give the reader the tools to understand all the prayers of these rites.

Prayers and Catechumens

The period of the catechumenate begins with the Rite of Acceptance into the Order of Catechumens, and continues with the various elements of formation described in RCIA 75. The rite gives a collection of prayers, both exorcisms and blessings, to be used during this period. In the section to follow, we will explore a prayer unit from the Rite of Acceptance into the Order of Catechumens, and comment on sample prayers from the repertoire.[14]

Signing of the Candidates

In the Rite of Acceptance into the Order of Catechumens (48–74), those who are not yet members of the Church are signed with the cross and become members—not yet fully, but as a member of the Order of Catechumens. This act is accompanied by words, actually a complex set of words. All, the faithful, candidates for the catechumenate, and their sponsors, have gathered outside the door of the church. After a greeting, the opening dialogue establishes their identity (name) and the purpose for their presence (baptism). The candidates make a first acceptance of the Gospel and receive affirmation by their sponsors and the community.

The signing of the candidates with the cross follows with this structure:

- Invitation by the celebrant (two options, depending on the number of candidates)
- Tracing of the sign of the cross with the recitation of a formula
- Acclamation of the people present
- [Signing of the other senses—optional]
- Concluding prayer (two options)

Briefly comparing this with the ideal form we explained above shows some similarities and differences. The invitation asks people to come forward rather than to pray. In place of silence, the celebrant signs the candidate with the cross, using a formula addressed to the candidate. The acclamation by the people at this point has no clear analogue in the ideal structure. The concluding prayer is introduced by another invitation, "Let us pray," but no indication of silent prayer is given. We will notice the relationship between performative texts and prayer texts in other moments of the RCIA.

The texts follow:

> Invitation: Come forward now with your sponsors to receive the sign of your new way of life as catechumens.

The sign of the cross is accompanied by:

> N., receive the cross on your forehead.
> It is Christ himself who now strengthens you
> with this sign of his love.
> Learn to know him and follow him.

The people sing: Glory and praise to you, Lord Jesus Christ!
The concluding prayer: Let us pray.
Option A:

> Lord,
> we have signed these catechumens
> with the sign of Christ's cross.
> Protect them by its power,
> so that, faithful to the grace which has begun in them,
> they may keep your commandments
> and come to the glory of rebirth in baptism.
> We ask this through Christ our Lord.

The people respond: Amen.

Option B:

> Almighty God,
> by the cross and resurrection of your Son
> you have given life to your people.
> Your servants have received the sign of the cross:
> make them living proof of its saving power
> and help them to persevere in the footsteps of Christ.
> We ask this through Christ our Lord.

The people respond: Amen.

This is a complex moment in the ritual. During this action and prayer, the candidates become catechumens. The change occurs with the action and words pronounced during the action. The words specify the meaning of the action (not just any cruciform marking, but signing with Christ's cross). This performative word is completed by a prayer addressed to God.

The prayers follow the second structure we described above. Option A begins by calling on God as "Lord." In place of a relative predicate describing some action or characteristic of God, the prayer recalls what we have just done: signed the catechumens with the cross of Christ. The second part of the prayer reveals the attributes of God that are pertinent: God has already given them grace and given commandments as part of his covenant love. Christ's cross is a sign of all that God will and can do. The petition asks, in the light of the cross received, for current protection, for the ability to keep God's commandments, and for future rebirth in baptism.

Option B invokes God as "almighty." There is a relative predicate: this is the God who gives life through the cross of Christ. After reminding us of the action just performed, the petition asks that the lives of the new catechumens reveal the power of the cross. Again, the prayer looks to the future by asking for perseverance in following Christ.[15]

In the ideal overall structure we identified above, the invitation is followed by silence in which the Holy Spirit leads all those present to prayer. In the ritual action we have just described, the invitation-silence moment becomes invitation–symbolic act. Note that in both cases, the Holy Spirit is understood to be acting: in the first case, in the silence, leading people to prayer; in the second case, in the symbol/verbal formula accomplishing the meaning of the act. In both cases, the invitation sets the context for the work of the Spirit.

Exorcisms and Blessings

The period of the catechumenate is described in the RCIA as marked by a comprehensive formation that includes intellectual, ecclesial, liturgical, and apostolic components (75). A key element is the gathering for catechetical sessions, which includes a Celebration of the Word (81–89). The model celebration concludes with a minor exorcism or with a blessing. If it concludes with a minor exorcism, a blessing may also be added to it.

Minor exorcisms. When we speak of exorcisms today, all too often it conjures up images from movies like *The Exorcist*, with lurid scenes of the devil possessing someone and a brave exorcist combating it.

The actual roles of minor exorcisms during the catechumenate and of the major exorcisms (the scrutinies) during the period of purification and enlightenment are of a vastly different character. These rites are rooted in the sense that the world is in fact rife with evil power and evil actions. These exorcisms are not designed to drive this evil away directly but rather to strengthen the catechumens for their daily struggle with sin, evil, and the devil.[16]

The overall structure of the Celebration of the Word is (85–89):

- Song
- Readings and responsorial psalms
- Homily
- Concluding rites

The concluding rites can be a minor exorcism or a blessing. If a minor exorcism is used, it can be followed by a blessing or on occasion by the rite of anointing (89).

The prayer of exorcism begins with the catechumens kneeling while the celebrant stretches hands over them. One of eleven prayers follows. We give two examples (94A and H):

> Let us pray.
> God of power,
> who promised us the Holy Spirit through Jesus your Son,
> we pray to you for these catechumens,
> who present themselves before you.
> Protect them from the spirit of evil
> and guard them against error and sin,
> so that they may become the temple of your Holy Spirit.
> Confirm what we profess in faith,
> so that our words may not be empty,
> but full of the grace and power
> by which your Son has freed the world.
> We ask this through Christ our Lord.
> Amen.

The structure is as we outlined above: introduction, prayer, response. There is no rubric to include silent prayer, but it may be presumed.

The prayer addresses the "God of power." In fact, the whole prayer reflects on power relationships: between good and evil, between God and the spirit of evil. God's power is specified in the relative predicate, "who promised us the Holy Spirit through Jesus your Son." God exercises his power through the Spirit. The petition sets up the conflict between the spirit of evil, with its concomitant error and sin, and God's protective guarding. The goal articulated in this first petition is that the catechumens eventually (in baptism) become temples of the Holy Spirit—that is, the antithesis of evil, error, and sin. The second petition continues this insistence. Here are contrasted empty words and words of grace and power, noting that the latter are the means of our having been freed by Christ. The prayer is heavily trinitarian, invoking God, stressing the role of the Spirit here and now, and relying upon the mediating work of Christ.

The second prayer example is a bit different (94H):

> Lord Jesus Christ,
> sent by the Father and anointed by the Spirit,
> when you read in the synagogue at Nazareth
> you fulfilled the words of the prophet Isaiah
> that proclaimed liberty to captives
> and announced a season of forgiveness.
> We pray for these your servants
> who have opened their ears and hearts to your word.
> Grant that they may grasp your moment of grace.
> Do not let their minds be troubled
> or their lives tied to earthly desires.
> Do not let them remain
> estranged from the hope of your promises
> or enslaved by a spirit of unbelief.
> Rather, let them believe in you,
> whom the Father has established as universal Lord
> and to whom he has subjected all things.
> Let them submit themselves to the Spirit of grace,
> so that, with hope in their calling,
> they may join the priestly people
> and share in the abundant joy of the new Jerusalem,
> where you live and reign for ever and ever.
> Amen.

This prayer is addressed not to the Father but to the Son, the Lord Jesus Christ. The relative predicate evokes the experience at Nazareth when Jesus participated in synagogue worship by reading from Isaiah and preaching (Luke 4:16-21). The consummation of the earth in God's kingdom is presented. The prayer makes the transition from remembering to asking by recognizing the catechumens who now hear the Word. The petition asks that they "grasp your moment of grace." The petitions continue with a double-negative prayer (do not let . . .): freedom is asked from troubled minds, from bondage to earthly desire, from estrangement from hope, and from enslavement to the spirit of unbelief. Note the sense of sin as personal (the spirit of unbelief) and as a form of involuntary servitude and isolation. To counteract this enslavement, the prayer asks for positive help. This will come through belief in Christ, who is Lord and ruler of all, and by submission to the Spirit, who will be the source of grace, of relationship with the priestly people, and thus lead them to joy in the new reality of the heavenly Jerusalem. The prayer does not ask for an absolute freedom but rather shifts the person from slavery to the base and earthly, the sinful and lonely, to free submission to hope, relationship, and joy in an unfathomable future.

Blessings. The Celebration of the Word may end with a blessing, or the blessing may be added after the prayer of exorcism. The RCIA gives nine texts from which to choose.[17] The blessing is offered by the celebrant who, as he prays, extends his hands over the catechumens. The catechumens may then approach the celebrant who imposes hands on them one by one, after which they then take their leave.

Two examples will stand for the whole. The first blessing is as follows (97A):

> Let us pray.
> Lord,
> form these catechumens by the mysteries of the faith,
> that they may be brought to rebirth in baptism
> and be counted among the members of your Church.
> We ask this through Christ our Lord.
> Amen.

The prayer follows the structure we outlined above, though once again, there is no mention of leaving time for silent prayer. God is addressed simply as "Lord," and there is no specific relative predicate. The petition asks that God "form" the catechumens by the "mysteries of the faith." This phrase most often refers to the celebration of the liturgy. Here it would seem to refer to the overall formational program detailed in RCIA 75, where the mysteries of the faith are expressed in intellectual, ecclesial, liturgical, and apostolic moments. The very Celebration of the Word, whether at Mass or as part of a catechetical session, is part of this formation by the "mysteries of the faith." That formation is seen to have a dual outcome: rebirth in baptism and membership in the Church.

A second example (97E):

> Let us pray.
> Almighty and eternal God,
> you dwell on high yet look on the lowly;
> to bring us your gift of salvation
> you sent Jesus your Son,
> our Lord and God.
> Look kindly on these catechumens,
> who bow before you in worship;
> prepare them for their rebirth in baptism,
> the forgiveness of their sins,
> and the garment of incorruptible life.
> Enfold them in your holy, catholic, and apostolic Church,
> that they may join with us
> in giving glory to your name.
> We ask this through Christ our Lord.
> Amen.

This prayer follows the structure we noted above. The address is expanded in this prayer and includes a relative predicate. God's majesty and power, imagined as "on high," contrasts with his concern for his creatures, "the lowly," which he bridges through the gift of Jesus. Again, there is a transition from memorial to invocation by means of the current worship of the catechumens. And again, there is a twofold petition: to prepare the catechumens and to enfold them. The preparation is for baptism, which will involve rebirth, forgiveness, and an orientation toward eternity ("the garment of incorruptible life"). This preparation is guarded ("enfolded") by the Church, which they will one day join in order to prolong God's praise with their brothers and sisters.

The role of the Holy Spirit, so prominent in the exorcisms, is not in the foreground in the blessings.

Prayers and the Elect

When the catechumens are ready for baptism, they enter the final stage of preparation, which coincides with the season of Lent. On the First Sunday of Lent, the bishop of the diocese hears testimony and enrolls them among the elect. The elect then participate in a series of final, intense celebrations: the scrutinies and the presentations. We will examine some representative prayers from each of these moments.

Rite of Election

The Rite of Election or Enrollment of Names takes place at Mass after the homily (RCIA 129–37).[18] The catechumens are presented, affirmed by their godparents, and invited to enroll their names (130–32). After their enrollment, the bishop admits them as members of the elect (133). The prayer we will explore is the intercessions for the elect with the prayer over the elect (134–35). The RCIA gives two choices for the intercessions and two choices for the prayer over the elect. A single invitation is given for either set of intercessions, which may be modified to fit the circumstances. It is an elaboration of the simple invitation, "Let us pray," adapted to the context. In place of a period of silence, in which all pray in silence, an assisting minister proposes a series of intentions to the faithful who have gathered for the celebration. Those present respond to each intention with "Lord, hear our prayer."

The prayer over the elect is the collect of this litanic prayer. The first version reads (135A):

> Lord God,
> you created the human race
> and are the author of its renewal.
> Bless all your adopted children
> and add these chosen ones
> to the harvest of your new covenant.
> As true children of the promise,
> may they rejoice in eternal life,
> won, not by the power of nature,
> but through the mystery of your grace.
> We ask this through Christ our Lord.
> Amen.

The address of the prayer sets us immediately in the context of Genesis 1: God creates us for paradise. Yet the man and woman sinned, and God set to the task of renewing them, as the rest of the Bible recounts. This summary is similar to the post-Sanctus of Eucharistic Prayer IV: "You formed man in your own likeness. . . . Even when he disobeyed you . . . you did not abandon him . . . but helped all . . . to seek and find you." The prayer heaps images on top of each other, as in the first petition: adoption and harvest are juxtaposed. Adoption refers to God's decision to join new members to his family (see Rom 8:12-17). Harvest is an image of abundance and of the kingdom (see

Matt 13:24-30, 36-43, the parable of the weeds and wheat with its explanation). The imagery continues with "children of the promise" (Rom 9:8; Gal 4:21-31, esp. 28 and 31). All is done, not by nature but by grace. The prayer emphasizes the character of election: God calling each person according to his own plan—not simply a Church ritual, but the unfolding of God's plan of salvation for individuals and the world.[19]

The other choice offers a different emphasis (135B):

> Father of love and power,
> it is your will to establish everything in Christ
> and to draw us into his all-embracing love.
> Guide the elect of your Church:
> strengthen them in their vocation,
> build them into the kingdom of your Son,
> and seal them with the Spirit of your promise.
> We ask this through Christ our Lord.
> Amen.

The address brings together two disparate images: love and power. Both are characteristics of God. The power is revealed in God's plan in Christ for the world; the love, in all being drawn to him. The petitions again begin with the current situation, the presence of the elect in this action. The threefold intercession looks to the near future (strengthen their vocation) and to the ultimate future (build them into the kingdom of your Son) all done in the Holy Spirit. The prayer uses scriptural phrases and images (establish all in Christ, Eph 1:10; Holy Spirit of your promise, Eph 1:13).

Scrutinies

The scrutinies are major exorcisms. They are an intensification of the desire of the Church to prepare the elect for the final step of their entering Christ in the Church at Easter. There are three scrutinies, intended for use on the Third, Fourth, and Fifth Sundays of Lent. The readings for each Sunday are specified: the Samaritan woman at the well (John 4), the healing of the man born blind (John 9), and the raising of Lazarus (John 11). The scrutinies draw on the imagery of these gospels as the foundation for their language and articulate a progressive attack on the forces of sin and evil in the lives of the elect.

The three scrutinies follow one ritual pattern:

- An invitation to silent prayer
- Intercessions for the elect (two possible sets of petitions, which can be adapted to circumstances)
- Exorcism (in two consecutive prayers; two options).

During the silent prayer, the elect may either bow their heads or kneel. All stand for the intercessions, during which the godparents place their right hands on the shoulders of the elect. At the midpoint of the exorcism, which follows the petitions, the celebrant lays hands on each of the elect in silence and then says the second prayer with hands outstretched over them.

Note that the basic structure we described above serves as a guide: invitation to prayer, silent prayer (expanded verbally with the intercessions), concluding prayer (here not simply a general collect but a prayer that specifies the kind of prayer that this is), and the final affirmation of the people.

We will examine one exorcism, which can serve as a guide for a deeper analysis of the other prayers.[20] Here is the text of the first option for the first scrutiny on the Third Sunday of Lent (154A):

> God of power,
> you sent your Son to be our Savior.
> Grant that these catechumens,
> who, like the woman of Samaria, thirst for living water,
> may turn to the Lord as they hear his word
> and acknowledge the sins and weaknesses that weigh them down.
> Protect them from vain reliance on self
> and defend them from the power of Satan.
> Free them from the spirit of deceit,
> so that, admitting the wrong they have done,
> they may attain purity of heart
> and advance on the way to salvation.
> We ask this through Christ our Lord.
> Amen.

This first part of the prayer of exorcism follows the typical pattern. God is addressed as a God of power, and that power is shown in the sending of his Son. The move from memorial to petition once again is via the current situation: this gathering of the elect (here referred to, anachronistically, as catechumens). The lengthy petitions highlight the aspect of sin that must be attacked: weakness, reliance on self, the web of deceit.

The remedy: reliance on God's power, honesty in self-accusation, attentiveness to the Word. The final goal is purity of heart and movement toward salvation. This prayer does not contrast the evil spirit with the Holy Spirit as do other prayers.

After the (optional) laying on of hands, the celebrant continues with the second prayer.

> Lord Jesus,
> you are the fountain for which they thirst,
> you are the Master whom they seek.
> In your presence
> they dare not claim to be without sin,
> for you alone are the Holy One of God.
> They open their hearts to you in faith,
> they confess their faults
> and lay bare their hidden wounds.
> In your love free them from their infirmities,
> heal their sickness,
> quench their thirst, and give them peace.
> In the power of your name,
> which we call upon in faith,
> stand by them now and heal them.
> Rule over that spirit of evil,
> conquered by your rising from the dead.
> Show your elect the way of salvation in the Holy Spirit,
> that they may come to worship the Father in truth,
> for you live and reign for ever and ever.
> Amen.

The second prayer of each scrutiny is addressed to Jesus Christ rather than to the Father. It takes the place of the traditional prayer that was directly addressed to the evil spirits residing in the person.[21] Christ is invoked under several titles: Lord, fountain, Master, Holy One. In each title we discover an aspect of Christ that the elect desire: protection from the powers of evil and from the thirst of the desert of sin, authentic teaching in the face of lies, and holiness in contrast to sin. The prayer describes the current state of the elect: conscious of sin and woundedness and in need of forgiveness and healing. The petition is clear: act with power—dominate evil, heal weakness, guide to safety. The final goal takes us back to the Samaritan woman and her conversation with Christ: worshiping the Father in truth, by the aid of the Holy Spirit. This prayer almost overwhelms us with its abundance of images and themes. It is a good example of the naming of sin and the begging for assistance that the scrutinies contain.

The first scrutiny has a second set of intercessions and a second set of exorcisms, and the second and third scrutinies have a double set as well. We invite the reader to a close reading of each of the scrutinies to gain a clear sense of the conversion that the Church is calling the elect to embrace as they approach the Easter sacraments.[22]

Presentations

The period of purification and enlightenment intersperses the presentations among the three scrutinies. After the first scrutiny, the Church presents the Creed to the elect. After the third scrutiny comes the presentation of the Lord's Prayer. The texts of the Creed and the Lord's Prayer are the keys to the presentations. In addition, there are prayers over the elect, which continue the themes we have seen so far.[23] (A commentary on the Creed and the Lord's Prayer exceeds the limits of this study.) The prayers for the elect are actually generic. The prayer for the presentation of the Creed (161) follows:

> Let us pray for these elect, that God in his mercy may make them responsive to his love, so that through the waters of rebirth they may receive pardon for their sins and have life in Christ Jesus our Lord.
> All pray in silence. Then the celebrant continues:
> Lord,
> eternal source of light, justice, and truth,
> take under your tender care
> your servants N. and N.
> Purify them and make them holy;
> give them true knowledge, sure hope, and sound understanding,
> and make them worthy to receive the grace of baptism.
> We ask this through Christ our Lord.
> Amen.

The invitation is extended to give the motives for our silent prayer. It does not seem adapted to the context of the presentation of the Creed.[24] The prayer opens "Lord," who is source of particular blessings. The petitions ask for strength. In particular, God is asked to give the elect knowledge and understanding, which may relate to the gift of the Creed.

The prayer for the presentation of the Lord's Prayer shares these characteristics (182): The invitation is identical to that employed for the presentation of the Creed. After silent prayer, the celebrant concludes:

Almighty and eternal God,
you continually enlarge the family of your Church.
Deepen the faith and understanding
of these elect, chosen for baptism.
Give them new birth in your living waters,
so that they may be numbered among your adopted children.
We ask this through Christ our Lord.
Amen.

Nothing in this prayer seems to take into account the context of the Lord's Prayer except, perhaps, for the mention of the "family of your church" and "your adopted children." Again, it is a prayer for the elect who are rapidly approaching the waters of baptism.

Celebrating Baptism

The celebration of the baptism of adults takes place at the Easter Vigil in the ordinary course of the rite. Other days may also be chosen, but the ideal time and place for baptism is within the Easter Vigil, following the service of light and the Liturgy of the Word as described above and leading to the Liturgy of the Eucharist.

Litany of the Saints

After the presentation of the candidates, all move to the font. This may occur in several ways, described in RCIA 219. At this point, there are some divergences between the RCIA and the Sacramentary: in the invitation to prayer and at the end of the litany. Here are the two texts of the invitation:

RCIA 220:

> Dear friends, let us pray to almighty God for our brothers and sisters, N. and N., who are asking for baptism. He has called them and brought them to this moment; may he grant them light and strength to follow Christ with resolute hearts and to profess the faith of the Church. May he give them the new life of the Holy Spirit, whom we are about to call down on this water.

Sacramentary, Easter Vigil, 38:

> Dear friends in Christ,
> as our brothers and sisters approach the waters of rebirth,

let us help them by our prayers
and ask God, our almighty Father,
to support them with his mercy and love.

The litany follows.[25] The litany joins this gathering of the Church to
the cloud of witnesses who form a venerable, glorious part of the community that those to be baptized are joining.

The Sacramentary gives a concluding prayer to the litany (39):

> Let us pray.
> *Pause for silent prayer, if this has not preceded.*
> Almighty and eternal God,
> be present in this sacrament of your love.
> Send your Spirit of adoption
> on those to be born again in baptism.
> And may the work of our humble ministry
> be brought to perfection by your mighty power.
> We ask this through Christ our Lord.
> Amen.

It is not clear why the RCIA does not include this prayer. The text is an
adaptation of the introductory prayer of blessing found in the *Old Gelasian Sacramentary* (444).[26] The address is conventional, calling upon the
almighty and eternal God. There is no extension in a relative predicate.
The first petition is that God actualize this event for those to be baptized.
The second part of the petition is a request for the gift of the Holy Spirit,
a sort of epiclesis. The third part of the petition touches on the complex
question of the relationship between our liturgical activity and God's action
through Christ and in the Holy Spirit. The prayer recognizes that what we
do in our ministry has an outcome because of God's presence and activity.

Prayer over the Water

In terms of liturgical structure, the prayer over the water functions as
the conclusion to the Litany of the Saints. (In the case of the structure
used in the Sacramentary, the previous prayer is one that historically
served as the introductory prayer to the long blessing of water.) This
prayer over the water is the key prayer text of the whole celebration of
baptism. It is analogous to the eucharistic prayer at Mass, the prayer of
consecration at ordinations, and the other major euchology of the sacraments.[27] Given that analogy, its theological importance far exceeds its
structural role as conclusion to the litany.

Since the prayer is so long, we will divide it according to the structure we described above.

Address to God

Father

The Latin is *Deus*, "God." The address is as simple as can be. The Latin text of the prayer uses *Deus* as a refrain, introducing each of the sentences of the relative predicate: "O God, who . . ." The sense is an emphasis on the involvement of God in each step of the plan of salvation that the prayer narrates.

Relative predicate 1: Sacramental signs in general, and water.

> you give us grace through sacramental signs,
> which tell us of the wonders of your unseen power.
> In baptism we use your gift of water,
> which you have made a rich symbol of the grace
> you give us in this sacrament.

This first relative predicate speaks in more general terms about how sacramental signs work: they are visible forms of invisible grace (Augustine). The prayer then specifies water as the privileged symbol of baptism. The following sections of the prayer specify the richness of the symbolism.

Relative predicate 2: Three images from the Old Testament.

> At the very dawn of creation
> your Spirit breathed on the waters,
> making them the wellspring of all holiness.
> The waters of the great flood
> you made a sign of the waters of baptism
> that make an end of sin
> and a new beginning of goodness.
> Through the waters of the Red Sea
> you led Israel out of slavery
> to be an image of God's holy people,
> set free from sin by baptism.

The initial image from Genesis 1:1-2 takes us to the founding story of our world, where we find water as the context for God's action. God's

Spirit is at the heart of holiness. The second image takes us to a second creation story, that of Noah and the flood (Gen 6–9): evil is washed away in a flood of regeneration and new beginnings. The third image takes us to the exodus event and the crossing of the Red Sea (Exod 14): by crossing the waters, the people move from slavery to freedom. Note that the creation story and the crossing of the Red Sea are among the Old Testament readings for the Easter Vigil.

Relative predicate 3: Three images from the New Testament.

> In the waters of the Jordan
> your Son was baptized by John
> and anointed with the Spirit.
> Your Son willed that water and blood should flow from his side
> as he hung upon the cross.
> After his resurrection he told his disciples:
> "Go out and teach all nations,
> baptizing them in the name of the Father, and of the Son, and of the
>   Holy Spirit."

We start at the beginning of Jesus' public ministry: his baptism by John in the Jordan. Each of the gospels offers a perspective on this event (Matt 3:13-17; Mark 1:12-13; Luke 3:21-22; John 1:31-34), but this image is actually from Acts 10:38, which specifies that in his baptism, God anointed Jesus with the Holy Spirit and power. The second image is from John's gospel (19:34). It is a favorite quote of the early writers of the Church who see this event as the inauguration of the sacraments of baptism and the Eucharist (water and blood) and therefore the birth of the Church (in baptism and Eucharist). The third image is from Matthew 28:16-18 and highlights the mission that baptism entails.

Petition 1: Actualization of this moment.

> Father,
> look now with love upon your Church
> and unseal for it the fountain of baptism.

As we have seen in so many prayers, the movement from memorial to petition is catalyzed by the current moment of celebration: God who is faithful will act for us during this celebration in a way consistent with his past actions. It is this move from memorial to petition that we designate by the term "actualization."

Petition 2: First epicletic moment.

> By the power of the Holy Spirit
> give to this water the grace of your Son,
> so that in the sacrament of baptism
> all those whom you have created in your likeness
> may be cleansed from sin
> and rise to a new birth of innocence
> by water and the Holy Spirit.

The role of the Spirit has been invoked several times: at creation as the source of holiness, at the Jordan as an anointing presence, and at the mission to make disciples of all nations. Now the Spirit's role receives even greater articulation: it is the source of the Son's grace that cleanses and gives new birth. We begin with the Spirit and the water, as in the book of Genesis. The water is now named as receptive of Christ's grace, perhaps alluding to the water and blood that flowed from his side on the cross. Creation in God's likeness (Gen 1:27), marred by sin, is now about to be restored ("cleansed"). The newness of life granted after the great flood serves as the image of this new birth. This is a reference to John 3:1-15, the dialogue between Jesus and Nicodemus. One cannot return to the mother's natural womb (v. 4), but one must be born again of water and spirit in order to have life (v. 5).

Petition 3: Second epicletic moment (with optional lowering of the Easter candle into the font one or three times, or, at occasions other than the Easter Vigil, touching the water with the right hand).

> We ask you, Father, with your Son
> to send the Holy Spirit upon the waters of this font.
> May all who are buried with Christ in the death of baptism
> rise also with him to newness of life.

The prayer becomes even more insistent, repeating the request for the gift of the Spirit. The dipping of the candle or touching of the water with the right hand highlights the desire not just for the presence of but also for the action of the Spirit.[28] The final phrase is a reference to Paul's Letter to the Romans (6:3-11). Dying and rising with Christ is the last image given us.

Doxology and response of the people.

> We ask this through Christ our Lord.
> Amen.

There is also the possibility of an acclamation by the people at this point to intensify the moment: "Springs of water, bless the Lord. / Give him glory and praise for ever." This is a reminiscence of the canticle of the three young men from Daniel 3:60.[29] All is done though Christ, while the work of the Spirit has been highlighted throughout the prayer.

Two Optional Prayers, for Use outside the Easter Vigil (RCIA 222)

The ritual also gives two other forms of the blessing of water that can be used, as well as two forms for using water that has already been blessed.

The beginning of the blessing unit is the same as the blessing we have just examined: the invitation to prayer, litany, and initial blessing/conclusion to the litany (found only in the Sacramentary). Both forms of blessing include several acclamations by the people.

In the first form, the prayer falls into two parts: memorial and praise of God and petition for the Spirit's action upon us and the water.

1. Memorial and praise.

> Praise to you, almighty God and Father,
> for you have created water to cleanse and to give life.
> *All*: Blessed be God.
> Praise to you, Lord Jesus Christ, the Father's only Son,
> for you offered yourself on the cross,
> that in the blood and water flowing from your side
> and through your death and resurrection
> the Church might be born.
> *All*: Blessed be God.
> Praise to you, God the Holy Spirit,
> for you anointed Christ at his baptism in the waters of the Jordan,
> that we might all be baptized in you.
> *All*: Blessed be God.

This first part of the blessing of the water is trinitarian, each of the three strophes addressed to a Person of the Blessed Trinity. The Father is associated with creation, the Son with his offering on the cross, and the Holy Spirit with Christ's baptism at the Jordan. Each of the actions of the Trinity is associated with some present desire: cleansing and life, the birth of the Church, the baptism of the faithful. Each memorial is punctuated by an acclamation of the people, which praises God for his good actions on our behalf.

2. Petition for the work of the Spirit.

> Come to us, Lord, Father of all,

and make holy this water which you have created,
so that all who are baptized in it may be washed clean of sin
and be born again to live as your children.
All: Hear us, Lord.
Make this water holy, Lord,
so that all who are baptized into Christ's death and resurrection by
this water
may become more perfectly like your Son.
All: Hear us, Lord.

The celebrant may touch the water with his right hand:

Lord,
make holy this water which you have created,
so that all those whom you have chosen
may be born again by the power of the Holy Spirit
and may take their place among your holy people.
All: Hear us, Lord.

The second part of the prayer is directed to the Father. Each petition begins the same way: make this water holy. What this holiness accomplishes is specified in the petitions that follow. The first petition asks for a holiness of cleansing and for life as God's children (see Titus 3:4-7). The second begs for a holiness that conforms one to Christ's dying and rising. The third asks for a holiness characterized by new birth and life among God's people. Again, the threefold petition is marked by a threefold acclamation of the people requesting God's hearing. There is no need for a final Amen after this series of acclamations of praise and petition.

The second option includes:

1. Fourfold memorial of God's saving work.

Father, God of mercy,
through these waters of baptism
you have filled us with new life as your very own children.
All: Blessed be God.
From all who are baptized in water and the Holy Spirit,
you have formed one people,
united in your Son, Jesus Christ.
All: Blessed be God.
You have set us free and filled our hearts with the Spirit of your love,
that we many live in your peace.
All: Blessed be God.

You call those who have been baptized
to announce the Good News of Jesus Christ to people everywhere.
All: Blessed be God.

The form is somewhat different in this second option. The first three strophes, while all addressed to the Father, are trinitarian. The first returns to the first moments of creation, the second ends with union in the Son, and the third looks to the Spirit of love. In fact the work and presence of the Trinity permeate each of these three strophes. The fourth strophe serves as the moment of transition, focusing again on those gathered here for the celebration and reminding all of what baptism entails: a missionary thrust.

2. Petition for blessing of the water.

You have called your children, N. and N.,
to this cleansing water and new birth,
that by sharing the faith of your Church they may have eternal life.
Bless + this water in which they will be baptized.
We ask this in the name of Jesus the Lord.
Amen.

If, later in the Easter season, baptism is celebrated with water blessed at the Easter Vigil, the petitions of the two prayers above are omitted (the last three strophes of the first option, or the last strophe of the second option) and the following is said:

You have called your children, N. and N., to this cleansing water,
that they may share in the faith of your Church and have eternal life.
By the mystery of this consecrated water
lead them to a new and spiritual birth.
We ask this through Christ our Lord.
Amen.

The first part of the petition is identical to the last petition of the second optional prayer. In place of the blessing of the water, the prayer substitutes a mention of the consecrated water and raises up again the image of new birth, the reflection of John 3.

From Prayer to Action

After the blessing of the water, the RCIA gives us a series of texts that are not, strictly speaking, prayers. There are the profession of faith, the sacramental formula, and a series of explanatory texts. Each has its own form and integrity.

Professing faith. The profession of faith has two parts: the renunciation of sin and the profession itself. While the renunciation can be made either individually or by the whole group, the profession is to be made individually, followed immediately by the baptism, though a large group can respond together followed by the baptism of each person.

There are three options for the renunciation:

- Do you reject sin so as to live in the freedom of God's children? I do.
  Do you reject the glamour of evil, and refuse to be mastered by sin? I do.
  Do you reject Satan, father of sin and prince of darkness? I do.
- Do you reject Satan, and all his works, and all his empty promises? I do.
- Do you reject Satan? I do.
  And all his works? I do.
  And all his empty promises? I do.

The renunciation is followed by the profession:

> N., do you believe in God, the Father almighty,
> creator of heaven and earth?
> I do.
> Do you believe in Jesus Christ, his only Son, our Lord,
> who was born of the Virgin Mary,
> was crucified, died, and was buried,
> and is now seated at the right hand of the Father?
> I do.
> Do you believe in the Holy Spirit,
> the holy catholic Church, the communion of saints,
> the forgiveness of sins, the resurrection of the body,
> and the life everlasting?
> I do.

The whole process of becoming a catechumen—the celebrations of the Word; the formation in the intellectual, ecclesial, liturgical, and apostolic life of the Church; the scrutinies and presentations—now reach their culmination. The elect are able, after all this preparation, after opening themselves to the work of the Spirit and the grace of the Son, to commit themselves to the faith that has taken root within them and approach the font. The process has had a dual focus as seen in these texts: turning from sin, evil, and the master of dark deeds and turning to grace, good, and God's dominion. The formulas are ancient, taking us back to the third century. They are the immediate doorway to the action of baptism.

Formula of baptism. Our earliest records of baptism reveal that the elect were immersed three times as they made their threefold profession of faith.[30] Today, the celebrant says the following words after the profession of faith:

> N. I baptize you in the name of the Father,
> and of the Son,
> and of the Holy Spirit.

The words follow closely the words of Jesus in Matthew 28:19.[31] The immersing of the person and the pouring of water takes place three times, once for each person of the Trinity, as it is mentioned. These are performative words that give the immersing or pouring their significance: not any refreshing, not any cleansing, not any bath, not any confrontation with life and death, but a participation in the new birth, in the dying and rising of Jesus Christ, that is the gift of our God who is one in three and three in one.

Explanatory rites. Despite the fact that so much time and energy have been consumed in reaching this moment, that so much has been learned and experienced, the Church realizes that the vast implications of what has just happened must be drawn out more at length. The three rites that follow explicate what has happened. The first is omitted if confirmation is celebrated.[32]

1. Anointing after Baptism

> This anointing is omitted if confirmation is celebrated:
> The God of power and Father of our Lord Jesus Christ
> has freed you from sin
> and brought you to new life
> through water and the Holy Spirit.
> He now anoints you with the chrism of salvation,
> so that, united with his people,
> you may remain for ever a member of Christ
> who is Priest, Prophet, and King.
> Amen.

The text is not a prayer, but a formula for the applying of the chrism on the crown of the newly baptized person's head. Baptism is also an anointing, but not any anointing: it is not an anointing like those of the catechumenate. It is a different oil, this one scented with balsam, a perfume. It has not received a simple blessing but has been solemnly consecrated by the bishop. The text states what has just happened. It repeats some themes, such as freedom from sin and new life in water and the Spirit. What is unique to this anointing is its emphasis on participation in Christ who is *the* anointed one: priest, prophet, and king. Membership in Christ's priesthood and participation in the priesthood of all believers is the result of baptism (1 Pet 2:9-10). Stipulating that it be done on the crown of the head reminds us of the anointing of Aaron, when the oil was so abundant that it flowed from the crown of his head into his beard (Exod 29:7; Lev 8:12; and especially Ps 133:2: "It is like the precious oil on the head, running down upon the beard, on the beard of Aaron, running down over the collar of his robes"). Elijah is called to anoint Elisha (1 Kgs 19:15-16), and Isaiah speaks of having been anointed to proclaim God's Word (Isa 61:1). The kings of Israel and Judah are anointed king (e.g., Saul by Samuel [1 Sam 10:1] and David by Samuel [1 Sam 16:13]) and filled with the power of the Spirit.

2. Clothing with a Baptismal Garment

This is also a moment that could be omitted depending on circumstances. Changing clothes, like pouring water and anointing, is an event that can have various meanings: preparing for work, or an event, or for bed. Guests at the wedding feast described in Matthew's gospel wear special garb (Matt 22:1-14). The words specify what this change of clothes means:

> N. and N., you have become a new creation
> and have clothed yourselves in Christ.
> Receive this baptismal garment
> and bring it unstained to the judgment seat of our Lord Jesus Christ,
> so that you may have everlasting life.
> Amen.

We note again that this is not a prayer, but a statement to the newly baptized about the meaning of this action. We find reminiscences of St. Paul (Rom 13:14; Gal 3:26-27; Col 3:9-10, 12-14): we have put on Christ! The admonition to bring the garment unstained to the judgment seat is unexpected within the context of eschatological joy that permeates most of the other texts, which focus on the victory rather than the ongoing task that awaits (see the saints robed in white garments, washed in the blood of the Lamb in Rev 7:9-17).

3. Presentation of a Lighted Candle
The Easter candle, so prominent earlier in the celebration of the Easter Vigil, now returns to center focus. The godparents are asked to present a candle lighted from the Easter candle to the newly baptized. The celebrant says:

> You have been enlightened by Christ.
> Walk always as children of the light
> and keep the flame of faith alive in your hearts.
> When the Lord comes, may you go out to meet him
> with all the saints in the heavenly kingdom.
> Amen.

Again, this is a statement to the newly baptized, not a prayer. Light is a favorite image in John's gospel, where Christ tells us "I am the light of the world" (8:12; 9:5). In his final discourse before the Last Supper, Jesus said: "Walk while you have the light. . . . While you have the light, believe in the light, so that you may become children of light" (John 12:35-36). The text also uses Pauline imagery, for instance Romans 13:12 and 14: "put on the armor of light. . . . put on the Lord Jesus Christ." Likewise, Paul talks about faith in the heart in Romans 10:9: "if you confess with your lips that Jesus is Lord and believe in your heart that God raised him from the dead, you will be saved." Finally, we are reminded of the parable of the wise and foolish bridesmaids (Matt 25:1-13): "'Look! Here is the bridegroom! Come out to meet him.' Then all those bridesmaids got up and trimmed their lamps" (vv. 6-7).

Confirmation

In the Western tradition, confirmation is a sacrament separate from baptism.[33] The RCIA and the Code of Canon Law, however, are clear that, in normal circumstances, someone baptized as an adult should also celebrate confirmation and share in eucharistic Communion for the first time within the same rite. These three sacraments constitute the initiation of an adult as a Christian. We leave the lion's share of the treatment of confirmation to the appropriate volume, but give a brief commentary on the prayers contained in the RCIA, in order to see the celebration in its completeness.

The celebration takes place wherever the baptism has occurred, highlighting the close connection between the two.[34] The celebrant invites the newly baptized to be confirmed. He then invites the faithful present to pray for those to be confirmed. All pray briefly in silence. Then the celebrant holds his hands outstretched over the newly baptized and prays:

> All-powerful God, Father of our Lord Jesus Christ,
> by water and the Holy Spirit
> you freed your sons and daughters from sin
> and gave them new life.
> Send your Holy Spirit upon them
> to be their helper and guide.
> Give them the spirit of wisdom and understanding,
> the spirit of right judgment and courage,
> the spirit of knowledge and reverence.
> Fill them with the spirit of wonder and awe in your presence.
> We ask this through Christ our Lord.
> Amen.

With this prayer we return to the pattern that we saw in the introduction to the chapter: invitation, silence, prayer, Amen of the people. The name given God is God and Father of Jesus. The prayer takes us to John 3 (water and the Spirit) and to freedom from sin, as in the prayer of the blessing of the water. There is a very explicit epiclesis: Send the Spirit! It is the Spirit that Jesus identified in John 14: the abiding Spirit who will teach them all things. Finally, the prayer incorporates the gifts of the Spirit, as named by Isaiah, to be the ultimate outcome of this act (11:2), inaugurating the final age of the messianic king.

Prayers and Mystagogy

The RCIA does not give any specific prayers to be used during the period of mystagogy other than the readings and prayers of the Easter season Masses. The prayers of the Octave of Easter in particular name various facets of what has been celebrated at the Easter Vigil. The collect for the Second Sunday of Easter stands for the whole:

> Let us pray.
> God of mercy,
> you wash away our sins in water,
> you give us new birth in the Spirit,
> and redeem us in the blood of Christ.
> As we celebrate Christ's resurrection
> increase our awareness of these blessings,
> and renew your gift of life within us.

We ask this through our Lord Jesus Christ, your Son,
who lives and reigns with you and the Holy Spirit,
one God for ever and ever.
Amen.

This ancient prayer[35] reiterates for the newly baptized and all those gathered the meaning of their new life together. Our merciful God (the address) washes away sin and gives new birth (John 3) and redeems us in Christ's blood (see, for instance, Rom 3:25; Eph 1:7; Heb 9; Rev 1:5). The petition is that we become aware of what has happened to us. While this seems simple, it is a constant theme in Paul's letters: the first part of his letters lays out the doctrine of who we are in Christ, the second (parenetic) part calls us to be what we are. This kind of integrity is not easy to achieve. We need God's help to achieve what he has won for us in Christ.

Prayers for the Baptism of Children

The texts in the celebration of baptism of children are similar to the prayers in the RCIA. Major differences include a move from a process over months and perhaps even years to assist in the conversion of adults to a celebration that compresses the ritual into a single event. The other major difference is that adults speak for themselves while the children envisaged as the subjects of the RBC cannot. The texts reflect these two major differences.

At the Door of the Church

The ceremony at the door of the church summarizes what happens for adults at the Rite of Acceptance into the Order of Catechumens. The dialogue in the RBC is conducted between the celebrant and the parents and godparents. After two questions about what name the parents give the child and what they want for the child, the celebrant continues with a brief instruction:

You have asked to have your children baptized. In doing so you are accepting the responsibility of training them in the practice of the faith.

It will be your duty to bring them up to keep God's commandments
as Christ taught us, by loving God and our neighbor. Do you clearly
understand what you are undertaking?
We do.

The intention here is to raise the question of faith, in a way analogous
to the first acceptance of the Gospel in the rite for adults. Whose faith
lies at the basis of this baptism? Can a child have faith? What is faith?
Is it relational? Intellectual? Both? These questions will return in the last
chapter on the theology of baptism. The Christian life is act and content:
keeping the commandments as Christ taught them.

At the Ambo

This section of the RBC compresses the periods of the catechumenate
and of purification and enlightenment into several minutes. The main prayer
event of the Celebration of the Word comes after the readings and homily.
After the invitation to prayer (no indication of a silent pause given), there
follow two sets of petitions: intercessions and a brief form of the Litany
of the Saints. The concluding prayer is an exorcism. The whole ends with
either an anointing with the oil of catechumens or an imposition of hands.
    The prayer of exorcism has two texts from which to choose. The first is:

Almighty and ever-living God,
you sent your only Son into the world
to cast out the power of Satan, spirit of evil,
to rescue man from the kingdom of darkness,
and bring him into the splendor of your kingdom of light.
We pray for these children:
set them free from original sin,
make them temples of your glory,
and send your Holy Spirit to dwell within them.
We ask this through Christ our Lord.
Amen.

We have returned to the world of exorcism that we studied earlier. God
is invoked in terms of his power and asked to exercise that power by
sending Jesus Christ to overcome Satan, end darkness, and bring about
the kingdom. The petition introduces a new image: original sin. Adults
have their own personal sins and their own personal battles that require
the help of God's power. Children have as yet no personal sin, but must
still contend with the forces of evil in themselves, their families, and

their world. Freedom from original sin makes them capable of becoming temples of the Spirit (1 Cor 3:16-17).

The second prayer is like the first:

> Almighty God,
> you sent your only Son
> to rescue us from the slavery of sin,
> and to give us the freedom
> only your sons and daughters enjoy.
> We now pray for these children
> who will have to face the world with its temptations,
> and fight the devil in all his cunning.
> Your Son died and rose again to save us.
> By his victory over sin and death,
> cleanse these children from the stain of original sin.
> Strengthen them with the grace of Christ,
> and watch over them at every step in life's journey.
> We ask this through Christ our Lord.
> Amen.

Several points differentiate the two prayers.[36] The Spirit is not accorded an explicit role. Christ's mediating role is mentioned twice, in two separate moments of memorial: He is sent to conquer sin, conceived of as slavery, and to give freedom. Second, Christ's dying and rising are remembered as the victory over all sin and death. The power of darkness evokes the image of Christ's harrowing of hell, breaking open the doors of death and letting in the light of life.[37]

At the Font

The prayers for blessing water are identical to those used at the Easter Vigil.

As happens in the RCIA, at this point we leave the genre of prayer and continue with the profession of faith, baptismal formula, and explanatory rites. Several texts are worth exploring.

The profession of faith has an extensive introduction tailored to the circumstance of children. The celebrant says:

> Dear parents and godparents:
> You have come here to present these children for baptism. By water
> and the Holy Spirit they are to receive the gift of new life from God,
> who is love.

On your part, you must make it your constant care to bring them up in the practice of the faith. See that the divine life which God gives them is kept safe from the poison of sin, to grow always stronger in their hearts. If your faith makes you ready to accept this responsibility, renew now the vows of your own baptism. Reject sin; profess your faith in Christ Jesus. This is the faith of the Church. This is the faith in which these children are about to be baptized.

This introduction is similar to the one given at the door of the church at the beginning of the ceremony. In fact, some phrases are identical. The children are being baptized in the faith of the Church, and the parents agree to the responsibility of making sure their children grow up in that faith. This key theological issue will return in our last section.

When adults are baptized, the act follows immediately upon the profession of faith with no further words. With children, once more the parents are questioned:

Is it your will that N. should be baptized in the faith of the Church, which we have all professed with you?
It is.

The repetition of this theme indicates its theological importance.

The explanatory rites follow (anointing of the crown of the head with chrism, clothing with the white garment, presenting with the lighted candle, and the Ephphetha ceremony). The text for the anointing with chrism on the crown of the head is identical to the one in the RCIA (though this rite is optional in the RCIA and the translations differ from one another). The clothing with the white garment is altered to highlight the role of the parents:

See in this white garment the outward sign of our Christian dignity. With your family and friends to help you by word and example, bring that dignity unstained into the everlasting life of heaven.

Note that the celebrant is addressing the children directly, though they cannot respond. The drumbeat of parental responsibility continues.

The presentation of the lighted candle is yet another opportunity to impress upon parents and godparents their responsibility:

Parents and godparents, this light is entrusted to you to be kept burning brightly. These children of yours have been enlightened by Christ. They are to walk always as children of the light. May they keep the flame of faith alive in their hearts. When the Lord comes, may they go out to meet him with all the saints in the heavenly kingdom.

The text expands the words given in the RCIA with the emphasis on how parents are to provide the context in which the light can burn.

A difference of the RBC is the placement of the Ephphetha or prayer over ears and mouth. For adults, this is a part of the final preparation for baptism on Holy Saturday morning and is a kind of exorcism. In the RBC, however, it functions as a pledge of future encounter with the Word:

> The Lord Jesus made the deaf hear and the dumb speak. May he soon touch your ears to receive his word, and your mouth to proclaim his faith, to the praise and glory of God the Father.
> Amen.

To hear with understanding and then to proclaim in faith are hallmarks of Christian life. The passive and active combine and constitute our prayer for the child.

At the Altar

The RBC ends with all gathered at the altar. One last time, the celebrant reminds those present of the special needs of the children and of their deepening involvement in the Church that subsequent sacraments will bring:

> Dearly beloved, these children have been reborn in baptism. They are now called children of God, for so indeed they are. In confirmation they will receive the fullness of God's Spirit. In holy communion they will share the banquet of Christ's sacrifice, calling God their Father in the midst of the Church. In their name, in the Spirit of our common sonship, let us pray together in the words our Lord has given us.

The Lord's Prayer follows. This instruction serves as a succinct summation of the theology of initiation: baptism, confirmation, and Eucharist together make one a member of the Church. Even though the children do not receive confirmation and do not share in sacramental Communion during this ceremony, and those celebrations may occur only after many years, it is one act of incorporation unfolding over time.

The RBC ends with a blessing, the first option for which is a threefold blessing of mothers, fathers, and all those present.

The mothers take the children in their arms.

> God the Father, through his Son, the Virgin Mary's child, has brought
> joy to all Christian mothers, as they see the hope of eternal life shine
> on their children. May he bless the mothers of these children. They
> now thank God for the gift of their children. May they be one with
> them in thanking him for ever in heaven, in Christ Jesus our Lord.
> Amen.

The incarnation of Jesus and the motherhood of Mary form the backdrop
for this first blessing. Joy and thanksgiving are the hallmarks of new life
and motherhood. What greater hope can a mother have for her child
than eternal life?

> God is the giver of all life, human and divine. May he bless the fathers
> of these children. With their wives they will be the first teachers of
> their children in the ways of the faith. May they be also the best of
> teachers, bearing witness to the faith by what they say and do, in Christ
> Jesus our Lord.
> Amen.

The blessing for fathers mentions creation in general as the starting
point. Husbands and wives are seen as cooperators. (It is curious that
this collaboration finds no mention in the blessing of mothers.) Fathers
are connected with giving life and teaching. The height of teaching is
example in word and deed, where the faith achieves its fullness. "Bearing
witness" implies that fatherhood—parenthood in general—is a form of
martyrdom, a radical way of following Christ and living out the faith.

> By God's gift, through water and the Holy Spirit, we are reborn to ev-
> erlasting life. In his goodness, may he continue to pour out his blessings
> upon all present, who are his sons and daughters. May he make them
> always, wherever they may be, faithful members of his holy people.
> May he send his peace upon all who are gathered here, in Christ Jesus
> our Lord.
> Amen.

The final blessing is for all who are present and are assumed to be baptized. The life we receive in baptism is lived in a relationship that is
familial. Peace is the blessing that ends the prayer and should characterize
family life, whether particular or ecclesial.

The final blessing offers a theology of parenting and family. The whole RBC reveals a particular understanding of faith and proposes a status to children in God's plan that needs careful reflection.

Conclusion

The last section of this book will take up the strands that we have laid out so far. The nonverbal elements that tie together and distinguish the Rite of Christian Initiation of Adults and the Rite of Baptism for Children, the Word of God proclaimed in the various moments of the rites, and the prayers and other nonscriptural words spoken and proclaimed now combine to help form a matrix in which we can come to a deeper understanding of what is the baptism that lies at the beginning, at the heart, and at the end of our Christian existence.

Notes, Chapter Four

[1] For an orientation to Christian prayer, see Lawrence S. Cunningham and Keith J. Egan, *Christian Spirituality: Themes from the Tradition* (New York: Paulist, 1996). The *Catechism of the Catholic Church* has a fine treatment of prayer in part 4, 2558–2865.

[2] See A. G. Martimort, "The Dialogue between God and His People," in Martimort, *Principles of the Liturgy*, 131–71, esp. 152–61; Renato De Zan, "Criticism and Interpretation of Liturgical Texts," in *Introduction to the Liturgy*, vol. 1, *Handbook of Liturgical Studies*, ed. A. J. Chupungco (Collegeville, MN: Liturgical Press, A Pueblo Book, 1997), 331–65; Kathleen Hughes, *NDSW*, s.v. "Prayer, Types of, in the Liturgy," 959–67.

[3] See, for example, Robert F. Taft, "The Structural Analysis of Liturgical Units: An Essay in Methodology," originally in *Worship* 52 (1978): 314–29; rev. version in *Beyond East and West: Problems in Liturgical Understanding*, 2nd ed. (Rome: Pontifical Oriental Institute, 2001), 187–202.

[4] The celebrant may be a bishop, a priest, or a deacon, depending on the rite involved. In some services the celebrant's role may be taken by a designated lay

minster (e.g., in services of the Word during the period of the catechumenate). The RCIA tends to use the word "celebrant" to translate the Latin *celebrans*, and we will follow the same pattern.

[5] See for example Jean Deshusses and Benoit Darragon, *Concordances et tableaux pour l'étude des grands sacramentaires*, 3 volumes in 6, Spicilegii Friburgensis Subsidia 9–14 (Fribourg: Éditions Universitaires, 1982–83).

[6] Sometimes the conclusion is shortened to "We ask this through Christ our Lord," or some similar variation.

[7] The eucharistic prayer, especially, has engendered a huge bibliography about prayer forms. Much of the following analysis follows the work of Cesare Giraudo, *La struttura letteraria della preghiera eucaristica*, Analecta Biblica 92 (Rome: Biblical Institute, 1981); *Eucaristia per la Chiesa: Prospettive teologiche sull'eucaristia a partire dalla "lex orandi,"* Aloisiana 22 (Rome: Gregorian University, 1989); *Preghiere eucaristiche per la chiesa di oggi: Reflessioni in margine al commento del canone svizzero-romano*, Aloisiana 23 (Rome: Gregorian University, 1993). Alternative approaches to structure can be found in Thomas Talley, "Sources and Structures of the Eucharistic Prayer," *Worship: Reforming Tradition* (Washington, DC: Pastoral Press, 1990), 11–34; and Paul F. Bradshaw, "The Evolution of Eucharistic Rites," *The Search for the Origin of Christian Worship: Sources and Methods for the Study of Early Liturgy*, 2nd ed. (Oxford: Oxford University Press, 1992, 2002), 118–43.

[8] See Burkhard Neunheuser, "Memoriale," *Nuovo Dizionario di Liturgia*, ed. Domenico Sartore and Achille M. Triacca (Rome: Edizioni Paoline, 1984), 820–38; Frank C. Senn, *NDSW*, s.v. "Anamnesis," 45–46; I. H. Dalmais, "Anamnesi," *Dizionario Patristico e di Antichità Cristiane*, 2 vols., ed. A. de Berardino (Casale Monferrato: Marietti, 1983), 1:178–79; Salvatore Marsili, "La liturgia, momento storico della salvezza," in *La Liturgia: momento nella storia della salvezza*, Anamnesis 1, ed. S. Marsili (Casale Monferrato: Maritti, 1974), 31–156; Kevin W. Irwin, "Euchology," in *Context and Text: Method in Liturgical Theology* (Collegeville, MN: Liturgical Press, A Pueblo Book, 1994), 176–218; Irwin, "Model Four: Memorial of the Paschal Mystery," in *Models of the Eucharist* (New York: Paulist, 2005), 122–44; Brevard S. Childs, *Memory in Ancient Israel*, Studies in Biblical Theology 37 (Naperville, IL: Allenson, 1962); David N. Power, "The Anamnesis: Remembering, We Offer," in *New Eucharistic Prayers: An Ecumenical Study of Their Development and Structure*, ed. Frank Senn (New York: Paulist, 1987), 146–68; Fritz Chenderlin, *Do This as My Memorial: The Semantic and Conceptual Background and Value of* Ἀνάμνησις *in 1 Corinthians 11:24-25*, Analecta Biblica 99 (Rome: Biblical Institute, 1982); John H. McKenna, "Eucharist and Memorial," *Worship* 79 (2005): 504–22.

[9] See, for example, Enrico Mazza, *The Eucharistic Prayers of the Roman Rite*, trans. Matthew J. O'Connell (New York: Pueblo, 1986), 154–90.

[10] See A. M. Triacca, "Spirito Santo," in Sartore and Triacca, *Nuovo Dizionario di Liturgia*, 1405–19; Anscar Chupungco, "Epiclesi," in Bernardino, *Dizionario Patristico e di Antichità Cristiane*, 1:1157–60; John H. McKenna, "The Epiclesis Revisited," in Senn, *New Eucharistic Prayers*, 169–94; Frank C. Senn, *NDSW*, s.v. "Epiclesis," 390–91.

[11] Concrete situations of liturgies in which the celebrant does not actually leave silent time for prayer, or prays the prayer in such a way that the faithful are not led into the acclamation "Amen" are not rare. Celebrants and people must grow into the need for and practice of silence and response as an integral part of prayer. See the treatment of silence in the General Instruction of the Roman Missal (2002), 45, 54, 56, 66, 88 (various editions; here, *The Liturgy Documents*, vol. 1, 4th ed., ed. David Lysik [Chicago: Liturgy Training Publications, 2004], 45–48, 50–51, 56); and the General Instruction of the Liturgy of the Hours, 201–3 (various editions; here, *The Liturgy Documents*, vol. 2, ed. David Lysik [Chicago: Liturgy Training Publications, 1999], 300–301). See also Michael Downey, *NDSW*, "Silence, Liturgical Role of," 1189–90; Lawrence S. Cunningham, "Silence," in *The Catholic Experience* (New York: Crossroad, 1985), 64–87.

[12] See the discussion from the point of view of the Eucharist in Xavier Léon-Dufour, *Sharing the Eucharistic Bread: The Witness of the New Testament*, trans. Matthew J. O'Connell (New York: Paulist, 1987; French orig. 1982), 46–76, esp. 69–72 on the temporal axis of the account of the Last Supper of Jesus with his disciples.

[13] See, for instance, Bruce T. Morrill, *Anamnesis as Dangerous Memory: Political and Liturgical Theology in Dialogue* (Collegeville, MN: Liturgical Press, A Pueblo Book, 2000); Kathleen A. Cahalan, *Formed in the Image of Christ: The Sacramental-Moral Theology of Bernard Häring, C.Ss.R.* (Collegeville, MN: Liturgical Press, A Michael Glazier Book, 2004); *Liturgy and the Moral Self: Humanity at Full Stretch before God: Essays in Honor of Don E. Saliers*, ed. E. Byron Anderson and Bruce T. Morrill (Collegeville, MN: Liturgical Press, A Pueblo Book, 1998).

[14] Rite of Acceptance into the Order of Catechumens, RCIA 48–68; Prayers of Exorcism, RCIA 94A-K (eleven prayers); Prayers of Blessing, RCIA n. 97A-I (nine prayers).

[15] See Morris, *The RCIA*, 100–115, esp. 108–9; Kathleen Hughes, "Acceptance into the Order of Catechumens," in Tufano, *Celebrating the Rites of Adult Initiation: Pastoral Reflections*, 1–13, esp. 8–9; Richard N. Fragomeni, "Acceptance into the Order of Catechumens," in Wilde, *Commentaries on the Rite of Christian Initiation of Adults*, 5–13, esp. 7, 9, 10–11.

[16] Robert F. Duggan, "Conversion in the Ordo Initiationis Christianis Adultorum," *Ephemerides Liturgicae* 97 (1983): 141–223, esp. 143–46. Paul Turner, "Exorcism in the Baptismal Rite," *The New Dictionary of Sacramental Worship*, 466–67; "Exorcism," *The Oxford Dictionary of the Christian Church*, ed. F. L. Cross and E. A. Livingstone, 3rd ed. rev. (Oxford: Oxford University Press, 2005), 592; Edward Foley, "Minor Exorcisms," in Tufano, *Celebrating the Rites of Adult Initiation*, 29–39; Morris, *The RCIA*, 138–39.

[17] Duggan, "Conversion," 146–47. Marguerite Main, "Blessings of the Catechumens," in Tufano, *Celebrating the Rites of Adult Initiation*, 41–48.

[18] Duggan, "Conversion," 159–68. See Rita Ferrone, *On the Rite of Election*, Forum Essays 3 (Chicago: Liturgy Training Publications, 1994), esp. 22–24; Morris, *The RCIA*, 150–65; Allen Bouley, "Election or Enrollment of Names," in Wilde, *Commentaries on the Rite of Christian Initiation of Adults*, 25–33. See also Ronald A.

Oakham, "Sending of the Catechumens for Election," in Tufano, *Celebrating the Rites of Adult Initiation*, 49–62.

[19] See Ferrone, *On the Rite of Election*, 55–58, 91.

[20] Balthasar Fischer, "Baptismal Exorcism in the Catholic Baptismal Rites after Vatican II," *Studia Liturgica* 10 (1974): 48–55; Duggan, "Conversion," 168–93, esp. for the first scrutiny, 171–78. See Morris, *The RCIA*, 171–76; Robert D. Duggan, "Coming to Know Jesus the Christ: The First Scrutiny," in Wilde, *Commentaries on the Rite of Christian Initiation of Adults*, 43–51; Mark R. Francis, "To Worship God in Spirit and in Truth: First Scrutiny," in Tufano, *Celebrating the Rites of Adult Initiation*, 63–72. For the other scrutinies see Robert D. Duggan, "God Towers over Evil: The Second Scrutiny," in Wilde, *Commentaries*, 53–59; Mark Searle, "For the Glory of God: The Third Scrutiny," in Wilde, *Commentaries*, 61–71; Michael Joncas, "I Once Was Blind and Now I See: Second Scrutiny," in Tufano, *Celebrating the Rites of Adult Initiation*, 83–92; and Rita Ferrone, "Lazarus, Come Out! Third Scrutiny," in Tufano, *Celebrating the Rites of Adult Initiation*, 105–14.

[21] See the discussion in Duggan, "Conversion," 171–78, esp. notes 323, 326, and 327.

[22] See the commentaries listed in note 20 above for guides to the scrutinies.

[23] See Duggan, "Conversion," 147–53; Morris, *The RCIA*, 176–80; Aidan Kavanagh, "The Presentations: Creed and Lord's Prayer," in Wilde, *Commentaries*, 35–42; Catherine Mowry Lacugna, "Presentation of the Creed" and "Presentation of the Lord's Prayer," in Tufano, *Celebrating the Rites of Adult Initiation*, 73–82 and 93–103.

[24] The Latin text, however, is more direct: "adaperiat aures praecodiorum ipsorum," which seems to speak more directly about the act of handing over a verbal text (OICA 187). The translation contains this in the phrase "make them responsive to his love," which does not capture as well the dynamic of handing over a spoken profession of faith.

[25] See "Litany of the Saints," *ODCC*, 991; S. A. van Dijk, "The Litany of the Saints of Holy Saturday," *Journal of Ecclesiastical History* 1 (1950): 51–62; Michael Lapidge, *Anglo-Saxon Litanies of the Saints*, Henry Bradshaw Society 106 (London: Boydel and Brewer, 1991), esp. the introduction, 1–61; Donald G. LaSalle, "The Litany of the Saints: Practicing Communion with the Holy Ones," *Liturgical Ministry* 12 (2003): 20–29.

[26] *Liber Sacramentorum Romanae Aeclesiae ordinis anni circuli*, RED, Series Maior, Fontes IV, 3rd ed., ed. Leo Cunibert Mohlberg (Rome: Herder, 1960, 1981), 72. See Dominic Serra, "The Blessing of Baptismal Water at the Paschal Vigil in the *Gelasianum Vetus*: A Study of the Euchological Texts, Ge 444–48," *Ecclesia Orans* 6 (1989): 323–44; "The Blessing of Baptismal Water at the Paschal Vigil: Ancient Texts and Modern Revisions," *Worship* 64 (1990): 142–56.

[27] In addition to the articles by Serra mentioned above, see Maxwell E. Johnson, *The Rites* (2007), 224–25; Adrien Nocent, "I tre sacramenti dell'iniziazione cristiana," in *La Liturgia, i sacramenti: teologia e storia della celebrazione*, ed. Anscar J. Chupungco, Anàmnesis, Vol. 3/1 (Genoa: Marietti, 1986), 9–131, here 52–56 and 83–84; Nocent, "Christian Initiation in the Roman Church from the Fifth Century until Vatican II," in Chupungco, *Sacraments and Sacramentals*, 49–90, here

55 and 70–71; Robert Cabié, "Christian Initiation," in Martimort, *The Sacraments*, 11–100, here 44–50 and 89–90; David N. Power, "Blessing of the Baptismal Water," in Wilde, *Commentaries*, 91–98; Morris, *The RCIA*, 200–201; Searle, *Christening*, 67–77; Kleinheyer, *Sakramentliche Feiern I*, 115–18, 178–80; Bryan D. Spinks, *Early and Medieval Rituals and Theologies of Baptism: From the New Testament to the Council of Trent*, Liturgy, Worship and Society Series (Burlington, VT: Ashgate, 2006), 111–12; Spinks, *Reformation and Modern Rituals and Theologies of Baptism: From Luther to Contemporary Practices*, Liturgy, Worship and Society Series (Burlington, VT: Ashgate, 2006), 170.

[28] Creating this movement in the water may be a reference to John 5:4, describing how the water was moved by the angel of the Lord as a sign of the healing properties of the pool of Bethesda. Note that John 5:4 is not found in the most ancient manuscripts and is not included in the main text of John's gospel in the most recent versions. It was, however, part of the popular imagination at the time that the prayers for the blessing of water were first composed. Chavasse dates the text of the blessing to the mid-sixth century in *Le sacramentaire gélasien*, 155–71, esp. 168–71.

[29] It is interesting to note that the Latin version of the OICA does not give the acclamation, though it is found in the 1975 and 2002 Latin text of the *Missale Romanum* and in the English versions of both the Sacramentary and the RCIA.

[30] See, for instance, the *Apostolic Tradition*, 21, in *La Tradition apostolique de Saint Hippolyte: Essai de reconstitution*, ed. B. Botte, 5th ed., Liturgiewissenschaftliche Quellen und Forschungen 39 (Münster: Aschenforff, 1989),48–50; and the *Old Gelasian Sacramentary* I:XLIV, in *Liber Sacramentorum Romanae Aeclesiae ordiniis anni circuli*, Rerum Ecclesiasticarum Document, Series Maior, Fontes IV, ed. Leo Cunibert Mohlberg, 3rd ed. (Rome: Herder, 1981), 74n449.

[31] The Eastern Churches have a slightly different formula: "The servant of God, N., is baptized in the name of the Father, and of the Son, and of the Holy Spirit."

[32] One of the goals of the Constitution on the Sacred Liturgy is that, in the reform of the rites, duplications be avoided. The group responsible for the reform of the rites of initiation thought that having two anointings after baptism would be such a duplication. Others have pointed out, however, that the two anointings are of two different parts of the body (the first of the crown of the head, the second of the forehead) and have two different orientations as pointed out by the prayers (the first Christic and the second Pneumatic). Regardless, the directions are clear that if confirmation is celebrated, the first anointing is to be omitted. We will study the text since it gives a particular emphasis to what has just happened.

[33] A separate volume of the *Lex Orandi* Series will treat the sacrament of confirmation.

[34] An exception comes when those previously baptized in another tradition are received into full communion in the Catholic Church. In that case, confirmation is separated from baptism by the renewal of the baptismal promises and the celebration of reception. See RCIA 562–94.

[35] *Missale Gothicum*, 7th/8th century, ed. Mohlberg (Rome, 1961), n. 309. The form of this prayer and its current English translation are quite divergent:

Deus misericordiae sempiternae,
qui in ipso paschalis festi recursu fidem sacratae tibi plebis acendis,
auge gratiam quam dedisti, ut digna omnes intellegentia comprehendant,
quo lavacro abluti, quo spiritu regenerati, quo sanguine sunt redempti.
Per Dominum.

A more accurate English translation might be:

God of everlasting mercy,
each year when the feast of Easter returns you enliven the faith of your holy people.
Increase in them the grace you have already bestowed,
that they may understand more fully
in whose font they have been washed, in whose Spirit they have been reborn,
and in whose blood they have found redemption.

Adapted from *Sunday Celebrations of the Word and Hours* (Ottawa, Ont.: Canadian Conference of Catholic Bishops, 1995), 71.

[36] The original English translation had the phrase "bring these children out of the power of darkness" to translate the Latin text "ab originalis culpae labe nunc eripias." The text was emended to that which we give in the text. Earlier English editions still have the original version.

[37] See the image of Christ breaking down the doors of hell and freeing those who have died, an important theme of Byzantine icons. An example was accessed on June 25, 2008, at http://www.rdrop.com/~/stmary/frk283.jpg.

Part Three

The Theology of Baptism

This third section of the book will explore the theology of baptism. Chapter 5 gives a brief overview of the doctrinal concerns that emerged over the course of the Church's history. Chapter 6 provides an approach to the theology of baptism that takes its origin from the Roman Catholic celebration of baptism today. The final chapter also serves as a conclusion to the whole work.

Chapter Five

Themes of Baptismal Theology in Historical Perspective

This chapter summarizes the Church's teaching about baptism throughout its history. The pertinent initial accounts about baptism in the apostolic community present us with several perspectives: the origins of baptism among the first followers of Jesus; his baptism by John; and the reflection on baptism that we find in the Pauline letters, the Catholic epistles, and the book of Revelation.

The early Christian community developed these New Testament practices and reflections on baptism, and they continued to evolve after the Peace of the Church under Constantine (313). The changing political, cultural, and intellectual climate led to shifts in practice (from baptizing mostly adults [and their households] to baptizing mostly children [and adult converts] during the years between 400 and 800) and to a certain theological synthesis about sacraments in general and baptism in particular (between 1100 and 1400). The European explorations of continents both known (Africa and East Asia) and newly discovered (the Americas) led to a renewed interest in adult baptism, while the Reformation led to a Catholic codification of theology and ritual practice (1500–1900). Publication of long-forgotten or neglected sources gave rise to a renewed understanding of the richness of the Church's practice and theology of baptism, culminating in significant statements formulated during the Second Vatican Council (1962–65). Revised rituals for the baptism of adults and of children sparked theological reflection and served as the basis for two further developments: (1) the *Catechism of the Catholic Church* (1992) articulated the theology of baptism that had emerged, and (2) ecumenical dialogues offered statements about agreement and areas for further reflection.

This presentation of the history of the theology of baptism reveals two primary catalysts for its development: the celebration of baptism itself, and controversies surrounding various dimensions of the theology and practice of baptism. This latter source forms the primary basis for scholastic systematic reflection. It is limited by the context of its origin and at times takes little account of the actual celebration of baptism.

The final chapter offers a theology of the celebration of baptism, drawing together the nonverbal and verbal elements of celebration (its time, space, acts, words, and actors) with an eye toward the history of the rites and theology of baptism.

Baptism in Scripture

Baptism in the New Testament is here considered under three headings: (1) Descriptions of baptism. The apostles baptized new believers. This baptism seems to have emerged from Jesus' own baptism by John. The connections and tensions that characterize these two aspects demand our attention first. (2) Hints of baptism. Sprinkled throughout the New Testament are references to baptism and to the images (e.g., clothing, light) that baptism evokes. Whether they were part of the ritual in New Testament times or not, they reveal how the early Church thought about baptism. (3) Reflections on baptism. John and Paul in particular developed approaches to understanding baptism consistent with their individual theologies. Paul saw participation in the dying and rising of Christ. John imagined a new birth. Are these competing or complementary visions? Both remain part of our theological and ritual tradition.[1]

Descriptions of Baptism

The Acts of the Apostles gives Luke's account of the growth of the Church from Jerusalem, to all Judea and Samaria, and to the ends of the earth (see Acts 1:8). This spread of the Church occurs through witnessing, preaching, and baptism. The celebration of baptism takes different shapes in the various scenarios presented in Acts. We will explore several to get a sense of the issues.

Acts 2

On the day of Pentecost, the Holy Spirit came upon the disciples who witnessed to the multilingual crowd. All heard and understood the preaching, no matter their native tongue (Acts 2:1-12). Peter then took up the word in the first of Luke's kerygmatic sermons (2:13-36). Those who heard were moved to conversion and to action. A dialogue between Peter and those who had heard the word ensued. What should they do? Repent, and be baptized in the name of the Lord Jesus, for the forgiveness of sins and to receive the gift of the Spirit. Four thousand received baptism and then devoted themselves to "teaching and fellowship, to the breaking of bread and the prayers" (Acts 2:37-42; here v. 42).

An analysis of the dynamics of this passage finds (1) preaching, (2) a response of conversion and a call to faith, (3) baptism (in the Lord Jesus, for the forgiveness of sin, and reception of the Spirit), and (4) entrance into Christian living. If this is a paradigm for becoming Christian,[2] it is not found in exactly the same shape in any other account in Acts.

Other Accounts in Acts

Acts teems with stories of the process of conversion to Christ. No two are the same. Great signs accompanied the preaching of the name of Jesus, and so many were baptized (Acts 8:9-13). Some Samaritans had been baptized in the name of the Lord Jesus but required the laying on of hands by Peter and John to receive the Spirit (Acts 8:14-18). An Ethiopian eunuch came to faith on the road home and received baptism from Philip who had been brought to him by an angel (Acts 8:26-40). The persecutor of Christ, Saul, met Jesus on the road and was blinded by the experience. He was taken to Damascus where Ananias mediated Saul's healing, after which he was baptized and became a mighty preacher in his own turn (Acts 9:1-22). Cornelius the centurion and his whole household in Caesarea received the gift of the Holy Spirit while Peter preached to them. He then had them baptized, for "Can anyone withhold the water for baptizing these people who have received the Holy Spirit just as we have?" (Acts 10:1-48; here v. 47; see also 11:1-18). Paul preached in Philippi where Lydia, a local dealer in purple cloth, and her whole household were baptized (Acts 16:14-15). A jailer and his whole family were baptized when Paul and Silas were freed from prison by an earthquake (Acts 16:25-34). Some in Ephesus had been baptized in John's baptism and so received the laying on of hands and the gift of the Holy Spirit though Paul (Acts 19:1-6).

The spread of the Church as recounted in Acts was not limited to stories of baptism, however. Each page tells of the power of the Word and of the Spirit and of the miracles and courage of the apostles, and how God worked through them all. Acts tells of the spread of the Church from Jerusalem to Judea and Samaria, and to the ends of the earth (that is, Rome, where Paul was imprisoned but eloquent in proclaiming the Good News).

This evidence indicates that the community's main goal was to bring people to Christ. That journey required conversion from sin, acceptance of the Lord Jesus (in baptism?) and the welcoming of the gift of the Spirit, lived out in the community of believers.

Jesus' Baptism by John[3]

The preaching in Acts indicates that the baptism of Jesus by John was a key moment. Acts described the event in Peter's words to Cornelius and his household: "That message spread throughout Judea, beginning in Galilee after the baptism that John announced: how God anointed Jesus of Nazareth with the Holy Spirit and with power" (Acts 10:36-38a).

Each evangelist relates the story of the beginning of Jesus' public ministry and his encounter with John the Baptist. It takes place in a context of eschatological expectation. John invokes the prophet Isaiah's call to prepare for the coming of the Lord (Isa 40:3-5; in Luke 3:4-6 and par.), and the people are "filled with expectation" (Luke 3:15).

The event of the baptism revealed Jesus' relationship to his Father ("This is . . ." or "You are my beloved Son") and involved the descent of the Holy Spirit in the form of a dove. That John's was a baptism for the forgiveness of sins (Mark 1:4; Matt 3:11-12; Luke 3:3, 7-17) led to consternation on the part of some of the evangelists. Mark, on the one hand, tells the story in a straightforward way (1:9-11). Matthew includes a dialogue between Jesus and John to explain why Jesus chose to be baptized ("to fulfill all righteousness"; see Matt 3:13-17). Luke mentions the baptism in a relative clause but clearly places the words of the Father and the descent of the Spirit within an event of prayer (Luke 3:21-22). John the Evangelist characterizes the Baptist as a witness to Christ, as someone who baptizes but not for the forgiveness of sins, and describes the words of the Father and the descent of the Spirit as something that the Baptist saw. John, however, includes no mention that Jesus was baptized.

The baptism of Jesus is pivotal. All four evangelists include John the Baptist in their accounts and place the encounter between Jesus and John at the beginning of Jesus' public life. All four see this event as a catalyst, projecting Jesus into his life of preaching, healing, and confronting the forces of evil in the world. Jesus' relationship to the Father and the Spirit emerges as foundational to all that follows.

The baptism of Jesus undergirds the individual baptisms that served as the ritual beginning of life in Christ as described in Acts. Yet the baptism of Jesus is also unique because of the unique relationship he bears to Father and Spirit. The baptism of Christ and the baptism of a Christian are both inaugurations, but the one inaugurates testimony to the relationship of life and love that characterizes Father, Son, and Spirit, while the other inaugurates a conversion from sin and a conversion to Christ in the same Spirit.

Hints of Baptism

References to baptism are not limited to the gospels and the Acts of the Apostles. The letters of Paul, the Catholic Epistles, and the book of Revelation all contribute images and hints about the celebration and role of baptism in the first Christian generations.

Washing

The Letter to Titus gives a clear reference to baptism as a washing.

> . . . he saved us, not because of any works of righteousness that we had done, but according to his mercy, through the washing of rebirth and renewal by the Holy Spirit. This Spirit he poured out on us richly through Jesus Christ our Savior, so that, having been justified by this grace, we might become heirs according to the hope of eternal life. The saying is sure. (Titus 3:5-8)

This image of washing or bath can be used as a prism for other references to baptism: a new birth in water and spirit (John 3:3-5), a funeral bath (Rom 6:1-11), a nuptial bath (Eph 5:26).[4] In an ancient bath, many things occurred. One gathered with friends; stripped off clothes; plunged into water that was hot, then tepid, and then cold; was cleansed and refreshed; was anointed and clothed anew.[5] While Jews and Christians were not always comfortable with the Roman baths, they formed a normal part of every Roman city.[6]

Clothing

A favorite image of Paul is to be clothed in Christ. "As many of you as were baptized into Christ have clothed yourselves with Christ" (Gal 3:27;

see Rom 13:14 and Col 3:10, 12). Paul combines this image of clothing with the notion of equality in Christ: "there is no longer Jew or Greek, there is no longer slave or free, there is no longer male and female" (Gal 3:28; see also Col 3:11). This "putting on" implies stripping off the old (Col 3:9) and taking on the image of the creator (Col 3:10).

Anointing

Jesus is the Messiah, the Christ, the Anointed One (see John 1:21). During his life his feet were anointed (Luke 7:36-50). In the context of the Last Supper (Mark 14:3-9; John 12:1-8), the anointing was interpreted as a preparation for his burial. Mark tells of Jesus sending his disciples who anointed the sick (6:13; see Jas 5:14). After the crucifixion, the women went to anoint the body of Jesus (Mark 16:1).

Luke highlights Jesus as the Anointed One. During his inaugural homily in Nazareth, Jesus cites Isaiah: "The Lord has anointed me to bring good news to the poor" (Luke 4:18). Jesus' anointing is again proclaimed in Peter's sermon to Cornelius and his household. After mentioning John's baptism, Peter says: "God anointed Jesus of Nazareth with the Holy Spirit and with power" (Acts 10:38).

But Christians are also anointed: "But it is God who establishes us with you in Christ and has anointed us, by putting his seal on us and giving us his Spirit in our hearts as a first installment" (2 Cor 1:21-22). The anointing is a seal, a promise of what is not yet complete but eventually will be.

Light

Light speaks about God and our relationship to God. "God is light and in him there is no darkness at all" (1 John 1:5). Christ proclaims: "I am the light of the world" (John 9:5). Christians are light: "For once you were in darkness, but now in the Lord you are light. Live as children of light" (Eph 5:8). Paul calls us to put on light as we put on Christ: "Let us then lay aside the works of darkness and put on the armor of light . . . put on the Lord Jesus Christ" (Rom 13:12, 14).

Reflections on Baptism[7]

Already a theology of baptism is emerging from the several passages of Scripture that we have presented above in summary. Two passages have served as particular focal points for thinking about the meaning of baptism: the image of baptism as dying and rising in Christ in Paul's letter to the Romans and the image of baptism as new birth in John 3.

Paul: Participation in Christ's Death and Resurrection (Rom 6:3-11)

In his letter to the Romans, Paul struggles with the question of our salvation in Christ. He poses the contrast between Adam and Christ: sin came into the world through the one man, Adam; now life is returned to the world by the one man, Christ. Where sin abounded, now grace abounds all the more. To the (rhetorical) question, "Should we sin more so that more grace abounds?" Paul answers, no, we have died to sin in Christ that we might be raised to life in Christ. This dying has taken place in baptism and presents us with the hope of rising with Christ at the end. The context of Paul's treatment of baptism is doctrinal (sin and salvation) and his conclusion is ethical (so you must consider yourselves dead to sin and alive to God in Christ). His treatment implies a ceremony in which the act of baptizing embodies such an immersion that it brings to mind dying or being buried, and an emersion that allows one to think of rising from the dead as did Christ.

John: Being Born Again of Water and Spirit (John 3:1-21)

In the discourse with Nicodemus, Jesus plays with words to lead Nicodemus to a deeper understanding of what God is doing in the world and especially in Jesus himself. There are two words with double meanings used in the text: Jesus tells Nicodemus that to see the kingdom, one must be born *anothen* (this Greek word means either "from above" or "again"). Nicodemus imagines reentering a mother's womb, so Jesus leads him to a deeper understanding of a birth in water and *pneuma* (the Greek word means either "Spirit" or "wind"), a *pneuma* that blows where it wills.

Subsequent reflection on these two passages has led to viewing them as reflecting on baptism as both a tomb from which the dead rise to new life, and a womb from which one is born anew.[8]

The descriptions, hints, and reflections presented above in summary form lay out for us some of the richness of theological reflection on baptism. Baptism is the means that most often brings someone to Christ. It is about forgiveness of sin, the presence of the Holy Spirit, and membership in the Christian community. It is about washing, light, clothing, and anointing. It changes us: we are born anew in water and the Holy Spirit, we die to sin so that we might rise again in Christ Jesus. The centuries that proceed from this point take these components as their starting point for further celebration and reflection.

Historical Development[9]

Baptism before the Peace of the Church (to 313)

From its scriptural origins during the first Christian centuries, the theology of baptism developed slowly. What little is known about baptism comes from sources widely separated in space and time from one another: the *Didache* (Egypt? Syria? ca. 90–110), Justin Martyr (a Samaritan philosopher teaching in Rome, +160), the *Apostolic Tradition* (compiled by the Roman Hippolytus? early third century?), and Tertullian (a North African, + after 220). The crisis of the persecutions by the Roman emperors Decius and Septimius Severus (251 and 257) and the painful reality that some Christians fell away from the faith during them, meant that questions had to be answered: does the community rebaptize those who have fallen away and now want to return? Similarly, what if someone is baptized while in a heretical group and then wants to join the true Church? Are they to be rebaptized or is there another way that we welcome them?

Celebration of Baptism

The *Didache*,[10] or the *Teaching of the Twelve Apostles*, contains a chapter on baptism. The text describes how those to be baptized were instructed according to the Two Ways, found in the first six chapters of the *Didache*. They were baptized in flowing water in the name of the Father and the Son and the Holy Spirit; if no flowing water was available, then they were immersed in cold or warm water, or water was poured on them. The one baptizing fasted before administering baptism. The candidates for baptism also fasted one or two days before the baptism, joined by members of the community who wished to fast with them (7). Later, chapter 9 on the Eucharist stipulates that only the baptized may join in the eucharistic meal.

Justin Martyr described the celebration of baptism in his *First Apology* (ca. 150).[11] In chapter 61 he described baptism: it is a consecration to

God, a regeneration through Christ. Those who have been convinced and who believe

> are taught in prayer and fasting to ask God to forgive their past sins, while we pray and fast with them. Then we lead them to a place where there is water, and they are regenerated in the same manner in which we ourselves were regenerated. In the name of God, the Father and Lord of all, and of our Savior, Jesus Christ, and of the Holy Ghost, they then receive the washing with water.[12]

Justin went on to cite John 3 about new birth and Isaiah 1 about being washed clean. He emphasized the trinitarian formula again and then said: "This washing is called illumination, since they who learn these things become illuminated intellectually."[13]

We note several features: faith is necessary; teaching precedes baptism but is also accompanied by prayer and upright living; there is forgiveness of sins in a washing; the Trinity is invoked, and the life lived after baptism is in relationship with the members of the Trinity; it is an illumination of the mind. Justin's philosophical search inclines him to focus on the intellectual dimension of the conversion experience.

The *Apostolic Tradition* gives an elaborate description of the celebration of baptism. While the place and date of its composition have become controversial, it seems to conform to the world of the third and fourth centuries.[14] Candidates are screened by teachers about their lifestyle and profession. Those admitted then "hear the word" for as many as three years, during which time they pray apart from the community and receive the laying on of hands. They are examined again and the chosen receive a more intense instruction in prayer with a laying on of hands. On the day before their baptism they receive an exorcism from the bishop and spend the night in prayer. At dawn, the water is blessed. Children, men, and women are baptized in that order. The bishop blesses oil of thanksgiving and oil of exorcism. The candidates renounce sin and Satan and are anointed with the oil of exorcism. They are led into the water where they profess their faith in three moments (in the Father, in the Son, and in the Holy Spirit) and are three times immersed in the water. The presbyter anoints them with oil of thanksgiving, they dress, and enter the church. The bishop prays over them, anoints them on their heads with oil of thanksgiving, and gives them a kiss. All then pray together for the first time. The oblations are presented and prayed over. The newly baptized receive communion of bread, water, milk, and wine (in that order). "They then hasten to do good works."[15]

Tertullian wrote a treatise *On Baptism* around the year 200.[16] It is a defense of baptism against certain heretics. Tertullian describes a washing from sin in the great IXTHUS (the Greek word for fish), a mnemonic device for "Jesus Christ, God's Son, Savior." The water is blessed for baptism, and Tertullian hints at some of the themes in the prayer, though he does not seem to quote it. The one substitute for baptism is martyrdom for the faith. Those baptized must be well prepared, so infants are not prime candidates for baptism. Easter and Pentecost are the best times for baptism, though every day is a day of resurrection.

Tertullian also introduces into Latin theology the word *sacramentum*. It is his way of articulating the Greek word *mysterion*, the celebration that engages Christians with God's saving plan in Christ. The *sacramentum* (among other meanings) is an oath that commits a soldier to the service of the emperor. The Christian's *sacramentum* is one's commitment to Christ in baptism.[17]

The Crisis

During the persecutions of the mid-third century, a crisis regarding baptism developed. On one side were the Novatians, a rigorist group, along with Cyprian of Carthage. On the other side were the bishops of Rome, especially Stephen. The question concerned how one should receive heretics back into the Church. Novatian and his followers, supported by Cyprian, held that they had completely abandoned the faith and thus needed to be baptized (again). Pope Stephen was adamant that this approach constituted a novelty. He said: "If, therefore, some come to you from any heresy whatsoever let no innovation be made except according to what has been handed down, namely, let an imposition of hands be made on them by way of penance; for the heretics themselves are right in not baptizing other heretics who come over to them but simply receiving them into their communion."[18] This first magisterial statement will find further development by Augustine in the following period. It is rooted in a sense of tradition, but ultimately focuses on the fact that there is only one baptism, and it is not (cannot be) repeated.

Baptism after the Peace of the Church (313–600)

In the period after the Peace of the Church, we learn of the celebration of baptism primarily from the Mystagogical Catecheses of Ambrose, John Chrysostom, Cyril of Jerusalem, and Theodore of Mopsuestia. Doctrinal issues emerge from the Church's conflicts with heretics. Augustine's conflicts with the Donatists and the Pelagians have tremendous impact on future thinking about the meaning of baptism.

Mystagogy[19]

The Mystagogical Catecheses reveal a baptismal practice and understanding that is rich and growing richer. They arise in a specific context of celebration: after the period of the catechumenate the newly baptized return to Church regularly after their baptism to hear an explanation of what they experienced in their baptism, confirmation, and first reception of Communion. These post-initiatory homilies are called Mystagogical Catecheses. Space limits dictate only a partial analysis of all that these authors say. What seems key is twofold: (1) the texts of Scripture are interpreted in such a way that they are seen as illustrative of present reality, and (2) the rituals themselves illuminate the plan of salvation revealed in the words of Scripture. When an Ambrose or a John Chrysostom preaches to the newly baptized during Easter week, he is revealing to them the reality that they have entered, the reality first promised in Scripture and now alive and present in their own lives by means of their participation in the awe-inspiring rites.

The mystagogical catecheses describe a celebration of baptism that still includes a lengthy period of catechetical preparation, a group of candidates who are primarily adults, an elaborate and richly symbolic celebration, and an entrance into Christian living mediated by the bishop's series of catechetical homilies.

A characteristic practice of the period indicates that some become catechumens at birth but their baptism is postponed until around age thirty. Augustine and Basil are examples of this tendency.

Response to Heresy

The legacy of the third century doctrinal crisis lingered into the fourth and fifth centuries. Augustine serves as a good guide, not only because his analysis and solutions were so cogent, but also because they helped determine future reflection on the theology of baptism.[20] There are two areas where Augustine's thought is especially important. In his debates with the Donatists[21] he helps develop the doctrine that the moral uprightness of the minister is not the deciding factor in the validity of baptism. The Donatists taught that if people had left the Church and formed a heretical group, those baptized within that heretical group were not really baptized. Augustine, on the contrary, taught that it is really Christ who baptizes. The effect of the baptism may be limited while the person is outside the Church, but the person has really entered Christ. This permanent conforming of the baptized person to Christ has come to be known in the tradition as character, the seal of the Spirit (see Eph 1:13).

The second controversy involved the Pelagians.[22] The followers of Pelagius taught that there is no original sin and that believers cooperate in their own salvation. Augustine rejected this approach. He used the fact of the baptism of infants to insist that there is an original sin: baptism is for the remission of sins, so the Church clearly baptizes infants because they participate, not in any actual sin of their own, but in the original sin of the parents of all people, Adam and Eve.

This period sees a dual development: a rich tradition of unfolding the experience of baptism for those adults (and the parents of children?) newly baptized and a more systematic development sharpened by controversy. The first method is one of mystagogy, using images and the ability to read multiple meanings into the ceremonies celebrated, juxtaposing them with passages of Scripture and everyday images to lead the newly baptized to an awareness of their participation in the life and love of God.

The second development springs from debate and the rhetoric of the law court. That baptism is permanent and cannot be repeated, and that it removes original sin from infants, are the two doctrinal points that emerge from the controversy. Both are corollaries of the principal facts that baptism is for the forgiveness of sins and necessary for salvation. Henceforth, these two points will form an essential part of Catholic teaching about baptism.

Baptism in the Early Middle Ages (600–1100)

The rapid Christianization of the late Roman Empire led to major changes in the celebration of baptism. The theology of baptism built on the consensus that had emerged out of the patristic period. On the one hand, missionary efforts led to the baptism of whole peoples, such as the baptism of Clovis and the Franks (ca. 498). On the other hand, in settled areas the more typical candidate was the child of parents already Christian.

The Celebration of Baptism

The celebration of baptism shows these effects. From this period liturgical books have survived that describe the celebration of baptism. The

Old Gelasian Sacramentary (ca. 750, with a core of material that dates back to sixth-century Rome) and the *Ordo Romanus XI* (*OR XI*; ca. 850, with material that also dates from the sixth century) display complementary rituals laying out the way someone enters the Church in baptism. The *Old Gelasian* describes three scrutinies administered on the Third, Fourth, and Fifth Sundays of Lent, but, combined with other material, also indicates that these Sunday scrutinies had migrated to weekdays. There are rites for handing on to the candidates the Creed, the gospels, and the Lord's Prayer. Holy Saturday morning provides a final exorcism, with baptism, confirmation, and Eucharist taking place at the Easter Vigil. The *OR XI* describes seven scrutinies celebrated on weekdays, which seem to be a combination of the three *Gelasian* scrutinies, the handing-over ceremonies, plus the Saturday preparatory material. Both the *Gelasian* and the *OR XI* seem to have infants in view as the primary recipients of the sacrament.[23]

A later development is the appearance of a ritual for use when someone is dying. This ceremony brings together into one all the elements that the *Gelasian* and *OR XI* describe as taking place over all the weeks of Lent. Eventually, under the impetus of the Augustinian teaching on original sin, the high infant mortality rate, and other factors, this celebration of baptism for those in danger of death became the usual way that baptism was celebrated.[24]

This period also sees a series of developments that affect the celebration of baptism: over time, baptism becomes detached from Easter, detached from confirmation, and detached from the reception of Communion.

The Doctrine of Baptism

Until the rise of scholasticism, theology was primarily a monastic endeavor. Baptism, and the sacraments in general, was not an important focus of monastic attention. Baptism rose to the fore, however, as part of a pastoral (rather than strictly theological) effort during the reign of Charlemagne to unify practice and catechetical teaching. A questionnaire was distributed throughout his realm asking his metropolitan bishops how baptism was celebrated in their particular area. The eighteen questions posed covered the celebration of the sacrament but also gave a sense of the kinds of answers being sought. The questions included: Why is an infant first made a catechumen? What is a catechumen? A scrutiny? A Symbol (the creed)? How is belief in the Trinity, as expressed in the Symbol, understood? What is the renunciation of Satan, and of his works and pomps? Why an exsufflation? An exorcism? Why do catechumens accept salt? Why are their nostrils touched? Why is the breast anointed with oil? Why are their shoulders signed? Why are they dressed in clothes? Why is the head anointed with holy chrism? Why covered with the holy veil (a chismal hat?)? Why confirmed with the Body and Blood of the Lord?[25]

Sixty-one responses were eventually gathered, some in direct response to the questionnaire, others later works based on the original responses. They reveal an understanding rooted in Augustine and Isidore of Seville, still much in the typological world of the mystagogical catecheses but also demonstrating the resurgence of interest in writing Latin in a newly rich and articulate way. Theodulph of Orléans comments on the celebration of baptism: "Thus we die to sin when we renounce the devil . . . ; we are buried with Christ when, with the invocation of the Holy Trinity and the threefold immersion in the font, we descend as into a grave; we rise with Christ when, freed from all sins, we come up from the font as from a grave."[26]

The celebration of baptism has begun to change, mainly by combining all the ceremonies into a single rite originally intended for a sick catechumen, now transformed to become the rite for a child—perhaps in danger of death by virtue of the high infant mortality rate of the time, and definitely in danger of spiritual death because of original sin. The theology of baptism continues to flow from the patristic world but now is slowly being rethought for a newly emerging intellectual world, soon to take shape in the rise of scholasticism and the university.

Baptism in Scholastic Thought (1100–1500):

Reflection on the New Ritual Reality

The form of baptism now in practice, that of a single ceremony derived from the situation of a sick catechumen, served as the ritual context for the development of the theology of baptism during the scholastic period. Theologians like Hugh of St. Victor (+ 1142) and Peter Lombard (+ 1160) developed a paradigm for understanding how sacraments work. The Augustinian dyad of *sacramentum* and *res* (the combination of matter and word on the one hand, and the reality symbolized on the other hand) was expanded to a triad: *sacramentum, res,* and an intermediate term, the *sacramentum et res,* which is both material and spiritual. Scholastic theologians saw the *sacramentum* as the water poured while reciting the trinitarian formula ("I baptize you in the name of the Father and of the

Son and of the Holy Spirit"). The *res* was the ultimate goal of baptism: membership in Christ, forgiveness of sin, gift of the Holy Spirit. The *sacramentum et res* was another outcome of the *sacramentum*, namely, the character that permanently conforms the person to Christ and therefore means that there can be no rebaptism. The minister of baptism is a bishop, priest, deacon, any Christian, or indeed anyone who intends to do what the Church does in celebrating baptism. The recipient of the sacrament is someone not baptized who believes or is capable of belief (i.e., a child).

The Council of Florence, among its various goals, intended to provide the basis for reunion with the Church of the Armenians. The Decree for the Armenians (1439) used a brief document of Thomas Aquinas (+ 1274) to summarize Catholic teaching on the sacraments. Regarding baptism it states:

> Among all the sacraments holy baptism holds the first place because it is the gateway to the spiritual life; by it we are made members of Christ and belong to his body, the Church. And since through the first man death has entered into all [cf. Rom 5:12], unless we are born again of water and the Spirit, we cannot, as the Truth said, enter into the kingdom of heaven [cf. John 3:5].

> The matter [*materia*] of this sacrament is true natural water; it does not matter [*nec refert*] whether it is cold or warm. The form is "I baptize you in the name of the Father and of the Son and of the Holy Spirit." We do not deny, however, that true baptism is also effected by these words: "May the servant of Christ, N., be baptized in the name of the Father and of the Son and of the Holy Spirit," or: "By my hands N. is baptized in the name of the Father and of the Son and of the Holy Spirit." For as the principal cause from which baptism derives its virtue is the Holy Trinity, while the instrumental cause is the minister who confers the sacrament externally, the sacrament is performed whenever the act carried out by the minister is expressed along with the invocation of the Holy Trinity.

> The minister of this sacrament is the priest, to whom by reason of his office it belongs to baptize. But in case of necessity not only priests or deacons, but also laymen or laywomen, or even pagans and heretics may baptize, provided they observe the Church's form and intend to do what the Church does.

> The effect of this sacrament is the remission of all guilt, original and actual, and also of all punishment due to the guilt itself. For this reason, no satisfaction is to be enjoined on the baptized for their past sins; and if they die before committing any fault, they immediately gain access to the Kingdom of heaven and the beatific vision.[27]

This is a good summary of scholastic teaching on baptism. The first paragraph situates the teaching within the scriptural data, speaking of the final goal of baptism. Note the citation of Romans and John, as noted above. The second paragraph describes the matter and form: water poured with the trinitarian formula, which can be articulated in several ways, both indicative (the Western, Latin way: "I baptize you . . .") and deprecative (the Eastern, Greek, and Armenian way: "The servant of God is baptized . . ."). The minister is normally a priest, though anyone can perform the rite as long as it is done in the way the Church intends; it is really the Holy Trinity who baptizes. The effect is forgiveness of guilt and punishment due to sin. Not mentioned is the character that baptism confers. The Decree had mentioned this earlier, in speaking of the sacraments in general: "Among these sacraments there are three, baptism, confirmation and Order, which imprint on the soul an indelible character, that is a certain spiritual sign distinguishing [the recipient] from others. Hence, these are not repeated for the same person."[28]

A distinctive addition to the patristic way of thinking about the sacraments was the adoption of Aristotle's understanding of causality. *Sacramentum* is now understood to be made up of two causes: the material cause (the water) and the formal cause (the trinitarian text). The primary cause is the Holy Trinity, while the secondary, instrumental cause is the priest. The focus on causes and the use of Aristotle are typical of late scholasticism.[29]

Baptism in Reformation and Tridentine Thought and Practice (1500–1700)

Protestant Reformers and the Emergence of Anabaptists

The Protestant Reformation emerged in the aftermath of Martin Luther's challenge to the Catholic Church. Several diverse currents can be distinguished, including Lutheran, Reformed, Anglican, and Anabaptist. One of Luther's desires was to be completely rooted in God's Word in Holy Scripture. This led him to consider the traditions of the Catholic Church not found directly in Scripture to be a distraction, or worse, a deviation from the true Word of God. A clear and brief summary of Luther's understanding of baptism is found in the *Small Catechism* (1529). In it, he follows a path very similar to that of the Council of Florence or Aquinas or Bonaventure, but with an evangelical emphasis. Baptism is washing with water using the Word of God. Baptism forgives sins and grants salvation. These effects are produced by God's Word in conjunction with water and the faith of the person, which is rooted in God's Word. It signifies the death of sin in us and the promise of new life, according to Romans 6:4.[30]

Certain reformers took a more radical stance than Luther, e.g., Thomas Müntzer and Balthasar Hubmaier, who in their evangelical zeal called for believer's baptism. This they saw as more faithful to the biblical practice as detailed in the Acts of the Apostles. Since they considered the baptism of infants to be no baptism at all because it lacked the personal faith of the one baptized, they practiced a baptism of believers only and "re"baptized those baptized as infants. Luther, Zwingli, and Calvin all reacted violently to the movement, which had many variations in the sixteenth century.[31] Mennonites and British and American Baptists are descendants of the sixteenth-century Anabaptists.

The Response of the Council of Trent

The Council of Trent took up the question of baptism in its seventh session (1547). The council provided no section of doctrinal exposition as it did for other topics, such as justification or the Eucharist, but treated baptism in fourteen canons (DS 1614–27). The canons affirmed the following: that the baptism of Christ is different from that of John (1); that water and the trinitarian formula are necessary (2); that the Roman Church has maintained the true doctrine and practice of baptism (3); that someone baptized need not be rebaptized, even if their baptism was administered by a heretic or performed while the recipients were still infants and not able to speak for themselves (4, 11, 12, 13, 14); that baptism is necessary for salvation (5); that one can sin after baptism and lose grace (6, 10); that baptism makes one a full member of the Christian community (7, 8); that baptism does not take the place of the sacrament of penance for sins committed after baptism (10).[32]

Crucial to the understanding of the Catholic doctrine on baptism as necessary for salvation is the Decree on Original Sin from the fifth session (1546) in which the council fathers make their own the decrees of the Council of Carthage (418). Adam is the source of an original sin conveyed to every person born of Adam, and Christ is the sole source of salvation for all, whether adults or children. Baptism is the means by which this sin is expiated and salvation gained.[33]

The Ritual of 1614

Flowing from the teaching of the Council of Trent, the popes took responsibility to oversee a complete reform of the liturgy. Various papal commissions issued a new Breviary (1568), Missal (1570), Martyrology (1584), Pontifical (1595/96), Ceremonial of Bishops (1600), and Ritual (1614).

The Ritual contains the Rite of Baptism. It follows the rite that had emerged in the early Middle Ages that combined all the rites of the preparation for baptism into a single ceremony. The Ritual begins its treatment with the essentials of the sacrament: matter and form, the minister, the baptism of children, godparents, and the other requisites (oil, candle, white garment, etc.).[34] There follow two rites, one for baptizing children,[35] the other for baptizing adults.[36] The basic shapes of these two rites appear in chapters 1 and 2 of this book. They codify late medieval baptismal practice and combine it with the theological concerns that had emerged from scholasticism and the Tridentine response to the reformers.

Baptism in a Changing World (1700–1962)

The theology of baptism remained fairly constant in the centuries after the Council of Trent. The outline in a typical theological manual of the early twentieth century[37] captures the issues that formed the Catholic mindset. The treatment was divided into four sections:

(1) *Baptism itself*, which included the institution of baptism by Christ and treatment of the matter and form of baptism.

(2) *The effects of baptism*: the permanent character of baptism, which makes one a citizen of the reign of God and fit to receive the other sacraments; the forgiveness of all sins, original and actual; the penalty due to sin; the grace and regeneration of someone in new spiritual life; but without removal of the tendency toward sin.

(3) *The minister of baptism*: The ordinary minister of baptism is the priest; a deacon is an extraordinary minister. Baptism can be administered privately in urgent situations by any legitimate minister, which would be anyone who intends to baptize as the Church intends, with water and the trinitarian formula.

(4) *The subject of baptism*: One must be baptized to be saved, although acts of charity or of perfect contrition, which demonstrate an implicit desire for the sacrament of baptism, can supply for the celebration of the rite. Martyrdom for the faith is likewise a sufficient substitute for baptism. Adult baptism requires proper intention and faith and hope to which is added supernatural attrition for sin. Infant baptism is possible (against Anabaptists and Walden-

sians), and necessary for salvation. Children of unbelievers cannot be baptized without their parents' consent, except in danger of death or when undergoing Catholic education and no one who has authority over them objects. Baptism, despite the teaching of Anabaptists, cannot be repeated. On the other hand, if there is doubt about baptism, it should be conferred conditionally.[38]

The ceremonies of baptism are treated in the manual's appendix:

(1) *The ceremonies and rites* were distinguished. Ceremonies included everything outside of the matter and form. The rite of baptism was the form (Latin or Oriental) in which the ceremonies were celebrated.

(2) *Godparents* were required in solemn celebrations, but in danger of death were not necessary. There should not be too many godparents so as to avoid creating too many spiritual relationships. Godparents were already to have been baptized, could not be the parents, were to have been at least fourteen years old, were to have known the basics of the faith, and were not to have been ordained unless they had the permission of the ordinary. The role of the godparent was to care for the spiritual upbringing of the child. The relationship was one of spiritual parenthood, which therefore prohibited marriage of the godparent to the child.

(3) *The time and place* of baptism: children were to be baptized as soon as possible after birth; children could be baptized at any time on any day; adults ideally were baptized at the Easter Vigil or the Vigil of Pentecost. Solemn baptisms were to be celebrated at the font in the parish church.

(4) *Baptisms had to be registered* in a book and kept safe in a parish house.[39]

Great change was under way, however, outside the world of post-Tridentine manual theology. On the level of practice, the discovery of the Americas by Europeans and the subsequent missionary impetus there and in Asia and Africa led to the call for a celebration of baptism that took the missionary context more into account. We treated this briefly in chapter 1.[40]

The rise of historical and critical methods in Protestant circles during the nineteenth century, and the return to the biblical, patristic, and liturgical sources in Catholic circles, led to a realization that the historical record contained more than was quoted in the manual texts and needed to be accounted for.

Historical-critical questions about the possible origin of Christianity from the myths and practices of ancient Greco-Roman religion prompted a number of reactions. The *Syllabus of Errors* and the *Decree against Modernism* were official reactions to historical-critical inquiries. Others, however, thought that the questions needed to be answered on their own terms. The most important voice in Catholic circles was to be Odo Casel, who saw affinities but not a direct dependence on ancient religion. His development of the idea of "the mystery of Christian worship," taking inspiration from the ancient mystery religions, was an important step in developing a theology of sacramental celebration that broke beyond the scholastic formulation of causal description (matter, form, minister, recipient). Casel developed a way of understanding the sacraments as a participation in the saving acts of Christ. The use of the term "participation" connected Casel's reflection to the teaching of Pius X in his letter *Tra le sollecitudini* on Church music.[41]

The growing realization that the early Church had celebrated the initiation of adults in stages led to missionaries experimenting with using the ritual in a similar way. Eventually, the Congregation of Rites issued a revision of the Rite of Baptism for Adults to be celebrated in stages.[42]

Baptism in Vatican II and Postconciliar Activity (Ritual Books, Catechism, Dialogues)

The Teaching of Vatican II

The fathers gathered for the Second Vatican Council issued *Sacrosanctum Concilium*, the Constitution on the Sacred Liturgy, as one of their first documents, on 4 December 1963.[43] Baptism forms the focus of SC 64–70, in which the constitution calls for several changes. A catechumenate for adults, in stages, is to be restored (64), initiatory elements from other cultures in congruity with the faith can be included, and the rites of baptism for adults, both the simple and the solemn forms, are to be revised, with a new formula "on the occasion of a baptism" to be inserted into the Missal (65–66). The Rite of Baptism for Children should be revised to highlight that it is children, not adults, being baptized and to emphasize the special role of parents and godparents in the rite (67). Rites for special circumstances should be developed: for large groups, for use by catechists, and in danger of death (68). Other special circumstances are also mentioned: when a child is baptized in an emergency, a new rite emphasizing that the child has already entered the Church is needed. In addition, a rite for welcoming already-baptized Christians into the Catholic Church must be devised (68). Finally, baptismal water should be blessed within the ceremony, except during the Easter season when the water blessed at the Easter Vigil is used (70).

No formal theology of baptism is presented, but theological implications underlie these practical norms. One is the principle of the truth of signs (see SC 7, 23, etc.): the celebration should flow out of the signs used. Hence the rites for adults and children need to manifest who exactly is being baptized. Another is that the prayer of blessing for baptismal water is too important to be heard only once per year at the Vigil: it should be prayed over water at every baptism. The prayer names what is happening in the celebration.

The Work of the Consilium and the New Ritual Books

Pope Paul VI established a special commission to implement the Constitution on the Sacred Liturgy.[44] The new rites of Baptism for Children (1969) and for Christian Initiation of Adults (1972) emerged through the hard work of the study group entrusted with this work by Pope Paul VI.[45]

The theology contained in "Christian Initiation: General Introduction" is important for understanding the theology of baptism and of all the sacraments of initiation.[46] Paragraphs 1–2 provide an overall view of the theology of baptism seen from the perspective of initiation.

> 1. In the sacraments of Christian initiation we are freed from the power of darkness and joined to Christ's death, burial, and resurrection. We receive the Spirit of filial adoption and are part of the entire people of God in the celebration of the memorial of the Lord's death and resurrection.
>
> 2. Baptism incorporates us into Christ and forms us into God's people. This first sacrament pardons all our sins, rescues us from the power of darkness, and brings us to the dignity of adopted children, a new creation through water and the Holy Spirit. Hence we are called and are indeed the children of God.
>
> By signing us with the gift of the Spirit, confirmation makes us more completely the image of the Lord and fills us with the Holy Spirit, so that we may bear witness to him before all the world and work to bring the Body of Christ to its fullness as soon as possible.
>
> Finally, coming to the table of the eucharist, we eat the flesh and drink the blood of the Son of Man so that we may have eternal life and show forth the unity of God's people. By offering ourselves with Christ, we

share in the universal sacrifice, that is, the entire community of the redeemed offered to God by their High Priest, and we pray for a greater outpouring of the Holy Spirit, so that the whole human race may be brought into the unity of God's family.

Thus the three sacraments of Christian initiation closely combine to bring us, the faithful of Christ, to his full stature and to enable us to carry out the mission of the entire people of God in the Church and in the world.

These two paragraphs offer a vision of baptism within the economy of life in the Church that goes beyond the categories of the scholastic and manual syntheses seen in the period before the Second Vatican Council. It takes into account the long history of the Church and the variety of practice that has characterized this life. By presenting a theology rooted in the Scriptures and the patristic age, the teaching contained here continues the style of the Second Vatican Council that chose to adopt a means of expression that was constructive rather than reactive.

The general introduction continues in five sections. The first section, The Dignity of Baptism (3–6), carries forth the tone set in the first two paragraphs. Baptism opens the door to life in the Church. It is a sacrament of faith that requires faith: in catechumens, in parents and godparents, incipiently in children. Since faith comes from hearing, catechesis and Celebration of the Word of God are requisites for this faith. Baptism is a permanent incorporation into the Body of Christ and into the temple of the Spirit: it is never repeated. Baptism cleanses from sin. Baptism is a participation in the dying and rising of Christ. The liturgical celebration embodies these various truths of baptism.

The next main section of the general introduction speaks of offices and ministries of baptism. First mentioned are the faithful members of the community, since they have a stake in the growth of the body. A particular expression of this concern is found in the role of godparents. The rules for godparents are laid out: designated by the candidate (or parents), sixteen years of age, having been baptized, confirmed, and having received Communion, members of the Catholic Church. Ordinary ministers of baptism are bishops, priests, and deacons. Pastors have a particular responsibility for the preparation of catechumens and parents and godparents. In danger of death, anyone can baptize with the right intention (of doing what the Church does in baptism).

The requirements for the celebration of baptism come next (18–29). These include the use of water, the font, a preference for immersion, the formula, the inclusion of the Word of God, the desire that there be a single ceremony that gathers all recently born children, the need to record the baptism in the parish register. The final two sections (30–35) detail the adaptations to be made by the conferences of bishops and by the minister of baptism.

Baptism in the *Catechism of the Catholic Church*

The *Catechism of the Catholic Church*[47] summarizes the teachings of the Church, in order to consolidate the approaches taken in the Second Vatican Council. It resembles the *Catechism for Pastors* that followed the Council of Trent (1566).

The *Catechism* has four parts, centering on the Creed, the seven sacraments, the Ten Commandments, and the Lord's Prayer. The treatment of the sacraments begins with an overview of the whole system of sacraments. They are the work of the Trinity and an ecclesial expression of the paschal mystery. This general introduction to the sacraments continues by laying out a liturgical way of understanding the sacraments, based on the participants, the words and actions, liturgical time, and liturgical space.

Baptism is one of the three sacraments of initiation (including confirmation and Eucharist). The *Catechism* blends the inherited treatment of the sacraments from the scholastic and manual tradition with an appreciation of the scriptural and patristic concerns that the previous period of historical, liturgical, patristic, and scriptural research had revealed.

After an introductory paragraph that gives an overview of baptism, there are seven sections. The introductory paragraph summarizes the magisterium's teaching on baptism, citing the Council of Florence, the 1566 *Catechism for Pastors*, and the 1983 Code of Canon Law:

> Holy Baptism is the basis of the whole Christian life, the gateway to life in the Spirit (*vitae spirtualis ianua*), and the door which gives access to the other sacraments. Through Baptism we are freed from sin and reborn as sons of God; we become members of Christ, are incorporated into the church and made sharers in her mission: "Baptism is the sacrament of regeneration through water and in the word."[48]

In part 1 of its treatment, the *Catechism* explores the various names of baptism (1214–16): "Baptism" is further explained as to "plunge" and to "immerse." Then Titus 3:5 and John 3:5 are mentioned to propose baptism as "the washing of regeneration and renewal by the Holy Spirit." A third name is proposed: enlightenment.

Part 2 explores baptism within the economy of salvation (1217–28). The prayer for the blessing of water at the Easter Vigil uses some Old Testament prefigurations: creation, the flood, the Red Sea. Christ's baptism is the fulfillment of these Old Testament figures. Baptism in the Church is explained in the light of the Acts of the Apostles.

Part 3 offers a mystagogical reading of the rite of baptism. It begins with a consideration of baptism as part of initiation (1229–33) and points out the difference between the baptism of an adult and the baptism of a child: catechumenate crowned by the three sacraments of initiation; or baptism followed by a postbaptismal catechumenate with confirmation and first Eucharist following later. There follows a "mystagogy" of the celebration of the sacrament (1234–45). The elements highlighted include the sign of the cross at the beginning, the Celebration of the Word of God, exorcisms and the professions of faith, the blessing of the baptismal water, the essential rite (threefold immersion or pouring of water with the trinitarian formula), anointing with sacred chrism, the presentation of a white garment and a lighted candle, First Holy Communion, and a final solemn blessing.

The treatment intersperses consideration of the uses of the Eastern liturgy: differences in the trinitarian formula ("The servant of God is baptized"), and the significance and importance of the anointing with chrism. In the East, this is the sacrament of chrismation. The *Catechism* curiously treats the anointing of children with chrism as an announcement of the later sacrament of confirmation. The text accompanying the Latin anointing is christological (Christ as priest, prophet, and king), while the confirmation anointing is pneumatic, invoking the gifts of the Holy Spirit. The *Catechism* omits mention of the fact that when an adult is baptized in the Latin Church, the christological anointing is omitted and replaced by the pneumatological anointing of the sacrament of confirmation. The celebration of Communion is also different in the East and West: in the East, all, including children, receive Communion at baptism. In the West, children receive Communion only after they have arrived at the age of reason.

Part 4 treats the recipient of baptism (1246–55). Both adults and children can receive baptism. Both do so in the context of faith. Adults receive after they have professed faith on their own behalf. Children receive to counter the forces of original sin and in the faith of the parents and godparents who speak for them. In both cases, faith is conceived as demanding a community of fellow believers and as a reality that continues to grow throughout life. It is here that the newly baptized most clearly encounter the sheer gratuity of God's salvific will—even before they ask they are granted grace.

Part 5 considers the minister of baptism (1256): the bishop, priest, and deacon. In necessity anyone with the required intention can baptize.

The necessity of baptism is the focus of part 6 (1257–61). The first point made is to articulate the tension in the teaching that baptism is required for salvation but that God is not bound by the sacraments he created. Hence we know that some who have not been baptized have access to salvation: those who have been martyred for the faith (called by tradition "baptism of blood"). There is also a recognition that catechumens and others who desired baptism but died before receiving it have the capacity to share in the benefits of baptism ("baptism of desire"). Regarding children who die before baptism, the *Catechism* says, "the Church can only entrust them to the mercy of God" (1261).[49] The 2007 statement of the International Theological Commission, *The Hope of Salvation for Infants Who Die without Baptism* offers a nuanced review of the tradition and a well-grounded hope that goes beyond the rather laconic statement of the *Catechism*.[50] Another topic not touched on by the *Catechism* is the fate of unbaptized adults who have lived a good life.

Part 7 deals with the graces of baptism (1262–74). It lists these as forgiveness of sins (both original and actual), becoming a new creature (justification), incorporation into the Body of Christ (the Church), a bond of unity with all Christians, and the imprinting of an indelible spiritual mark (character).

A strength of the *Catechism* is its combination of the more recent scholastic and magisterial heritage with the scriptural, patristic, and liturgical language and celebration of the first millennium. The inclusion of the liturgy of both East and West is an enrichment of its consideration. As noted above, however, it does leave questions that will have to be answered through further reflection and dialogue.

Baptism in Ecumenical Statements

One of the new realities of Church life after the Second Vatican Council is the work of various ecumenical dialogues. One of the most important statements on baptism is contained in a convergence statement published by the Commission on Faith and Order of the World Council of Churches: *Baptism, Eucharist and Ministry* (BEM).[51] The document, developed through more than several drafts over many years, is organized in five sections: the institution of baptism, the meaning of baptism, baptism and faith, baptismal practice, and the celebration of baptism.

Baptism is "rooted in the ministry of Jesus" (1). It centers on Jesus' death and resurrection and makes his followers part of the New Covenant. It is God's gift that Jesus' followers are meant to offer to new believers (see Matt 28:18-20).

The meaning of baptism is summarized in five themes: participation in Christ's death and resurrection; conversion, pardoning, and cleansing; the gift of the Spirit; incorporation into the Body of Christ; and the sign of the kingdom (2–7). The development of each of these themes is supported by numerous citations of Scripture. The document also has one note of commentary on the theme of incorporation into the Body of Christ. The text mentions that "one Lord, one faith, one baptism" remains an ideal and constitutes "a call to the churches to overcome their divisions and visibly manifest their fellowship" (6). The comment states that this lack of unity "has seriously compromised" the witness of the Church to the world (Commentary 6).

The section on baptism and faith recognizes that baptism is a gift and demands a response. The faith of Christians must continue to grow and develop. Ultimately, baptized faith must reveal itself in a life of Christian witness (8–10).

The section on baptismal practice raises three issues: baptism of believers and infants, baptism-chrismation-confirmation, and mutual recognition of baptism (11–16). The division between those who baptize a new member at any age and those who baptize only those capable of professing personal faith remains a difficult one (11–13). BEM attempts to find common ground between the two practices. The statement itself begins with a recognition of historically divergent practices. Faith, whether professed personally or by parents or godparents, must always grow from where it is into a more mature faith. The commentary on this paragraph highlights the two emphases: infant baptism is about "corporate faith" shared with community and family; believers' baptism is about the "explicit confession of the person." Yet both infants and believers require the nurturing of their faith with the help of others. The comment ends by recalling that some communities baptize infants and have an adult profession of faith later, and others welcome and bless infants and baptize them when they are ready to profess their faith—perhaps all the communities of faith need to reflect on this duality (Commentary 12).

The reflection on baptism-chrismation-confirmation (14) revolves around the gift of the Spirit in baptism. The various faith communities all agree that baptism takes place in water and the Spirit (John 3:5), but have various practices that emphasize it. The commentary raises two issues, both revolving around the relationship of baptism and Eucharist. The first is whether there should be anything that interposes between baptism and Eucharist—would not that make it more difficult to see how Eucharist flows directly from baptism? The second issue is about the wisdom of separating Eucharist from baptism by age—why should someone wait to receive the Eucharist that seems to flow so naturally from baptism? Finally, the commentary commends the renewal of baptismal promises at various celebrations during the Church year (Commentary 14).

In reflecting on mutual recognition of baptism (15–16), BEM acknowledges the divisive issue of believers' versus infant baptism. It calls for more explicit mutual recognition and challenges the communities of believers to open their understandings: proponents of believers' baptism to recognize God's protection of children; proponents of infant baptism to guard against indiscriminate baptism.

In describing the celebration of baptism (17–23), BEM concludes its treatment. It mentions water and the trinitarian formula; the value of the symbolism of water and of immersion; symbolizing the gift of the Spirit by a laying on of hands or anointing; the reading of the Word of God; invoking the Spirit; renouncing Satan; a profession of faith in Christ and the Trinity; a declaration of membership in the Body of Christ. Some groups also see anointing in the Spirit and the sharing of Communion as essential to the celebration of baptism. The normal minister is someone ordained, though others can also baptize in certain circumstances. Baptism is normally celebrated during public worship of the believing community. BEM offers two comments on the text. In commenting on the use of water (Commentary 18), the dual symbolism of new life and participation in the dying and rising of Christ is emphasized. Three cautions are raised in the Commentary on paragraph 21 (the various meanings of baptism as contained in the previous section): that baptism must be differentiated from naming; that indiscriminate baptism must be avoided; and that baptism with water is essential, though the African custom of baptizing by the laying on of hands should be further studied.

The Roman Catholic response to BEM[52] is positive but with some reservations. In general, there is a concern that BEM does not adequately include an ecclesiological perspective.[53] Before making specific comments on the treatment of baptism in BEM, the Roman Catholic response highlights some overarching concerns of the treatment in general: the lack of an adequate theology of sacrament and sacramentality, the role of apostolic tradition, and the place of authority in the Church.[54] Within a context of overall appreciation for the nature of the document that BEM is (a convergence statement that tries to articulate what the churches believe in common) and the quality of the expression of the faith that it contains, there are a number of cautions raised in the Roman Catholic response. The section on the institution of baptism is well done. The section on the meaning of baptism does not deal with the necessity of baptism for salvation nor the related topic of original sin. While the text speaks of the "seal" of baptism, it does not deal with "character" and the permanence of baptism. The section on baptism and grace offers a deep theology of grace and an invitation to a profound spirituality of baptism. The ecclesial dimension of baptism, however, is lacking. The section on baptismal practice raises concerns. The text speaks of "believers" and "infants." A better terminology would be "adults" and "infants." Infants too live within the faith and their baptism is a result of faith. The concern about "indiscriminate" baptism of infants does not take into account the need for parents and godparents to accept the responsibility for the formation of infants, helping them advance into a deeper appropriation of faith. In addition, the Catholic Church celebrates confirmation as a separate sacrament and sees this as a "normative development." The section on the celebration of the sacrament is well done. "Thus in the text on baptism we find much we can agree with, as well as points to be studied further in the Faith and Order process."[55]

An important treatment of baptism is contained in the Joint Declaration on the Doctrine of Justification made on 31 October 1999 by the Roman Catholic Church and the World Lutheran Federation.[56] Some key paragraphs follow:

> 28. We confess together that in baptism the Holy Spirit unites one with Christ, justifies, and truly renews the person. But the justified must all through life constantly look to God's unconditional justifying grace. . . .
>
> 29. Lutherans understand this condition of the Christian as a being "at the same time righteous and sinner." Believers are totally righteous, in that God forgives their sins through Word and Sacrament and grants the righteousness of Christ which they appropriate in faith. In Christ, they are made just before God. Looking at themselves through the law, however, they recognize that they remain also totally sinners. . . .
>
> 30. Catholics hold that the grace of Jesus Christ imparted in baptism takes away all that is sin "in the proper sense" and that is "worthy of damnation" (Rom 8:1; see Council of Trent, Fifth Session, Decree on Original Sin, DS 1515). There does, however, remain in the person an inclination (concupiscence) which comes from sin and presses toward sin. . . .

Baptism is the way that sin is washed away. Baptism does not make someone by that fact free from the tendency to sin. Sin is, in fact, the doorway to right relationship with God.

Notes, Chapter Five

[1] Some helpful treatments of baptism in the New Testament include: G. R. Beasley-Murray, *Baptism in the New Testament* (Grand Rapids, MI: Eerdmans, 1962); Rudolph Schnackenburg, *Baptism in the Thought of St. Paul: A Study in Pauline Theology* (Oxford: Basil Blackwell, 1964); Adela Yarbro Collins, "The Origin of Christian Baptism," *Studia Liturgica* 19 (1989): 28–46; Stanley E. Porter and Anthony R. Cross, *Dimensions of Baptism: Biblical and Theological Studies*, Journal for the Study of the New Testament, Supplement Series 234 (New York: Sheffield Academic Press, 2002); Maxwell E. Johnson, "The Origins of the Rites of Christian Initiation," in *The Rites* (2007), 1–40; Bryan D. Spinks, *Early and Medieval Rituals and Theologies of Baptism: From the New Testament to the Council of Trent* (Burlington, VT: Ashgate, 2006), 3–13. See also Michael G. Witczak, "Baptismal Imagery: The Meeting of Two Worlds," *Liturgical Ministry* 8 (1999): 22–30.

[2] See Aidan Kavanagh, *The Shape of Baptism: The Rite of Christian Initiation*, Studies in the Reformed Rites of the Catholic Church, vol. 1 (Collegeville, MN: Liturgical Press, A Pueblo Book, 1978), 14–23.

[3] In addition to the works mentioned in note 1, see Kilian McDonnell, *The Baptism of Jesus in the Jordan: The Trinitarian and Cosmic Order of Salvation* (Collegeville, MN: Liturgical Press, A Michael Glazier Book, 1996).

[4] See Kavanagh, *Shape of Baptism*, 29.

[5] See Garrett G. Fagan, *Bathing in Public in the Roman World* (Ann Arbor, MI: University of Michigan Press, 1999); D. S. Potter and D. J. Mattingly, eds., *Life, Death, and Entertainment in the Roman Empire* (Ann Arbor, MI: University of Michigan Press, 1999).

[6] See O. Pasquati, "Terme (Bagni)," in *Dizionario patristico e di antichità cristiane*, ed. Angelo di Berardino (Casale Monferrato: Marietti, 1983), 2:3411.

[7] See Witczak, "Baptismal Imagery," 24–26.

[8] Some have interpreted the text of John 13:1-15, the washing of the feet of the apostles by Jesus at the Last Supper, as a baptismal text. See, for instance, Ambrose, *De sacramentis* 3.4-7, where he comments on the custom of the Church of Milan to wash the feet of the newly baptized as part of the initiation rites. This custom was not widespread. See the text in Yarnold, *The Awe-Inspiring Rites*, 121–23, with a brief commentary on the practice on 30–31.

⁹ Helpful treatments of the history of the theology of baptism include: Burkhard Neunheuser, *Baptism and Confirmation*, trans. by John Jay Hughes, The Herder History of Dogma (New York: Herder and Herder, 1964). This is the translation of Neunheuser's *Taufe und Firmung*, Handbuch der Dogmengeschichte 4.2 (Freiburg i. Breisgau: Herder, 1956). He prepared a revised second edition in 1983, never translated into English. It updates bibliography and gives an account of the post–Vatican II developments. Also helpful are Johann Auer, "Das Sakrament der Taufe," in *Die Sakramente der Kirche*, vol. 7, *Kleine katholische Dogmatik*, 21–78 (Regensburg: Pustet, 1978); Michael Schmaus, "Die Taufe," in *Der Glaube der Kirche: Handbuch katholischer Dogmatik*, vol. 2, 391–423 (Munich: Max Hueber Verlag, 1970); Liam G. Walsh, *The Sacraments of Initiation: Baptism, Confirmation, Eucharist* (London: Geoffrey Chapman, 1988), 76–110; Kenan Osborne, *The Christian Sacraments of Initiation: Baptism, Confirmation, Eucharist* (New York: Paulist, 1987), 9–104; Regis A. Duffy, "Baptism and Confirmation," in *Systematic Theology: Roman Catholic Perspectives*, vol. 2, ed. Francis Schüssler Fiorenza and John P. Galvin, 213–30 (Minneapolis: Fortress, 1991); Spinks, *Early and Medieval Rituals and Theologies of Baptism*, 14–158. Key texts are found in H. Denzinger and A. Schönmetzer, *Enchiridion Symbolorum, definitionum et declarationum de rebus fidei et morum*, ed. 36 rev. (Freiburg i. Breisgau: Herder, 1976); English translation of many texts in J. Neuner and J. Dupuis, *The Christian Faith in the Doctrinal Documents of the Catholic Church*, 6th rev. and enlarged ed. (New York: Alba, 1996).

¹⁰ Text in Willy Rordorf and André Tuilier, eds. and trans., *La Doctrine des douze apôtres (Didachè)*, Sources Chrétiennes 248bis (Paris: Cerf, 1998). See also Kurt Niederwimmer, *The Didache: A Commentary*, trans. Linda M. Maloney, ed. Harold W. Attridge, Hermeneia Series (Minneapolis: Fortress, 1998); and Aaron Milavec, *The Didache: Text, Translation, Analysis, and Commentary* (Collegeville, MN: Liturgical Press, A Michael Glazier Book, 2003).

¹¹ Text in E. J. Goodspeed, *Die ältesten Apologeten* (Göttingen, 1914). ET in *The Writings of Saint Justin Martyr*, trans. Thomas B. Falls, *The Fathers of the Church: A New Translation*, vol. 6 (Washington, DC: Catholic University of America Press, 1948), 33–111; hereafter cited as FC 6. See Johannes Quasten, *Patrology, Volume I: The Beginnings of Patristic Literature* (Westminster, MD: Christian Classics, 1983; orig. ed. 1950), 196–219, esp. 199–201.

¹² FC 6, 99.

¹³ Ibid., 100.

¹⁴ See the text in Bernard Botte, *La Tradition apostolique de Saint Hippolyte: Essai de reconstitution*, ed. Albert Gerhards, Liturgiewissenschaftliche Quellen und Forschungen 39, 5th ed. (Münster i. Westfalen: Aschendorff, 1961, 1989). A helpful English translation is Geoffrey J. Cuming, *Hippolytus: A Text for Students*, Grove Liturgical Study 8 (Bramcote, Nottinghamshire: Grove Books, 1976). The controversy about author, date, and place can be found in Paul F. Bradshaw, Maxwell E. Johnson, and L. Edward Phillips, eds., *The Apostolic Tradition: A Commentary*, ed. Harold W. Attridge, Hermeneia Series (Minneapolis: Fortress, 2002); with alternative arguments in Alistair Steward-Sykes, ed., *Hippolytus: On the Apostolic Tradition*, Popular Patristic Series 22 (Crestwood, NY: St. Vladimir's Seminary Press, 2001). See Charles Whita-

ker, "Baptism," in *Essays on Hippolytus*, ed. Geoffrey J. Cuming, Grove Liturgical Study 15 (Bramcote, Nottinghamshire: Grove Books, 1978), 52–60; Peter Cramer, *Baptism and Change in the Early Middle Ages, c. 200–c. 1150* (Cambridge: Cambridge University Press, 1993), 9–45; Johnson, *Rites*, 96–110.

[15] Chapters 15–22. See Bradshaw edition, pp. 82–135, here chapter 22, p. 122.

[16] Text in A. Reifferscheid and G. Wissowa, eds., *Quinti Septimi Florentis Tertulliani Opera*, Corpus Scriptorum Ecclesiasticorum Latinorum (CSEL) 20 (Vienna, 1890), 201–18. See also Johannes Quasten, *Patrology, Volume II: The Ante-Nicene Literature after Irenaeus* (Westminster, MD: Newman, 1953; repr. Westminster, MD: Christian Classics, 1983), 278–81. See Cramer, *Baptism and Change*, 46–63; Johnson, *Rites*, 84–90.

[17] See Neunheuser, *Baptism and Confirmation*, 92–99.

[18] Text in Denzinger and Schönmetzer, *Enchiridion Symbolorum*, 110. ET in Neuner and Dupuis, *The Christian Faith*, n. 1401, p. 539. It is quoted in Cyprian, Ep. 74.1, in W. Hartel, ed., *S. Thrasci Caecilii Cypriani Opera Omnia*, CSEL 3.2 (Vienna: Giraldi, 1871).

[19] See Yarnold, *The Awe-Inspiring Rites*; Enrico Mazza, *Mystagogy: A Theology of Liturgy in the Patristic Age*, trans. Matthew J. O'Connell (New York: Pueblo, 1989). See Cramer, *Baptism and Change*, 64–72; Johnson, *Rites*, 121–24 (Cyril of Jerusalem), 129–32 (John Chrysostom), 132–34 (Theodore of Mopsuestia), 169–75 (Ambrose); Neunheuser, *Baptism and Confirmation*, 111–16 (Ambrose). See also Hugh M. Riley, *Christian Initiation: A Comparative Study of the Interpretation of the Baptismal Liturgy in the Mystagogical Writings of Cyril of Jerusalem, John Chrysostom, Theodore of Mopsuestia, and Ambrose of Milan*, Studies in Christian Antiquity 17 (Washington, DC: Catholic University of America Press, 1974).

[20] See the overview of Augustine's treatment in Neunheuser, *Baptism and Confirmation*, 107–34; Johnson, *Rites*, 185–98.

[21] See the overview of the texts related to the Donatist controversy in Quasten, IV:383–86. Particularly important is *De baptismo libri VII*, in M. Petschenig, ed., CSEL 51, 145–375; ET LNPF 4, ser. 1 (1887), 411–514.

[22] See the overview of the texts related to the Pelagian controversy in Quasten, IV:386–92. See especially *De peccatorum meritis et remissione et de baptismo parvulorum ad Marcellinum libri III*, in C. F. Urba and J. Zycha, ed. CSEL 60 (1913), 3–151; ET in LNPF 5, ser. 1 (1887), 15–78.

[23] *Old Gelasian* text in Leo Cunibert Mohlberg, Leo Eizenhöfer, and Petrus Siffrin, *Liber sacramentorum romanae aeclesiae ordinis anni circuli (Cod. Vat. Reg. Lat. 316/Paris Bibl. Nat. 7193, 41/56) (Sacramentarium Gelasianum)*, 3rd ed., Rerum Ecclesiasticarum Documenta, Series Maior, Fontes IV (Rome: Herder, 1960, 1981), nn. 193–328 (Sundays of Lent, becoming a catechumen, scrutinies, the handing over of the Creed and the Lord's Prayer), 419–62 (Holy Saturday morning, Easter Vigil), pp. 32–53, 67–77. *Ordo Romanus XI* text in Michel Andieu, *Les Ordines Romani du haut moyen age II: Les Textes (Ordines I–XIII)*, Spicilegium Sacrum Lovaniense, Études et Documents 23 (Louvain: Spicilegium Sacrum Lovaniense Administration, 1948; repr. 1971), Ordo XI, pp. 417–47; see also Andrieu's commentary on pp. 365–413. See the commentaries in Antoine Chavasse, *Le Sacramentaire Gélasien*

(Vaticanus Reginensis 316): Sacramentaire presbytéral en usage dans les titres romains au VIIe siècle (Paris: Desclée, 1957), 140–76; Mario Righetti, *Manuale di storia liturgica, Vol. IV: I sacramenti – i sacramentali*, (Milan: Áncora, 1959; repr. 1998), 51–138; Johnson, *Rites*, 222–32; Kleinheyer, *Sakramentliche Feiern I*, 102–21; Adrien Nocent, "L'organizzazione liturgica del catecumenato e l'iniziazione cristiana dal IV al IX secolo," in *La Liturgia, i sacramenti: teologia e storia della celebrazione*, vol. 3/1 of *Anàmnesis: Introduzione storico-teologica alla Liturgia*, ed. Anscar J. Chupungco (Genoa: Marietti, 1986), 41–63; Nocent, "Christian Initiation in the Roman Church from the Fifth Century Until Vatican II," in Chupungco, *Sacraments and Sacramentals*, 49–90, esp. 49–60; Cabié, "Initiation in the West Until the Twelfth Century," in Martimort, *The Sacraments*, 64–70.

[24] The earliest text for the baptism of a catechumen in danger of death seems to be that found in the *Gellone Sacramentary* of the mid-eighth century; see A. Dumas, *Liber Sacramentorum Gellonensis: Textus*, Corpus Christianorum, Series Latina CLIX (Turnhout: Brepols, 1981), "Incipit ordo ad infirmum caticuminum faciendum siue baptizandum," nn. 2344–86, pp. 339–47; see Dumas's commentary in CCL CLIXA:xxx–xxxii.

[25] The text of the questions can be found in Glenn C. J. Byer, *Charlemagne and Baptism: A Study of Responses to the Circular Letter of 811/812*, (Lanham, MD: International Scholars Publications, 1999), 51.

[26] *De ordine baptismi*, 13, PL 105: 232D, as quoted by Neunheuser, 182.

[27] Neuner and Dupuis, *The Christian Faith*, nn. 1412–15. See also Denzinger and Schönmetzer, *Enchiridion Symbolorum*, nn. 1314–16. The work of Aquinas is *De articulis fidei et Ecclesiae sacramentis*, ed. P. Mandonnet, *S. Thomae Aquinae Opuscula omnia*, t. 3 (Paris, 1927), 11–18, cited in Denzinger and Schönmetzer, *Enchiridion Symbolorum*, notes to nn. 1310–28, p. 332. In contrast, in the *Summa Theologiae* Aquinas dedicates six questions with sixty articles to baptism, which requires 185 pages in the Blackfriars edition with notes and commentary: *Summa Theologiae, Volume 57: Baptism and Confirmation (3a. 66–72)*, trans. and ed. James J. Cunningman (New York: McGraw-Hill, 1975).

[28] Neuner and Dupuis, *The Christian Faith*, n. 1308; Denzinger and Schönmetzer, *Enchiridion Symbolorum*, n. 1313.

[29] See Kenan Osborne, *Sacramental Theology: An Introduction* (New York: Paulist, 1988), 49–68; Herbert Vorgrimler, *Sacramental Theology*, trans. Linda M. Maloney (Collegeville, MN: Liturgical Press, 1992), 50–55; Neunheuser, 199–220.

[30] Text in Timothy F. Lull, ed., *Martin Luther's Basic Theological Writings* (Minneapolis: Fortress, 1989), 484–85.

[31] See G. H. Williams, *The Radical Reformation* (Philadelphia: Westminster, 1962), 3rd ed., Sixteenth Century Essays and Studies 15 (Kirksville, MO: Sixteenth Century Journal Publishers, 1992). See Luther's "Concerning Rebaptism," in *Martin Luther's Basic Theological Writings*, ed. Timothy F. Lull, 341–74 (Minneapolis: Fortress, 1989), for a flavor of the response. See also Bryan D. Spinks, *Reformation and Modern Rituals and Theologies of Baptism: From Luther to Contemporary Practices* (Burlington, VT: Ashgate, 2006), 3–133.

[32] See Kenan Osborne, "Holy Baptism: The Teaching of the Roman Catholic Church," in *The Christian Sacraments of Initiation: Baptism, Confirmation, Eucharist* (New York: Paulist, 1987), 11–23; Neunheuser, *Baptism and Confirmation*, 221–25; Vorgrimler, *Sacramental Theology*, 111–13.

[33] Sixteenth Council of Carthage (418), in Denzinger and Schönmetzer, *Enchiridion Symbolorum*, n. 222; Council of Trent, fifth session (1546), Decree on Original Sin, nn. 1513–14; ET in Neuner and Dupuis, *The Christian Faith*, nn. 501, 510–11; Vorgrimler, *Sacramental Theology*, 113.

[34] See the text in Manlio Sodi and Juan Javier Flores Arcas, *Rituale Romanum: Editio Princeps (1614)*, Monumenta Liturgica Concilii Tridentini 5 (Vatican City: Libreria Editrice Vaticana, 2004), 13–47; introductory material, 13–20. 1925 edition in Philip T. Weller, *The Roman Ritual in Latin and English with Rubrics and Planechant Notation, Volume I: The Sacraments and Processions* (Milwaukee, WI: Bruce, 1950), 20–195; introductory material, 20–37. 1952 edition in Manlio Sodi and Alessandro Toniolo, *Rituale Romanum: Editio Typica 1952*, Monumenta Liturgica Piana II (Vatican City: Libreria Editrice Vaticana, 2008), 13–105; introductory material, 13–25.

[35] Text found in 1614 edition, Sodi and Flores Arcas, *Rituale Romanum*, 21–26; 1925 edition, Weller, *The Roman Ritual*, 36–57; 1952 edition, Sodi and Toniolo, *Rituale Romanum*, 25–37.

[36] Text found in 1614 edition, Sodi and Flores Arcas, *Rituale Romanum*, 27–44; 1925 edition, Weller, *The Roman Ritual*, 57–119; 1952 edition, Sodi and Toniolo, *Rituale Romanum*, 37–70.

[37] J. M. Hervé, *Manuale Theologiae Dogmaticae*, 4 vol. (Paris: Berche et Pagis, 1929).

[38] Hervé, *Manuale Theologiae Dogmaticae, Vol. III: De Gratia Christi—De Virtutibus Theologicis—De Sacramentis in genere, Baptismo et Confirmatione* (Paris: Berche et Pagis, 1929), 504–57.

[39] Ibid., 558–65.

[40] For a brief account, see Turner, *Highway*, 139–55; Turner, *Ages of Initiation*, 37–48 with the documentation found on the accompanying CD-ROM. Jaime Lara presents some interesting perspectives in *Christian Texts for Aztecs: Art and Liturgy in Colonial Mexico* (Notre Dame, IN: University of Notre Dame Press, 2008), 90–96.

[41] See Odo Casel, *The Mystery of Christian Worship and Other Writings*, ed. Burkhard Neunheuser, foreword by Charles Davis (Westminster, MD: Newman, 1962; repr. with a new foreword by Aidan Kavanagh, New York: Crossroad, Herder and Herder, 1999). See the discussion by Neunheuser in *Taufe und Firmung*, Handbuch der Dogmengeschichte IV, 2, 2nd ed. (Freiburg: Herder, 1983), 124–28. See Pius X, *Tra le sollecitudini*, Motu proprio, on sacred music, 22 November 1903, in *Documenta Pontificia ad instaurationem liturgicam spectantia (1903–1953)*, ed. A. Bugnini, Bibliotheca "Ephemerides Liturgicae" Sectio Practica 6 (Rome: Edizioni Liturgiche, 1953), see the introduction, 3–4. ET in James J. McGivern, *Worship and Liturgy*, Official Catholic Teachings (Wilmington, NC: McGrath, 1978), 17–18.

[42] See *AAS* 34 (1962): 310–38.

⁴³ Text found in David Lysik, ed., *The Liturgy Documents: A Parish Resource*, vol. 1, 4th ed. (Chicago: Liturgy Training Publications, 2004), 3–30.

⁴⁴ Motu proprio *Sacram Liturgiam*, 25 January 1964, in *Documents on the Liturgy 1963–1979: Conciliar, Papal, and Curial Texts* (Collegeville, MN: Liturgical Press, 1982), 84–87.

⁴⁵ See an account of this work in Annibale Bugnini, *The Reform of the Liturgy 1948–1975* (Collegeville, MN: Liturgical Press, 1990), 584–612.

⁴⁶ Text in *The Rites of the Catholic Church*, vol. 1 (Collegeville, MN: Liturgical Press, A Pueblo Book, 1990), 3–12.

⁴⁷ *Catechism of the Catholic Church*, 2nd ed. (Washington, DC: United States Catholic Conference, 1994, 1997, 2000). We cite the paragraph numbers of this edition.

⁴⁸ N. 1213, citing *Roman Catechism* II, 2, 5; cf. Council of Florence: DS 1314; CIC, cann. 204, 1; 849; CCEO, can. 675,1.

⁴⁹ There is no mention of "limbo," a place for unbaptized children to enjoy a state of natural happiness for eternity, but separated from the beatific vision.

⁵⁰ Accessed 12 March 2010 at http://www.vatican.va/roman_curia/congregations /cfaith/cti_documents/rc_con_cfaith_doc_20070419_un-baptised-infants _en.html#top. See especially the conclusion on hope, nn. 102–3.

⁵¹ *Baptism, Eucharist and Ministry*, Faith and Order Paper No. 111 (Geneva: World Council of Churches, 1982). See also Max Thurian, ed., *Ecumenical Perspectives on Baptism, Eucharist and Ministry*, Faith and Order Paper 116 (Geneva: World Council of Churches, 1983); and Max Thurian and Geoffrey Wainwright, *Baptism and Eucharist: Ecumenical Convergence in Celebration*, Faith and Order Paper 117 (Geneva: World Council of Churches, 1983); Max Thurian, ed., *Churches Respond to BEM: Official Responses to the "Baptism, Eucharist and Ministry" Text*, 6 vols., Faith and Order Papers 129, 132, 135, 137, 143, and 144 (Geneva: World Council of Churches, 1986–88). The official commentary of the WCC is found in *Baptism, Eucharist and Ministry 1982–1990: Report on the Process and Responses*, Faith and Order Paper 149 (Geneva: World Council of Churches, 1990). For recent reflection see Thomas F. Best and Tamara Grdzelidze, eds., *BEM at 25: Critical Insights into a Continuing Legacy* (Geneva: World Council of Churches, 2007).

⁵² The response is found in Max Thurian, ed., *Churches Respond to BEM: Official Responses to the "Baptism, Eucharist and Ministry" Text*, vol. 6, Faith and Order Paper 144 (Geneva: World Council of Churches, 1988), 1–40. The general response is on pp. 1–9, and the response to the section on baptism on pp. 9–16.

⁵³ The Commission on Faith and Order is currently preparing a document on the topic of ecclesiology and baptism. See the working paper, "Ecclesiological and Ecumenical Implications of a Common Baptism: A JWG [Joint Working Group] Study," in *Joint Working Group Between the Roman Catholic Church and the World Council of Churches: Eighth Report 1999–2005* (Geneva: WCC Publications, 2005).

⁵⁴ Thurian, *Churches Respond*, 6–9.

⁵⁵ Ibid., 9–16, here 16. The issues raised have continued to evolve in Faith and Order commission texts. See *Becoming Christian: The Ecumenical Implications of Our Common Baptism*, Faith and Order Consultation, Faverges, France,

January 17–24, 1997, downloaded from http://www.oikoumene.org/en/resources /documents/wcc-commissions/faith-and-order-commission/ii-worship-and-baptism /becoming-a-christian-the-ecumenical-implications-of-our-common-baptism .html, accessed on 19 June 2009; *One Baptism: Toward Mutual Recognition [a text in progress]*, from the Faith and Order Commission meeting at Faverges, France, 14–21 June 2006, downloaded from http://www.oikoumene.org/en/resources /documents/wcc-commissions/faith-and-order-commission/ii-worship-and-baptism /one-baptism-towards-mutual-recognition-a-text-in-progress.html, accessed 19 June 2009. See also "Ecclesiological and Ecumenical Implications of a Common Baptism: A JWG Study," in *Joint Working Group Between the Roman Catholic Church and the World Council of Churches: Eighth Report* (Geneva: WCC Publications, 2005), 45–72; Thomas F. Best, ed., *Baptism Today: Understanding, Practice, Ecumenical Implications*, Faith and Order Paper 207 (Collegeville, MN: Liturgical Press, A Pueblo Book, 2008). See the helpful summary chapter by Bryan D. Spinks, "Cross-curents: Some Baptismal Theologies of the Twentieth Century," in *Reformation and Modern Rituals and Theologies of Baptism*, 137–63.

[56] Joint Declaration on the Doctrine of Justification, 31 October 1999, found at http://www.vatican.va/roman_curia/pontifical_councils/chrstuni/documents /rc_pc_chrstuni_doc_31101999_cath-luth-joint-declaration_en.html (accessed 5 July 2009).

Chapter Six

A Theology of the Celebration of Baptism

T he previous chapter presented an overview of the history of the theology of baptism. Many of the key issues emerging out of controversy were highlighted. The desire to safeguard the fundamental act of participating in God's saving plan for humanity led the Church to articulate concepts that were essential for any orthodox understanding of baptism.

This chapter will take those hard-won truths as a given and in that context offer an account of the theology of baptism that emerges from its celebration rather than conflict about it. The first four chapters present the initiation of adults and the baptism of children from the point of view of the nonverbal and verbal. This chapter will presume that presentation, but ask a different set of questions of the celebration. The resulting account will revolve around time, space, act, word, and participants. We will conclude each section with a reflection on themes that emerge.

Time is one of the contexts in which the celebration occurs. In particular, we are looking at two aspects of time: duration and quality. Regarding duration, both initiation of adults and baptism of children come into play. The duration question for adults is especially important for the first two periods: how long a time is needed for their preparation? They may require years to be ready. For children, the duration is more focused on the preparation needed by the parents: how long a time do they need to be able to make the commitment on behalf of their child?

The quality of time is affected by the connection of the celebration of baptism to certain seasons and days of the Church year. Lent is the time for the period of purification and Enlightenment; the Easter Vigil for initiation of adults and children; Sunday for baptizing children, Easter season for the period of mystagogy. On the other hand, as Tertullian comments, every day is the Lord's day and a good day to baptize.[1]

Space is the other contextual element for the celebration. For adults the space requirements begin in a very unfocused way. The first two periods can unfold almost anywhere: homes, classrooms, offices, the rectory, or church basements. The last two periods are more focused on Church, and we see a movement within the church from the door, to the ambo, to the font, to the altar—and then out of the church into the world. As the formation of the candidate becomes more formal, so does the space: catechesis seems to require a space dedicated to it. Some churches have created a "catechumenon" for the use of adults preparing for initiation.

The preparation of parents for presenting their child for baptism does not garner much attention in the ritual. The preparation could take place at the parish or the home or someplace else. The space for the ritual celebration of baptism for children follows the pattern just described for adults: the movement from the door of the church, to the ambo, to the font, and ending at the altar.

The temporal and spatial context helps shape what the participants say and do. Their words and actions interact with the season and day, and with the place where the events of the ritual occur. The liturgical celebration of the initiation of adults and the baptism of children is a complex and rich moment in which God, the Christian community, and the individual believers, with their godparents and family, enter into a relationship. That relationship changes everything for the believer and for the community. Neither will be the same again.

This chapter will name some aspects of this saving reality and lead the reader and participant in baptism to a deeper appropriation of the event for the person and the Church.

Baptizing Adults

Our treatment will follow the overall structure of the celebration of the Rite of Christian Initiation of Adults, as outlined in chapter 1. As mentioned above, we will explore the dimensions of time, space, act, word, and participants in the ritual. The time and the space provide the physical context in which the words and actions are performed by the participants. The themes that emerge from this reflection conclude each period and rite.

Welcome: Outsiders Become Insiders (RCIA 36–40)

The fundamental context for welcoming new members to the Church is the understanding of God as triune: God's creative exuberance and desire that all be saved and join the divine life, as manifested by Jesus Christ and sustained by the Holy Spirit. Furthermore, there is a conviction expressed that the Church is the sacrament of Jesus Christ and thus of the people of God, who are the Body of Christ and the temple of the Holy Spirit. This community of believers, hungry to share this Good News, reaches out to those who are not yet members and invites them into this life.

The appropriate time for this part of the rite is open-ended. Enough time must be taken to allow the work of the Holy Spirit to begin and to unfold in the lives of those who are seeking faith.

The place for this to occur also is not defined. Someone becomes a seeker for many reasons, and place may play a role. A sunrise or sunset at a mountain lake, a star-studded sky deep in a woods, a life-changing conversation over a meal table, the wedding of a friend, or the funeral of a colleague at a church, a friend's spontaneous invitation at a ball game to come with them to Mass—all of these are places where the grace of God may begin to move someone to faith. Once someone has responded to this movement—for instance, by contacting a rectory and participating in an inquiry process—the place can be a meeting room at a parish, the home of a catechist, a local restaurant, or wherever the group decides to meet.

The acts associated with this period are narrating and welcoming. There is no ritual action prescribed for this period (39).

The words of this period once again are not set or established. They are for the most part narratives. The story of God's plan of salvation as contained in the Bible becomes the framework for the story of how salvation is working itself out in the lives of the individuals now involved in the process of coming to faith. Particularly important are the stories of Christ. Penetrating his life, message, and allure and beginning to follow him takes place through hearing the stories of his life, death, and resurrection. The prayers of blessing and exorcism can be used by the pastor when he meets with these inquirers (40).

The period ends with the first step: Acceptance into the Order of Catechumens (RCIA 41–74). When is the proper time to celebrate this rite? It is when inquirers have shown "the beginning of the spiritual life," that the "fundamentals of Christian teaching have taken root" in them, that they possess "first faith," "an initial conversion," that they have an "intention to change . . . and enter into a relationship with God in Christ," "first stirrings of repentance," along with a "start to the practice of calling on God in prayer," "a sense of the Church," and "some experience of . . . Christians" (42). These are the signs of the proper time for celebration of the Acceptance into the Order of Catechumens. This list of criteria indicates the kind of storytelling that should have been taking place up to this point. Since so much is at stake here, additional time must be given to the evaluation and purification of motives and intentions (42). Once this discernment has taken place, the time for the ritual celebration has come. It takes place on "specified days during the year" (44), perhaps quarterly.

Two places are crucial for this celebration: the door of the church and the ambo where the Word of God is proclaimed. The door is a multivalent place. It closes out and welcomes in. It is the means of passing from outside to inside. It is a threshold, where believers, those to be married and buried, cross to celebrate membership and cross again to live that membership outside the Church. The door of the church building represents the entry into the Church community.

The main actions of this rite are at the door: signing the senses of the candidates with the cross then entering the church. The cross is the vehicle of Christ's death and the sign of his victory over death. It is a brand-mark that identifies the person as now belonging to Christ.

The words of the rite specify the actions. At the door, the candidates identify themselves and their desire for faith. The Gospel message of Jesus Christ forms the next way station: the candidate accepts this Gospel for the first time in public. The words accompanying the signing of the senses with the cross identify the cross with a relationship and a way of life: "It is Christ himself who now strengthens you with this sign of his love. Learn to know him and follow him" (55). The concluding prayer of the signing indicates that it is the cross that changes candidates into catechumens: "Lord, we have signed these catechumens with the sign of Christ's cross" (57). The words name the act of entering the church as approaching a place of nourishment: "N. and N., come into the church, to share with us at the table of God's word" (60).

The actors in this period are those who respond to the Gospel they have heard. Others are those who proclaim the message, welcome the responders, and offer discernment regarding the movement of the Spirit in their lives. Those who hear are old enough to understand the message and mature enough to allow the message to change them. Those who proclaim the Good News are a diverse lot. They can be bishops, priests, and deacons in their formal preaching and teaching. They can be family members, neighbors, and colleagues who by word and example reveal a message of a life worth living. The Gospel is preached in many ways and in different contexts. The welcomers may be the same as the preachers or may be others. Those privileged to learn of the initial impact of the Word on the life of someone must learn how to nurture this initial growth of the Spirit by attentive listening and hospitable welcome: to a home, to a meeting, to an introduction to a priest or catechist. Those entrusted with evangelization and hospitality must also take seriously the need to discern the movement of the Spirit and to judge when is the right time to move to the next stage of coming to Christ. These actors are the Church for the person. All preaching of the Gospel, the response to it, and the discernment of it, is ecclesial.

Three themes seem to emerge from reflection on this period and rite: evangelization, hospitality, and discernment of the Holy Spirit.

Evangelization is at the heart of the Gospel: Jesus proclaims the kingdom and invites others to change their lives in order to enter it. The message is so compelling that those who hear it begin to follow Jesus. With him they find a welcome. They also find that a halfhearted response is not enough. Some go away sad. Some betray Jesus. Often they do not understand the full depth of the message of the Gospel. But Jesus keeps proclaiming the message and followers keep engaging him in dialogue.

That same dynamic is at play today. The Christian community lives with the drive to share the good news of the kingdom, the good news of Jesus' death and resurrection, and to welcome those who hear this and are moved to respond. On a concrete level, Christian communities are challenged to take seriously the need to proclaim the Gospel effectively and to welcome those who respond. The welcome always needs to be wholehearted but can never be without discernment. Coffee and doughnuts are not sufficient. The welcome must include asking the question: how deeply has the Spirit entered the life of this person? The criteria mentioned above serve to outline how the community needs to judge the way the new relationship with Christ is developing. Only then can inquirers begin to bear the sign of the cross, receive the Gospel as their own, and enter the life of the Church.

Evangelization is about Good News. This news is found in the Bible and is distilled in the *Catechism*. Bible is the heart of the story of salvation. The *Catechism* lays this narrative out in a way that leads to a more systematic appropriation of the story. This Good News, the Gospel, is so good that it demands that those who have believed it should share it with others and call them into relationship with the community of believers. The telling of the Good News leads to a response to it, and that response requires some kind of welcome.[2]

Hospitality is about welcoming the stranger. Someone who may be totally unknown comes into a place and into a community. Those who are there make a place for the guest. When inquirers are called to join a community of believers, there must be some place into which they can come. The most important guest welcomed into the community is God himself (see Gen 18:1-15, the three visitors to Abraham). To receive the guest is to receive Christ (see Matt 25:31-46; Rule of Benedict 53.1: "All guests who present themselves are to be welcomed as Christ.").[3]

Discernment involves learning to see the work of the Holy Spirit in the lives of people. It is related to discipleship: those who have learned become followers. It is related to discipline: those who follow begin to follow a particular way of life, with rules and expectations. The role of those who proclaim the Good News and welcome the guests who come requires learning how the Spirit is at work in the person and naming that presence for them and for the community.[4]

Catechesis: Echoing Church Life as Intellectual, Spiritual, Liturgical, and Apostolic (RCIA 75–117)

The period of the catechumenate also has an open-ended time frame. It takes as long as is necessary for the catechumen to be ready for full entrance into the Church. The bishops of the United States require at least one year for the catechumenate (National Statutes for the Catechumenate 6).[5] All, however, "will depend on the grace of God and on various circumstances. . . . Nothing can be settled a priori" (RCIA 76).

The space for this period includes various places at the church, including meeting rooms and classrooms. The various forms of catechesis will determine the appropriate space (75). Intellectual formation may best take place in a class or meeting room. Celebrations of the Word may take place in church, in a chapel, or in a meeting room. Moments of prayer may take place in church or in class. Apostolic formation takes place at soup kitchens, food banks, homeless shelters, or wherever the program directs.

Two related acts dominate this period: the laying on of hands and anointing the breast or hands with the oil of catechumens. The laying on of hands is a gesture of power and of comfort. As a gesture of power, it functions in two directions: against the forces of evil and sin and to impart strength from God and the Church. As a gesture of comfort, it assures catechumens of the love and support of the catechist, priest, and of the whole Church. The anointing is analogous to the imposition of hands. It is part of the arsenal for combating the forces of sin and ignorance. The anointing is done on the breast or the hands, to hearten them and to give direction to their work.

The words of this period are, first, those of the Gospel and the *Catechism*. The catechumens continue to interrelate the stories of the Old and New Testaments with their own life journeys. In addition, they learn the rich reflections of the Church on the mysteries of the faith that are codified in the *Catechism*. They likewise discern how this wisdom affects their lives. The words of the exorcism, blessings, and prayers of anointing name and orient these actions toward the enrichment of the process of the catechumenate.

During the period of the catechumenate, various persons are involved. First and foremost are the catechumens themselves who participate in the fourfold catechesis. During this period, the catechumens have "undergone a conversion in mind and in action" and have "developed a sufficient acquaintance with Christian teaching as well as a spirit of faith and charity." They must develop the "intention to receive the sacraments of the church" (120). Catechists, priests, deacons, godparents, sponsors, and others play roles at various times and moments in the period to help the candidates arrive at this point of discernment. At the Rite of Election, which concludes the period, the bishop is the usual presiding minister. His presence symbolizes his guiding role for the whole process of the catechumenate.

The period of the catechumenate is completed by the Rite of Election (RCIA 118–37). This rite normally occurs on the First Sunday of Lent, when the temptation of the Lord is the gospel proclaimed. The place of the Rite of Election is the cathedral, although another church more pastorally suitable could serve. The act of the rite consists of the catechumens enrolling their names onto a sheet of paper or into a book. Godparents may do this on behalf of the catechumens, or the minister of the rite may inscribe the names. In certain circumstances the inscription can be done ahead of time, and the names presented to the presiding minister during the ceremony. The action of inscribing is preceded by the presentation of the catechumens by someone responsible for their preparation, and by their godparents' affirmation of their readiness. The presiding minister concludes the enrollment by declaring them now to be "members of the elect" (133). The prayer over the elect calls them "true children of the promise" (135).

The theme that seems to characterize this period is that of sponsoring and godparenting (see CIGI 8–10 and RCIA 10–11). The work of many persons sets the context for catechumens to arrive at the maturity needed to become members of the elect and declare their intention to be baptized. But those who are already members of the community must serve as companions, guides, and witnesses of readiness. The sponsors become acquainted with the catechumens and provide help along the way. The relationship should be close enough that the sponsors can testify at the proper time to the catechumens' "moral character, faith, and intention" (10). Sponsors are often chosen by the catechumens, but can be chosen by the pastor or director of the catechumenate. At the Rite of Election, the catechumens themselves choose individuals to serve as godparents to accompany them during Lent and at the Easter Vigil. The godparents may be those who have served as sponsors, or others may be chosen.

Purification and Enlightenment: Scrutiny of Life and Presentation of Foundational Words (RCIA 138–205)

The period of purification and enlightenment is associated with Lent. The General Norms for the Liturgical Year and Calendar characterize the season in this way: "Lent is a preparation for the celebration of Easter. For the Lenten liturgy disposes both catechumens and the faithful to celebrate the paschal mystery: catechumens, through the several stages of Christian initiation; the faithful, through reminders of their own baptism and through penitential practices."[6] This context colors the celebrations that take place during the period. The season is characterized by a somber color (violet or purple), somber music, somber readings and prayers. Its mood is one of "more intense spiritual preparation, consisting more in interior reflection than in catechetical instruction" (RCIA 139). Some ritual moments happen at the parish Mass on the Third, Fourth, and Fifth Sundays, others during the Third and Fifth Weeks. A final moment of preparation begins on Holy Saturday morning.

The activities that take place during this period occur in the parish church.

Two main types of action characterize the period: scrutinies and presentations. This solemn exorcism (scrutiny) involves silence, kneeling by the elect, and an imposition of hands on the elect by the priest. The presentations of the Creed and of the Lord's Prayer are primarily verbal moments. On Holy Saturday morning, the Ephphetha (= "be open") Rite includes the touching of the ears and the lips of the elect.

The gospel readings shape the mood and meaning of the Third, Fourth, and Fifth Sundays of Lent: the Samaritan woman, the man born blind, and the raising of Lazarus. The scrutiny prayers flow from these gospel texts and ask that the elect make the transition from dryness to living water, from blindness to light, from death to life. The presentations of the Creed and the Lord's Prayer offer the elect the foundational texts that should shape their lives as members of the Christian community: faith in the triune God and a life of prayer.

The elect spend this Lenten retreat accompanied by their godparents, who stand by them, hands on their shoulders during the scrutinies. The priest leads these services. The whole community of believers accompanies and supports the elect at each moment, particularly at the scrutinies.

A theme that emerges during this period is that of the journey of conversion. Conversion is a theme that is part of the whole process. The persons caught up in God's call and action in their lives come to recognize that nothing can remain the same. This new relationship with God and these new relationships with sponsors, godparents, catechists, priests, the whole community of this parish, and beyond, draw them into new ways of thinking, believing, acting, praying, deciding. The gospel story of Jesus healing a blind man in stages seems apt:

> He took the blind man by the hand and led him outside the village. Putting spittle on his eyes he laid his hands on him and asked, "Do you see anything?" Looking up he replied, "I see people looking like trees and walking." Then he laid hands on his eyes a second time and he saw clearly; his sight was restored and he could see everything distinctly. (Mark 8:23-25)

This process of conversion, of turning from one way of life to another, is rooted in the Gospel. Following the lead and example of Jesus Christ, guided by the Holy Spirit, in the company of the community of the Church, it is a lifetime journey. It begins at a certain point in time; it grows deeper in the light of learning and experience; it touches the lives of others at home, neighborhood, school, church, town; it moves to new levels of insight and possibility at certain key moments marked by ritual celebration; it begins definitively at baptism; it continues in the sacraments, the decisions, the prayers of daily life; it achieves its end at the day of judgment before God's throne when the whole journey ceases.[7]

Studies of journey literature note that the journey occurs in three phases: the setting out, the adventures, and the return home. The setting out can be precipitated by any number of events: dissatisfaction, argument, expulsion, a dare. The adventures are many and varied and form the heart of the story. There are battles (with enemies external as well as internal); encounters with characters fascinating, ugly, and beautiful; sometimes a falling in love and a departure; deeds of derring-do; moments of quiet reflection and prayer. At the end, the journeyer returns home. But the return is of a person now changed, by life and events, from the person who had left. And those left behind are changed, too, by the absence and now by the return.[8]

Incorporation: Light, Word, Bath and Anointing, Communion (RCIA 218–43)

> The preferred time for the celebration of the initiation of adults is the Easter Vigil: . . . the holy night when Christ rose from the dead, ranks as the "mother of all vigils" (Augustine, *Sermo* 219). Keeping watch, the Church awaits Christ's resurrection and celebrates it in the sacraments. Accordingly, the entire celebration of this vigil should take place at night, that is, it should either begin after nightfall or end before the dawn of Sunday.[9]

The Easter Vigil takes place at the church, in several locations. It begins outside, with all gathered around a large fire. The congregation then passes through the door of the church and gathers to focus on the ambo where first the Easter light is praised and then the history of salvation is unfolded in a series of readings. The action shifts to the baptismal font. Finally, the celebration culminates at the altar upon which the bread and wine are consecrated and from which the community, now including the newly initiated, are nourished by Christ's Body and Blood.

The acts of the Vigil include blessing the fire, entering the church in procession, gathering at the ambo to hear the Word, going to the font in procession for the rites of initiation (washing in water and anointing with the oil of chrism), and then gathering around the altar to obey Christ's command at the Last Supper to "do this in memory" of him. Here the journey is experiential: from door to altar, the final goal.

The words of the Vigil include the prayer blessing the fire, the hymn of praise to Christ the Light (the Easter Proclamation or *Exsultet*), and the series of readings. They recount the history of salvation from creation, freedom in the Exodus event, and the prophetic challenge. The mystery culminates in Christ who brings salvation to its fullness in his death and resurrection. The rites of initiation include the Litany of the Saints, recalling the participation of the Church past and present in this event. The blessing of the water rehearses the salvation history unfolded earlier in the readings and names the water present as yet another moment of God's salvific intervention in Christ. Performative words accompany the washing and anointing to name the reality that God is accomplishing in them. The liturgical action culminates in the words of the eucharistic prayer wherein the lifetime of nourishment in Christ finds origin and continuation. The words are rich in their content and impact. They place the movement of the rite within the movement of God's plan of salvation. They narrate the plan and then make the plan actual in the lives of the elect and in the community when it is celebrated in the sacramental action.

The participants in the Vigil include the elect who through their time of preparation as catechumens and members of the elect are now chosen for this new life. Their godparents walk with them and support them in this journey from fire to ambo to font to table. The priest and other ministers lead and ensure the proper celebration of the rites. The whole assembly of believers celebrates the end of their own Lenten path and welcomes those who make a new beginning of life in Christ.

The themes of the Easter Vigil are many and varied. They pull together in one night and one celebration all that has been occurring in the lives of these individuals and this community over the past months and even years. The Vigil is first of all about *light*. Light is God's first creation and the mark of his constant presence in the world he has created. Jesus Christ is the Light of the world and the one whom all follow even in a world that seems ready to be overcome by darkness. This part of the ceremony ritualizes the initial light of faith that reveals to the elect and to all present their need for salvation in Christ.

The Vigil is about *the history of salvation*. God reveals himself to the men and women he has created, and they tell the story of that relationship under the inspiration of the Holy Spirit. Despite selfishness, greed, hypocrisy, and even murder, God's love continues to be made manifest in the events that transpire and are told. The story of creation, of Abraham and Isaac, and of the Exodus; the prophetic musing on and proclamation of God's plan; all then come to completion in the dying and rising of Christ. The stories of Scripture and of individuals and of the whole community come together and illuminate each other. The ceremony recapitulates the months and years of catechesis.

The Vigil is about *washing and anointing*. The stain of sin must be washed away. The dry earth must be watered. The watered garden must lead to joy. The refreshment of the bath must be crowned with the rich scent of consecration in the Holy Spirit. This part of the ceremony is the pivot. All life has led to this moment. All Christian life flows from it.

The Vigil is about a *sacrificial meal*. The newly enlightened, newly instructed, newly baptized and confirmed and their companions now approach the altar of sacrifice and the table of life. From this altar table all that has begun receives nourishment for the life of Christ in the Spirit. This part of the ceremony is oriented to the future. Food for the journey—of life and eternal life.

The Vigil is about *a people*. The journey is never completed alone. One is born from parents. One comes to faith through God's inspiration and most often through the words and deeds of other believers. Companions and teachers and priests and others fill the canvas of this life. These participants in the ceremony ritualize the life of community that is the constant and necessary context of the Christian life.

Integration with the Body: The Period of Mystagogy (RCIA 244–51)

This final period of the process of adult initiation takes place during the Easter season. This "week of weeks" strives to live the fifty days as one "great Sunday."[10] The Sundays of Easter are the ritual focus. The time needed for integration of a new member into the life of the community needs more than fifty days and becomes the task of the rest of one's life.

The space used for this integration is first of all the church where the community gathers to celebrate the Sundays of Easter and each Sunday. On the other hand, the integration occurs wherever the Church gathers and acts.

The acts of this period are the celebration of the Eucharist, meditation on the gospel, and deeds of charity (RCIA 244). In other words, since the integration is into the life of a Christian believer, it begins to take on the day-to-day aspects of Christian life. This embraces the daily joys and trials—the grind—of human existence.

The words of this period are the readings and prayers of Sunday. First, the accounts of the meetings of the disciples with the risen Lord shape the time. The images of the Good Shepherd, the vine and the branches, the gift of the Paraclete, and the priestly prayer for unity pave the way for the gift of the Holy Spirit. The Spirit then becomes the one who will continue to mark the lives of Jesus' followers from then on.

The participants of this period are the neophytes and the members of the community, head and members. The community rearranges itself to make room for the new arrivals. New potential is discovered. New tensions emerge as everyone must shift to make room for the newcomers. The community of believers discovers a renewed and reinvigorated life now present among them.

The fundamental theme of this period is living the Eucharist. All the periods and steps lead to this moment: becoming a member of the eucharistic people, nourished for life in community and for the journey of life in this world by the eucharistic bread and wine, transformed by the Holy Spirit into Christ's Body and Blood. Day by day the Eucharist converts those who have become Christ's Body and the Spirit's temple more and more into those very realities until, at last, Christ will be all in all (Col 3:11).

Baptizing Children

The baptism of children incorporates many of the same issues that we have seen in the initiation of adults, but, of course, with differences.

Time (RBC 8–9)

The time for the celebration of the baptism of children is determined in a complex way. The first concern mentioned is the child's good: the child should have the benefit of the sacrament. On the other hand, the parents (the mother is mentioned in particular) should be present and should likewise be well-prepared for the celebration of the sacrament. In danger of death, baptism should be performed without delay. At least one parent must consent to the baptism and receive sufficient preparation. While children should receive baptism "within the first weeks after birth" (RBC 8.3), the need for the child to receive a Catholic formation must also be taken into account. In fact, the conference of bishops can determine a longer period of time between birth and baptism if that will help the child's upbringing as a Catholic (RBC 25). These concerns about time revolve around theological concerns: that baptism is necessary for salvation, the reality of original sin, and the desire that the child not be denied sacramental grace. Danger of death trumps every other consideration.

A second temporal concern centers on the paschal character of baptism (RBC 9). The Easter Vigil or any Sunday is an appropriate day for baptism, since these themselves are celebrations of the Lord's resurrection. A further recommendation states that, in addition to Sunday in itself, the community's Sunday celebration of Mass would be an appropriate time, so that "the relationship between baptism and eucharist may be clearly seen" (RBC 9). An immediate caution continues: "but this should not be done too often." The fear seems to be that too frequent celebration of baptisms at Sunday Mass would become burdensome for the community. In addition, there is no clear rite presented for celebrating baptism at Mass. The priest must apply rubrics found in the introduction in order to take what is presented and "adapt" it for Mass (RBC 29–30). Celebration during Mass is not a norm supported by the ritual text.

The order of the paragraphs and the detail of their exposition indicates the primacy of safeguarding the child's salvation over the liturgical aptness of Easter and/or Sunday as the day of celebration.

Space (RBC 10–13)

The parish church is the normal place for the celebration of baptism. This location manifests the appearance of baptism "as the sacrament of the Church's faith and of incorporation into the people of God" (RBC 10).

Within the church, certain places are focal: the church entrance (door), the ambo, the font, and the altar. In this, the ceremony draws together the key places found also in the Rite of Christian Initiation of Adults.

Acts

The acts of the Rite of Baptism for Children center on the key places just mentioned. Place and action shed light on each other's meaning. At the door the child is signed with the cross and welcomed into the Church (RBC 35). All enter in procession and go to the ambo (RBC 42), where, after readings and prayers, the child receives an anointing on the chest with oil of catechumens (RBC 50–51). (In the United States, the minister may lay his hands on the child instead.) All move in procession to the font (RBC 52). There, after the blessing of the water and the profession of faith, the washing of baptism and the explanatory rites follow: anointing of the crown of the head with chrism, clothing with a white garment, presenting a lighted candle, and touching the child's ears and mouth in the Ephphetha ceremony. (Note that the Ephphetha is postbaptismal in the rite for children. For adults it is celebrated on Holy Saturday morning as part of the preparation for initiation.) All move in procession to the altar, where the mothers hold their children during the blessing.

The overall action of the rite is a procession with stations: ambo, font, altar. Each station highlights an aspect of the unfolding reality of baptism.

Words

The words of the ceremony sometimes address the child. The usual addressees, however, are the parents and godparents. At the door, parents and godparents are questioned about their readiness and willingness to take on their duties (RBC 37–40).

The Word of God forms part of and ritualizes the totality of the necessary catechesis of the parents and godparents so they can understand their role in the Christian life of their child. The prayers that follow the homily wrestle with original sin (RBC 47–50). The child needs the help of both God and the community to become free of sin's power.

The prayer blessing the water is the same as at the Easter Vigil and rehearses God's plan of salvation for the whole world (RBC 53–55).[11] The renunciation of sin and profession of faith are made by the parents and godparents on behalf of the child (RBC 57–59). The introduction to the baptismal promises makes explicit again, in words sometimes identical to those spoken at the door of the church, that parents and godparents understand and accept the responsibilities of bringing a child for baptism.

The words that accompany the baptismal bath and the explanatory rites name the various outcomes of the rite (RBC 60–65): incorporation into the life of the Trinity; identification with the consecrated life of Christ; spotless new creation, now enlightened by Christ. These latter two symbols are explained as taking their full meaning only with the assistance of parents, godparents, family, and friends (in other words, the Church: the whole Christian community that they represent). The Ephphetha ceremony rewords the text to look to the future: "May he soon touch your ears" (RBC 65).

The words of the concluding rite, including the introduction to the Lord's Prayer and the solemn blessing, project the rite into the future (RBC 68–71). Confirmation and First Communion will complete the action. Mothers, fathers, and the whole Christian community need God's strength to ensure that the child will arrive safely at this fullness.

Participants (RBC 4–7)

The key participants in the Rite of Baptism for Children include first of all the child to be baptized. The parents and godparents are often the focus of the words and actions. The priest or deacon presiding has a key role to play in guiding the actions and processions. The community of believers, whether represented by the family and friends gathered or by the Sunday community of the parish, has an almost silent but clear and important role to play. Its members provide a context of support and prayer for the child and for the parents and godparents in their respective responsibilities.

Themes

The themes that emerge in the Rite of Baptism for Children are similar to but different from the themes addressed above in the Rite of Christian Initiation of Adults. Three that seem crucial are: journey, child of God, and nurturing parent.

Journey

Because the Rite of Baptism for Children takes place in a single ceremony, it brings together all the journey elements of initiation into one experience. The journey begins outside the door of the church and proceeds to the ambo for the stories of faith; to the font for baptismal washing and anointing, vesting and enlightening; and finally to the altar for the promise of completion of initiation in the sevenfold gift of the Spirit through the sacrament of confirmation and in the eventual nourishing participation at the altar table of the Eucharist.

This journey has several levels. It is a temporal journey, beginning at creation and the growth of the world and of God's people as recounted in Scripture and prayer. The journey continues today in this celebration. The journey opens onto a future nearer (confirmation and Eucharist) and more remote (final possession of the kingdom).

It is a sacramental journey, starting with baptism and oriented to confirmation and Eucharist.

It is a journey toward maturity, beginning with the life of a young child, but placed in the hands of parents and godparents to be brought safely to a future of mature participation in the life of Christ and the Church.

Child of God

The Rite of Baptism for Children reflects on the role of the child. The child is helpless and passive. Parents and godparents carry the child and answer for it. The child is malleable and open to formation into a mature believer. The child must be fed by others and cannot yet feed itself. On the other hand, from the moment of birth, the child is also an actor. The child has a history and a story, though the child may not be able to tell that story itself. The child has experienced the trauma of birth, moving from the environment of the mother's womb to the harsh open air of the world outside the mother. The child has reconfigured the life of its family and in the celebration of baptism reconfigures the parish community simply by being present. The child draws from others responses that would not exist but for the child. Whereas the great theme for adults is conversion, for the child it is the total gift that is salvation. Not earned in any way, it is a free expression of God's continually expansive love and creativity that must express itself and then draw all back to itself.[12]

Christian Parents

Christian parenting is another theme that emerges from the rite. The parenting involved begins before the celebration. Parents must decide to bring the child for baptism. Their care for the new life that they have conceived includes the child's welfare, not just physical, intellectual, and moral, but also spiritual. The child is their child but also God's child. They need to acknowledge the divine within their child. The priest works with the parents to help them understand the implications of this dimension of their childbearing and child rearing.

During the ceremony, the role of the parent arises at several points. At the door of the church, while holding the child, they promise to bring the child up in the practice of the faith: to love God and show that love of God in love of neighbor. Similar words are pronounced at the renunciation of sin and profession of faith, which takes place within the context of their own baptismal promises.

The parents do not only make promises about their responsibilities on behalf of the child. They also perform actions on behalf of their child. They sign the child with the cross on the forehead. They shared with God the creative love that brought forth this child. Now they place the child under the symbol of God's own Son, a further sharing in God's own creative parental love. They clothe the child in white and hope, by word and example, to help the child bring the garment to heaven unstained. They receive a lighted candle in the hope of helping to sustain the light throughout the child's life.

A review of the readings in the Lectionary for the baptism of children reveals what the Church proposes as instruction for parents. At several points in the ceremony, especially in the intercessions, they are also called to pray. Parents should be examples of faith to inspire their children.

The final blessing contains an ideal portrait of the mother and the father. The mother is full of joy as she looks on her child. She is thankful for the gift of this child. Mother and child are one in giving thanks to God. The father is a sharer in God's giving of life. He is a coworker with his wife as a teacher, a witness in word and deed to the faith for their child.

Notes, Chapter Six

[1] *De baptismo* 19. See E. C. Whitaker/Johnson, *Documents*, 10.

[2] See James Dunning, *Echoing God's Word: Formation for Catechists and Homilists in a Catechumenal Church* (Arlington, VA: National Forum on the Catechumenate, 1993).

[3] Timothy Fry, ed., *RB 1980: The Rule of St. Benedict in Latin and English with Notes* (Collegeville, MN: Liturgical Press, 1981), 255. See also Henri Nouwen, *Reaching Out: The Three Movements of the Spiritual Life* (New York: Doubleday Image, 1975), esp. 63–109; Sylvia Cirone Deck, *Ministry of Hospitality* (Kansas City: Sheed & Ward, Santa Clara University Pastoral Ministries Program, 1996).

[4] See Michael Buckley, "The Structure of the Rules for Discernment," in *The Way of Ignatius Loyola: Contemporary Approaches to* The Spiritual Exercises, ed. Philip Sheldrake (St. Louis, MO: Institute of Jesuit Sources, 1991), 219–37; see also the brief article by Buckley, "Discernment of Spirits," in Michael Downey, ed., *The New Dictionary of Catholic Spirituality* (Collegeville, MN: Liturgical Press, A Michael Glazier Book, 1993), 274–81.

[5] Found in *The Rites*, vol. 1, 342. The pastoral reality found in most parishes, however, is that the preparation lasts about six months.

[6] General Norms for the Liturgical Year and Calendar 27, in *The Liturgy Documents: A Parish Resource*, vol. 1, ed. David Lysik, 4th ed. (Chicago: Liturgy Training Publications, 2004), 168.

[7] "Conversion" and "journey" have both generated ample reflection. For starters, see Robert Duggan, ed., *Conversion and the Catechumenate* (New York: Paulist, 1984); and Mark Searle, "The Journey of Conversion," *Worship* 54 (1980): 35–55.

[8] See Searle, "Journey of Conversion"; Joseph Campbell, *The Hero with a Thousand Faces* (Princeton, NJ: Princeton University Press, 1949). The number of literary works that revolve around the theme of journey is mammoth and includes Homer's *Odyssey*; from the Bible, the book of Exodus and the two-part Luke-Acts; Thomas Mallory's *Morte d'Arthur* on the legend of the seeking of the Grail; Dante's *Divine Comedy* on a journey through hell and purgatory to heaven; Chaucer's *Canterbury Tales*, set during a pilgrimage to the tomb of Thomas à Becket in Canterbury; and contemporary novels such as Hermann Hesse's *Steppenwolf* and J. R. R. Tolkien's *The Hobbit* and *The Lord of the Rings*.

[9] General Norms of the Liturgical Year and Calendar 21, in *The Liturgy Documents*, 1:167.

[10] General Norms of the Liturgical Year and Calendar 22, in *The Liturgy Documents*, 1:168. The quotation is from Athanasius, *Epist. fest.* 1, cited in the notes.

[11] Note that optional prayers can substitute for the Easter Vigil prayer. These prayers contain options for a community refrain during the sections of the prayer (RBC 223–24).

[12] See the reflections on childhood in Mark Searle, "Infant Baptism Reconsidered," in *Alternative Futures for Worship: Volume 2, Baptism and Confirmation*, ed. Mark Searle, 15–54 (Collegeville, MN: Liturgical Press, 1987); reprinted in Maxwell Johnson, ed., *Living Water, Sealing Spirit: Readings on Christian Initiation* (Collegeville, MN: Liturgical Press, A Pueblo Book, 1995), 365–409. See also Kurt Stasiak, *Return to Grace: A Theology for Infant Baptism* (Collegeville, MN: Liturgical Press, A Pueblo Book, 1996), esp. 115–25. See also Nathan Mitchell, "The Once and Future Child: Towards a Theology of Childhood," *Living Light* 12 (1975): 422–36; Karl Rahner, "Ideas for a Theology of Childhood," in *Theological Investigations 8: Further Theology of the Spiritual Life 2*, trans. David Bourke, 33–50 (New York: Herder, 1971); Hans Urs von Balthasar, *Unless You Become Like This Child*, trans. Erasmo Leiva-Merikakis (San Francisco: Ignatius, 1991).

Conclusion

W hat kind of book is this? It is a commentary on the ordinary form of celebration of baptism as it exists in the Roman Catholic Church today.

To label more exactly what kind of commentary it is, it will be helpful to use the categories developed by John W. O'Malley in *Four Cultures of the West*.[1] He identifies four "cultures" that characterize some aspects of life in today's Western culture. He names them as (1) prophetic, (2) academic, (3) humanist and rhetorical, and (4) performative.

The prophet calls people to believe the one truth that the prophet sees. Those with the prophet are in; those who are against are out. The second culture is that of the university and of exacting, systematic study, aiming at the truth. The third culture revels in poetry, literature, and above all in rhetoric and persuasion, aiming to convince people to choose the good. The fourth culture is primarily wordless: music, dance, architecture, painting, mosaic, and theatrical representation understood as performance (not text).

To help understand each culture, O'Malley gives examples and exemplars. Martin Luther, the great Protestant reformer, would exemplify the first culture. Thomas Aquinas, the Dominican scholastic theologian, would stand for culture two. Erasmus, the renaissance humanist, would be an example of the third culture. Michelangelo, Italian sculptor, painter, architect, and poet, would reveal an approach to the fourth culture.

O'Malley sees these cultures as embodying, more or less, the four transcendentals: the one, the true, the good, and the beautiful. They overlap at times, and at times are mutually exclusive. Someone deeply immersed in one culture may not have any appreciation for another culture.

One reflection on this commentary can see it primarily as a work out of the third culture, a rhetorical and literary exploration, and at times a plea, to understand baptism. Of course, it is more complicated than that. Baptism as a liturgy is firmly enmeshed in what O'Malley would call culture four, performance. Theology has studied baptism for centuries out of the world of culture two, the rigorous, systematic, academic theological model. Some have seen baptism from the point of view of culture one: one must choose baptism to express one's faith—one cannot simply study it, or be brought to it, or obfuscate it with ceremony. Culture three uses images and plot and the rhythms of speech to appreciate baptism's beauty and meaning, not rigorously but impressionistically.

An intention of this book has been to lead the reader to a sense of the richness, complexity, depth, joy, amazement, and much more besides, that are a part of the celebration of baptism as members of the People of God, of the Body of Christ, of the Temple of the Holy Spirit, in the Catholic Church.

Notes, Conclusion

[1] John W. O'Malley, *Four Cultures of the West* (Cambridge, MA: Belknap Press of Harvard University Press, 1994).

Index of Documents

Apostolic Tradition, 5–6, 11, 50, 152, 153

Aristotle's *Poetics*, x

Augustine, *Sermo* 219, 189

Baptism, Eucharist, and Ministry (BEM), 169–72
   Roman Catholic response, 171

Castellani's *Liber sacerdotalis*, 9

Catechism of the Catholic Church, 145–46, 167–69, 184–85, 186

Christian Initiation: General Introduction (CIGI), 10, 11–15, 27, 57, 165, 166

Code of Canon Law (1917), 54

Code of Canon Law (1983), 14, 129, 167

Constitution on the Sacred Liturgy (*see also Sacrosanctum Concilium*), 12–14, 23, 52–53, 164

Didache, 5, 152

Divino Afflante Spiritu, 12

Eucharistic Prayer IV, 102, 113

First Apology, 152–53

The Hope of Salvation for Infants Who Die without Baptism, 169

Joint Declaration on the Doctrine of Justification, 172

Lectionary, 92

Lectionary for the baptism for children, 197

Lenten Lectionary, 80

Mediator Dei, 12

Mystagogical Catechesis, 9, 37, 154–55

Mysterium Fidei, 19

Mystici Corporis, 12

Nicene Creed, 11

Old Gelasian Sacramentary, 7, 11, 119, 156–57

Ordo Romanus XI, 8, 157

Rite of Baptism for Children (RBC; 1969, 1972), xv, 13–14, 37–39, 52–55, 56–67, 131–32, 135–37, 164

RBC 4, 57

RBC 5, 56
RBC 6, 57
RBC 7, 57
RBC 9, 193
RBC 25, 192–93
RBC 29–30, 193
RBC 32–71, 55
RBC 35, 193
RBC 37–40, 194
RBC 42, 193
RBC 50–51, 193
RBC 52, 193
RBC 53–55, 194
RBC 57–59, 194
RBC 60–65, 194
RBC 83, 193
Rite of Christian Initiation of Adults
    (RCIA; 1972), xiv, 14–15, 39,
    125, 130–31, 133–34, 165, 181,
    193
and the Code of Canon Law, 129
prayers, 105–8
RCIA 10–11, 187
RCIA 36, 74
RCIA 36–40, 182
RCIA 38, 74
RCIA 39, 118
RCIA 73, 108
RCIA 75, 24–25, 77, 83–89, 106,
    108
RCIA 94A and H, 108–9
RCIA 97A, 127
RCIA 97E, 112
RCIA 104–5, 66
RCIA 118–37, 81, 186–87
    or Enrollment of Names, 113
RCIA 120, 78
RCIA 129–37, 113
RCIA 134–35, 113

RCIA 135A, 113
RCIA 135B, 114
RCIA 139, 187
RCIA 154A, 115
RCIA 161, 117
RCIA 185, 85
RCIA 218–43, 189
RCIA 219, 118
RCIA 220, 118
RCIA 222, 123
RCIA 243, 41
RCIA 244, 42
RCIA 244–47, 88
RCIA 244–51, 191
RCIA 247, 42
RCIA 249, 42
RCIA 250, 42
Rite of Christian Initiation of Adults
    and the Rite of Baptism for
    Children, 81, 99–110
Rituale Romanum (1614), 10, 51

Sacramentary, 118, 119
    Easter Vigil, 38, 118
Sacrosanctum Concilium (*see also*
    Constitution on the Sacred
    Liturgy), 12, 164
SC 7, 71
SC 7, 23, 165
SC 33, 72
SC 35, 73
SC 51, 73
Santori's *Rituale*, 9–10
Small Catechism, 160
Syllabus of Errors, The, 164

The Teaching of the Twelve Apostles
    (*see Didache*)
Tra le sollecitudini, 164

Index of Scripture References

Genesis
1   101, 113
1:1-2   120–21
1:3   75
1:27   122
1:28-30, 2:16-17, 3:8-19   75
2   59
2:7-9; 3:1-7   79
6–9   121
9:8-15   79
11:1-9   90
12:1-4a   76
12:1-40   20
22:1-18a   86

Exodus
13:8   72
14:15–15:1   86
14   61
15   86
17:1-7   61
17:3-7   82, 92
19:3-3a, 16-20b   90
29:7   128

Deuteronomy   81
6   84
6:23   72
26:4-10   7

Joshua
3:7-17   61

1 Samuel
10:1   128
16:1b, 6-7, 10-13a   82
16:13   128

1 Kings
9:15-16   128

2 Kings
5   61

Nehemiah
8–9   102

Psalms
16   86, 88
19   86, 90
23   88, 93
23:1-3a, 3b-4, 5-6   82, 84
24:4-9   79
27   93
30   86
33   20, 86, 87, 90
33:4-5, 12-13,
    18-19, 20 and 22   76
34   93
42   86
47   87
51   86
51:3-6, 12-13, 17   79
66   89
91:1-2, 10-15   79

95:1-2, 6-9	82	13:24-30, 30-43	114
103:1-2, 8 and 10, 11-13, 18	84	16	84
104	86, 90	16:13-17	85
107	90	16:13-18	84
118	88	16:13-20	59
130:1-8	82	22:34-40	41
133:2	40, 128	22:35-40	93
		25:1-13	35, 129
Isaiah		25:31-46	41
1	153	25:31-46	42
6:1-1	128	28:1-10	87
11:2	130	28:16	5
12	86	28:16-18	9
40:3-5	148	28:16-20	89
54:5-14	86	28:18-20	92, 93
55:1-11	86	28:19a, 20b	89
Baruch		**Mark**	
3:9-15, 32–4:4	86	1:4	148
		1:9-11	4, 92, 148
Ezekiel		1:12-15	77
36:16-17a, 18-28	86	1:16	3
36:24-28	93	2:13	3
37:1-14	90	3:11-12	148
37:12-14	82	6:13	150
47:1-9, 12	93	7:31-37	85
		8:23-25	188
Daniel		10:13-16	73, 92
3	90	12:28b-34	93
3:60	123	14:3-9	150
		16:1	150
Hosea		16:1-7	87
11:16, 3-4, 8c-9	84		
		Luke	
Joel		2:2-19	102
3:1-5	90	3:3, 7-17	148
		3:4-6	148
Matthew		3:15	148
3:13-17	148	3:21-22	148
4:1-11	79	4:1-13	79
4:4b	79	4:16-21	110
6:9-13	85	4:18	150
9:9	3	7:36-50	150

10:25-37	41	15:1-4	93
24: 1-12	87	17:1-11a	90
24:13-35	42, 88	19:31-35	93
24:32	88	20	3
		20:19-23	90
John	83–84	20:19-31	88
1:21	150	20:29	88
1:35-42	20, 76		
1:35-37, 40-42	37	Acts of the Apostles	4, 91
3	125, 130–31, 153	1:8	146
3:1-6	93	1:1-11	89
3:3-5	149	1:2-11	90
3:5	167, 190	1:8	50
3:16	84, 92	1:12-14	89
3:22	40	2	3, 4
4	114	2:1-12	147
4:1-3	4	2:4a, 36-41	88
4:5-14	93	2:13-36	147
4:5-32	82	2:14, 22-23	88
4:42, 15	82	2:36-40	4
6:35, 63-71	85	2:37-42	147
6:44-47	93	2:42-47	88
7:37-39	90	6:1-7	89
7:37b-39a	93	8:5-8, 14-17	89
8:12	82	8:9-13	147
8:12; 9:5	129	8:14-17	4
9	114	8:14-18	147
9:1-7	93	8:26-40	4, 147
9:1-41	82	10:1-48	4, 147
9:5	150	10:24	49
10:1-10	88	10:38	150
10:44	88	10:44	49
11:1-45	82	10:44-48	4
11:25a, 26	83	10:48	49
12:1-8	150	16:14-15	4, 49, 147
12:35-36	127	16:19-34	69
12:44-50	84	16:25-34	4, 147
14	130	19:1-6	47
14:1-12	89	19:1-7	4
14:6	89		
14:15-21	89	Romans	81
14:18	90	3:25	131
14:23	89	5:1-2, 5-8	82

5:12-19	79	1:13	114, 156
6	5	1:17-23	89
6:1-11	149	4:1-6	93
6:3-5	93	5:8	150
6:3-11	86, 122, 151	5:8-14	82
6:4	161	5:26	149
8:1	172		
8:8-11	82	**Colossians**	
8:12-17	113	3:9-10	150
8:14-17, 26-27	85	3:9, 10, 12, 14	128
8:15	85	3:10, 12	150
8:22-27	90	3:11	192
8:28-32	93		
9:8	114	**Titus**	149
10:8-13	79, 84	3:4-7	124
10:9	129	3:5	167
13:12-14	129, 150		
13:14	128	**Hebrews**	
		9	131
1 Corinthians			
1:16	49	**James**	
3:16-17	133	5:14	150
11:23-24	102		
11:24	102	**1 Peter**	90
12:36-37, 12-13	90	1:3-9	88
12:12-13	93	1:17-21	88
15:1-89	84	2:4-5, 9-10	93
		2:4-9	89
2 Corinthians		2:9-10	128
1:21-22	150	2:20b-25	88
		3:15-18	89
Galatians		3:18-22	79
3:26-27	128	4:13-16	87, 89
3:27	149		
3:28	150	**1 John**	
4:4-7	85	1:5	150
4:21-31	114		
		Revelation	
Ephesians		1:5	131
1:7	131	7:9-17	128
1:10	114		

Index of Proper Names

Abraham (Abram), 75, 76, 86, 87,
    104, 190
  and Sarah (Sarai), 59
Adam, 8, 80, 161
  and Christ, 151
  and Eve, 80, 156
Aland, Kurt, 12
Ambrose, 7, 154–55
Ananias, 147
Andrew, 76
Anointed kings of Israel and Judah,
    128
Antoninus Pius, 5
Aquinas, Thomas, 159, 199
Augustine, 7, 8, 50
  about heretics, 154
  and the Donatists, 155–56
  grace, 120
  and Isidore of Seville, 158

Barth, Karl, 12
Basil, 7, 155

Calvin, John, 10, 161
Casel, Odo, x, 164
Charlemagne, 157
Congregation for the Doctrine of the
    Faith, 14
Constantine, 6, 9, 145

Cornelius, 49, 147, 150
  and his household, 148
Cullman, Oscar, 12
Cyprian of Carthage, 50, 154

David, 82, 128
Dominicans, 9
Donatists, 154–55

Elijah and Elisha, 128
Erasmus, 199
Ethiopian eunuch, 4–6, 147

Fink, Peter, xiii
Franciscans, 9

Gregory Nazianzen, 7

Hippolytus, 5, 152
Hubmaier, Balthazar, 161
Hugh of St. Victor, 158

Isaiah, 128, 130, 148, 150

jailer of Ephesus, 49, 147
Jeremias, Joachim, 12
John the Baptist, 3, 4, 76, 121, 145,
    146, 147, 148–49
John Chrysostom, 154–55

John the Deacon, 7, 50–51
John the Evangelist, 83, 146, 147, 151
Justin Martyr, 5, 151, 152–53

Lazarus, 83, 114, 188
Leo the Great, 51
Luke, 49–50, 80–81, 146–47, 148, 150
Luther, Martin, 10, 160–61, 199
Lydia, 49, 147

Mark, 80–81, 85, 148, 150
Mary, the Mother of God, 64, 80, 136
Mary and Martha, 83–84
Matthew, 80–81, 128, 148
Mennonites, 161
Messiah, the, 76, 150
Michelangelo, 199
Müntzer, Thomas, 161

Nicodemus, 92, 122, 151
Noah and the flood, 75, 80, 121

O'Malley, John, 199–200
Origen, 50

Paul, 5, 49, 80, 81, 102, 128, 129, 146, 147–48, 149–51, 151

Pelagians, 8, 50, 155, 156
Peter, 4, 49, 59, 76, 80, 147, 148, 150
Peter Lombard, 158
Philip, 147
Pope John XXIII, 12
Pope Paul V, 10, 14
Pope Paul VI, 14, 53, 165
Pope Pius V, 10
Pope Pius X, 164
Pope Pius XII, 12
Pope Stephen, 154

Ricoeur, Paul, xiv

Sacred Congregation of Rites, 12, 13, 164
Satan and the angels, 8, 79, 126, 132, 153, 158, 171
Saul, persecutor of Christ, 147

Tertullian, 5, 6, 152, 154
  in North Africa, 50
  when baptism occurs, 58
  when to baptize, 181
Theodulph of Orléans, 158
Thomas, 88

Zwingli, Ulrich, 161

Index of Subjects

adults' vs. children's baptisms, 50–51, 131, 168
already-baptized Christians, 14
American and British Baptists, 161
Anabaptists, 10, 160–63
anointing, 5, 6, 7, 8, 11, 24–25, 29, 38, 39–40, 51–52, 55, 61, 62, 66, 109, 121, 127–28, 132, 134, 149, 150, 153, 168, 171, 185–86, 190, 191, 193, 195
apostles, 3, 4, 50, 146, 148
appropriate day for baptism, 193
Augustine's controversy with the religions, 50–51

baptism, 4, 8, 9, 10, 34, 125, 147, 156, 167, 170, 171
  of adults, 10, 145, 182–89
  of blood, 169
  of children, 8, 10, 49, 50, 195–96
  Church teaching about, 145–50
  of Clovis and the Franks, 50
  of desire, 169
  in emergency, 6–9, 54, 55, 58, 65, 157, 158, 163, 164, 165, 192
  of households, 49
  of infants, 48–50, 52
  of Jesus, 92, 148–49

according to Protestant reformers, 161
  in scholastic thought, 158–59
  in Scripture, 146–51
baptismal,
  font, 6, 8, 10, 11, 34, 35, 36–37, 55, 56, 57, 58, 118, 126, 133–35, 163, 166, 181, 189, 193, 195
  promises, 4, 40, 56, 171, 194, 196
  water, 4, 5, 6, 8, 11, 14, 34, 37, 38, 40, 53, 55, 61, 62, 83, 94, 99, 118, 119, 120, 121, 122, 123, 124, 125, 127, 133, 149, 151, 152, 153, 160, 165, 168, 171, 190, 194
bishop, 6, 8, 24, 27, 28, 29, 34, 37, 39, 78, 112, 113, 153, 159, 186
Body of Christ, 4, 18, 36, 59, 91, 166, 169, 170, 171, 182, 200
bread and wine, 40–41

catechesis, 12, 21–22, 77, 87–90, 166, 181, 185–87, 190
catechumenate, 9, 13, 21–22, 24, 77, 78, 106, 108, 132, 164, 168, 185–87, 186
catechumenon, 22, 181

catechumens, 7–8, 17, 19, 20, 21, 22, 23, 24, 27, 28, 29, 61, 77, 78, 106, 108, 110, 111, 112, 126, 158, 186
  Order of, 15–17, 35, 76, 131, 182–83
causality, 160
celebrant, the, 16, 18, 32, 36, 57, 59, 62, 63, 76, 85, 99, 100, 104, 109, 111, 115, 129, 131, 134
Celebration of the Word, 22–24, 77–78, 78–87, 84–86, 108–12, 132, 166
  inside/outside Mass, 77–78
"character," the seal of the Spirit, 156
children,
  who die before baptism, 169
chrism, 7, 36, 38, 39–40, 41, 53, 62–63, 66, 127, 134, 168
chrism Mass, 39
Christ raised from the dead, 86
Christ's presence in the event, 93–94
Christ's public ministry, 80
Christian journey of life, 77
Church of the Armenians, 159
Communion, 7, 41, 50, 64, 129, 135, 155, 157, 168, 171, 194
community (*koinonia*), 4
community of believers, a, 16, 21, 25, 29, 30, 35, 56, 59, 66, 92, 182, 185, 192
confession of faith, 79
confirmation, 9, 34, 39–40, 62, 64, 129–30, 135, 157, 168, 172, 195
Consilium, the, 14, 53, 165
conversion, 4, 15, 23, 26, 34, 74, 78, 81, 91, 147, 170, 183, 186, 188, 196
Cornelius's household, 4
Council of Carthage (418), 161
Council of Florence, 159, 167
Council of Trent, 161–62, 167
covenant, 102, 104

Creed, 6, 30–32, 84, 85, 117, 167

decline of adult baptism, 6–10
dismissal of the catechumens, 20, 22, 78
duration of preparation for baptism, 180

Easter, 5, 6, 26, 50, 154
Easter season, 14, 42, 53, 88–90, 91, 117, 125, 130, 165, 181, 191
Easter candle, 36, 37, 39, 63, 86, 122, 129
Easter Vigil, 8, 12, 30, 33–36, 40, 54, 58, 61, 65, 81, 84, 86, 87, 90, 168, 180–81, 189
Eastern liturgy, 168
economy of salvation, 168
ecumenical dialogues, 146, 169
elect, the, 8, 27, 29, 30, 78–79, 81, 82, 85, 87, 112–18, 186–87, 188
  approach the font, 126
  in the Easter Vigil, 35
enlightenment, 29, 81, 87, 108–9, 117, 132, 167, 180, 187
Enrollment of Names, 25, 29, 78–81, 113–14, 186–87
entering the church, 19–20
Ephphetha ceremony, 8, 29, 31–32, 85, 66, 135, 188, 193–94
epiclesis (invocation), 103, 130
Eucharist, 5–6, 40–41, 42, 73, 121, 135, 171, 191, 192, 195
eucharistic, 40–41
evangelists, 80, 148
evangelization, 74–75, 87, 184
exorcism, 6, 8, 23, 30, 55, 106, 108–11, 132, 153, 157, 186
  prayer, 82
  scrutiny, 187

faithful, the, 18, 27–28, 35, 57, 84, 88, 100, 166, 187

fasting, 6, 152
fire, 35–36, 39, 86, 189
First Holy Communion, xv, 41, 84
First Pentecost, 3–4
First Sunday of Lent, 26, 78–79, 112, 186
  readings of, 80
flood and baptism, 80–81, 121, 122, 168
font, the (*see* baptismal, font)
forgiveness of sins, 4, 8, 112, 116, 147, 148, 151, 153, 156, 159, 162, 169

gift of the Holy Spirit, xiv, 3–4, 6, 39, 91, 119, 122, 147, 148, 159, 168, 170, 191, 195
God's Word, ix, x, 17, 21, 22, 34, 41, 55, 60, 73, 74, 75, 79, 94, 98, 160–61
godparents, the, 12, 14, 27, 28, 30, 35, 38–39, 40, 51–52, 56–57, 59, 65–66, 92, 115, 166, 115, 163, 172, 186, 190, 194
  help him/her into new white garments, 39
  present a candle, 39, 63, 129
Good Shepherd, 91, 191
Gospel, 9, 16, 17, 21, 24, 31, 74, 76–77, 81, 93, 106, 132, 183–85, 188
grace, 30, 32, 66, 110, 114, 122, 126, 151, 161, 169, 172

healing, 24, 94, 105, 116
heart, 24, 26, 42, 74, 77, 82, 87, 116
Holy Saturday, 34, 85
  morning, 8, 29, 31, 66, 84, 135, 157, 187–88
  preparatory rites, 32, 85
Holy Spirit, 4, 6, 23, 30–31, 34, 36, 37, 39, 41, 61, 74, 76, 91, 103, 108, 112, 114, 119, 147, 151, 182, 184, 185, 190, 192

Holy Week services, 12

illumination, 153
immersion, 7, 8, 34, 38, 62, 85, 127, 152, 153, 167, 171
  as a symbol, 151
  in water, 6
imposition of hands, 8, 23, 30, 31, 82, 132, 185–86
infants, 7, 49, 50, 52, 154, 156, 161, 170, 172
  as primary recipients of the Sacrament, 157
intercessions, 30, 81, 82, 113, 115, 117, 132

Jerusalem, 81
Jesus' anointing, 150
Jesus' baptism by John, 4, 121, 145, 146, 148–49
Jordan River, 4, 61, 121–23

Last Supper, 102, 129, 150, 189
laying on of hands, 4, 23, 153, 171, 185–86
  in exorcism, 116
legalization of Christianity, 6, 9
Lent, 27, 29, 82, 84, 157, 180–81, 187
light, 34, 36, 39, 41, 63, 75, 86, 94, 129, 133–35, 150, 189, 190
little children and Christ, 60, 92
liturgy, xiii–xiv, 12, 24, 72, 77, 80, 99, 103, 200
Liturgy of the Eucharist, 40–41
Litany of the Saints, 8, 34, 37, 100, 118–19, 132, 190
Liturgy of the Word, 18, 20, 22, 25–26, 34, 60, 76, 86–87
  and Liturgy of the Eucharist, 118
living waters, 90
Lord's Prayer, 10, 29, 31, 55, 135
Lutherans, 160, 172

major euchology, 99, 100, 102, 119
    vs. minor euchology, 99, 103
Marian shrine, 64
martyrdom, 154, 162
Mass, 8, 13, 29, 54, 58, 67, 73, 88,
    92, 99, 113, 130, 187, 193
matter and form, 159–60, 162
mercy, 30, 76
    for sinners, 79
minor euchology, 99, 100, 102,
    103
mission countries, 13, 14, 50, 52
missionary impetus, 125, 156, 163
missionary zeal, 9
mothers' roles, 136
mystagogy, 41–42, 87–91, 130–31,
    155, 181, 191–92
mysterion, 154

naming, 59
necessity of baptism, 169
neophytes, 40–42, 91
new birth, 127, 146
newly baptized, 41
New Testament, 9, 39, 49, 92–93, 94,
    98, 121, 145, 146
Novatians, 154

object of faith, 81
oil,
    anointed with, 5, 6, 7, 24, 39
    of catechumens, 7, 8, 29, 61, 132,
        185, 193
    of sanctification, 7
    significance of applying, 24, 94
    of thanksgiving, 6, 153
Old Testament, 92–94, 98, 120–21,
    168
original rite, 52
original sin, 8, 9, 50, 51, 53, 61,
    132–33, 156, 157, 158, 161,
    172–73, 194
origins of Christianity, 164

paganism, 7
Paraclete, the, 91, 191
parents, 7, 8, 12, 49, 53–54, 56–57,
    58, 59, 62, 63, 64, 66, 92, 131–
    32, 133–34, 135–37, 163, 164,
    166, 180, 181, 192, 194, 195,
    196–97
paschal character of baptism, 5, 53,
    54, 58, 67, 193
Passover Haggadah, 71
patristics, 11, 50, 156, 158, 160, 163,
    166, 167, 169
Peace of the Church under
    Constantine, (313), 5–6, 145,
    152, 154
Pentecost, 3, 90, 147, 154
    Vigil of, 90, 163
period of the catechumenate, 13,
    21–25, 77, 78, 106, 108, 132,
    155, 185–87
period of evangelization and
    precatechumenate, 74–75, 87
period of mystagogy, 41–42, 87–91,
    130, 155, 191–92
period of purification and enlighten-
    ment, 24, 29–32, 34, 81–87,
    108–9, 117, 132, 187–89
pneuma, 151, 168
prayer over the water, 119–29
preparation of the altar and gifts, 40
presentations, 30–31, 35, 43, 81, 84,
    117
    of the Bible, 17
    of the Creed, 30–31, 84, 117,
        187–88
    of a lighted candle, 63, 129,
        134–35
    of the Lord's Prayer, 30–31, 84–
        85, 117–18, 187–88
    of a white garment, 168
profession of faith, 34, 37, 40, 57, 81,
    84, 85, 125, 126–27, 133, 134,
    170, 171, 194, 196

Protestant Reformation, 9, 50, 145, 160–61

rebaptism, 14, 159, 161, 162
reception of heretics back to the church, 154
reconciliation (after baptism), 7
record of baptisms, 163
reform of the liturgy, 12, 52
renewal of baptismal promises, 40, 171
renunciation of sin and profession of faith, 34, 37, 40, 85, 126, 194, 196
requirements for baptism, 166–67
res, 158–59
responsorial psalm, 18, 20, 36, 75–76, 85, 93, 94
revised rites, 12–13
Rite of Acceptance into the Order of Catechumens, 15–17, 106, 131
rite of baptism, 10, 37–39
Rite of Baptism for Children, xv, 12–13, 53–64, 91–94, 99, 131–37, 164, 165, 193, 195, 196
Rite of Becoming a Catechumen, 20, 24, 32, 43
Rite of Christian Initiation of Adults (RCIA), xiv, 14–15, 39, 74–77, 105–31, 164, 181, 193
Rite of Election, 25–31, 43, 78–87, 186–87
rite for infants, 9
rites of initiation, 190
ritual, xiv–xv, 7–8, 9, 11, 55

Sacraments of initiation, 26, 30, 42, 43, 82, 86–87, 165, 167, 168
Sacraments of Initiation of an Adult, 129
  pray for, 130
  when it occurs, 129
sacramentum, 154, 158–59, 160

sacramentum et res, 158–59
sacrificial meal, 190–91
saliva, 10, 51
salt, 7–8, 10, 11, 51, 158
salvation history, 34, 36, 37, 80, 190
scrutinies, the, 7, 27, 29–30, 35, 81, 82–84, 114–17, 157, 187–89
Second Vatican Council, x, 12–14, 26, 52–53, 71, 145, 164–65, 166, 169
Seder, the, 71
serpent, the, 80
sign of the cross, 17, 19, 40, 59, 106, 107, 168, 183–84
sign of peace, 6, 8, 40, 49
signs, 13, 19, 23, 61, 120, 147, 183
  and symbols, 17
silence, 20, 76, 82, 87, 100, 108, 113
  purpose of, 105
sin,
  described, 173
  and ignorance, 186
  and grace, 79
space for baptism, 181
special circumstances for baptism, 164–65
Spirit, the (*see* Holy Spirit)
Spirit and the water, 122
spittle, 8
sponsors, 5, 17–18, 20, 23, 59, 79, 106, 186, 187
Sundays of Easter, 42, 88–90, 130, 191

temptation of Christ, 79–81, 179, 186
theology of baptism, 143, 150, 165, 180
  from the perspective of initiation, 165
  and scholasticism, 157
Third, Fourth, and Fifth Sundays of Lent, 81, 114, 157, 187

Third Sunday of Lent, 115–16
trinitarian formula, 38, 101, 110,
    125, 153, 158–60, 161, 162,
    168, 171
Trinity, 104–5, 123, 127, 167, 194

Upper Room, 3

washing, 38, 149, 151, 153, 154, 160,
    190, 193

and anointing, 191, 195
water, 14, 38, 53, 82, 83–84, 94, 130,
    152, 165
white garment, 5, 6, 38–39, 55, 63,
    134, 168, 193
Word, the, 98
Word of God, 16, 18, 20, 22, 24–25,
    41, 60, 73, 74–77, 81, 91–94,
    137, 160, 171, 183, 194 (*see also*
    God's Word)